Also by Donald Goddard

BLIMEY! ANOTHER BOOK ABOUT LONDON

JOEY

THE LAST DAYS OF DIETRICH BONHOEFFER

EASY MONEY

EASY MONEY

Donald Goddard

Farrar, Straus and Giroux
New York

Published simultaneously in Canada by
McGraw-Hill Ryerson Ltd., Toronto
Printed in the United States of America
Designed by Constance Fogler
Second printing, 1978

Library of Congress Cataloging in Publication Data
Goddard, Donald. Easy money.
1. Heroin. 2. Narcotics and crime—United States.
3. Organized crime—United States. I. Title.
HV5822.H4G62 364 77-29120

TO Natalie

FOREWORD

This is the true story of George Ramos, who conspired with Frank Matthews, the black Luciano, to smuggle into the United States a shipment of European heroin equivalent to about three *tons* of junk in dose form.

In the narcotics famine that addicts still remember as "the panic of '72," this meant a gross take of about $100 million at street level.

More significant, perhaps, is the inside view it affords of a social revolution. In the past ten years, the so-called Black Mafia and its Spanish-speaking counterparts have largely taken over the inner-city street rackets from the Mob, upsetting a balance of power unchallenged since the thirties, when the original Luciano first organized crime into a mainly Italian cartel.

In telling the story, I have tried to skirt the statistical wrangle about the extent of drug misuse. In 1977, Edward Jay Epstein argued, in *Agency of Fear,* that Richard Nixon for political reasons had deliberately overstated the problems of narcotics addiction. In 1975, George C. Richardson argued, in *Get Up, You're Not Dead,* that Richard Nixon for political reasons had deliberately *understated* the problems of narcotics addiction.

As each supported his contention with a wealth of persuasive evidence, I am very willing to believe that Nixon did both. He was not the first politician to abuse statistics for private, even sinister, purposes, and drug misuse is by no means the first social issue to be used as a political football. No one can possibly deny, however, that the illegal drug traffic *is* an issue, and I am here concerned more with the nature of it than with the size of it (although the figures mentioned are often astounding).

My chief "connection" for the book has been George Ramos himself, who came to know Frank Matthews well while planning the $100 million deal—so well, in fact, that the "Black Caesar" felt obliged to flee the country. (The most wanted man since John Dillinger, Matthews is still a fugitive, having comfortably eluded an international manhunt for five years.) As George is rarely at a loss for words, I have let him tell his own part of the story, breaking it off at intervals to fit each chapter of his narrative into the larger context.

I am also deeply indebted to William P. Callahan, president and director of United Intelligence, Inc. (Unitel), the New York-based international private investigative agency specializing in "white-collar" crime. Formerly New York Regional Counsel, Criminal Division, of the U. S. Department of Justice, he ran the federal grand jury that unraveled the Matthews affair, and with great kindness and patience steered me through the tangles of a case involving some two hundred city, county, state, and federal law-enforcement agencies across the nation and overseas.

My thanks are also due to Assistant U. S. Attorney David De Petris, Eastern District, New York, and Special U. S. Attorney Charles Jaffee, Southern District, Florida, who were both as helpful as the circumstances of a continuing investigation allowed them to be.

For the rest, I am grateful to those many former government attorneys, agents, witnesses, and police officers who gave freely of their time and recollections but prefer to remain anonymous for reasons that are readily understandable with Matthews still at large.

They will forgive me, I hope, for not matching their discretion in the text. No names have been changed to protect the innocent, because no one is innocent.

D.G.
January 1978

EASY MONEY

1

Orlando said, "I run into Ricardo Morales."

"Yeah?"

"Yeah. We had breakfast at Isabelita's."

I could tell from his face he was already into something, but I didn't say nothing.

"So like I asked him what's happening, and you know Ricardo. Jesus. That guy never stops."

I waited some more.

"That guy. He's always got something going down. And I figured you might be interested in this one."

"Then you figured wrong."

"No, wait a minute."

"For Christ's sake, Orlando," I said. "How many times do we got to go through this? Hang out with him? Sure. Do business with him? No. Not with *his* connections."

"No, listen," he said. "No deals, Georgie. This is political."

I looked at him. Orlando had been a cop in Cuba before coming to Miami. He had fought in the underground against Castro, and liked to think of himself as a patriot. Morales was no Flagler Street commando either. He worked for the CIA.

"Political?"

"Yeah," said Orlando. "Some guys showed up. Ricardo says they're here to make trouble."

That was different. I'm not political, and ordinarily I don't have time for "the cause" and all that bullshit. Dealing dope is a hard enough game as it is. But I was still waiting for my godfather to come up with another connection. It had been a quiet summer. And I don't like terrorists.

"So what's he want to do? Blow them away?"

Orlando just smiled.

"Okay," I said. "So he wants to blow away a couple of scumbags. That's fine with me. Basically, I like the idea. But I'm not going on no suicide mission. I want to know what I'm getting into."

That night, I dropped Anna off at her sister's and went on over to see Ricardo at Orlando's house.

Orlando had latched on to us a couple of months before this. He was out on bond. The vice squad had busted him on the corner of SW 8th Street and 18th Avenue with a little marijuana in his pocket. Every morning, nine o'clock, you could find him there. They used to call him the "Mayor." But he was strictly a nickel-and-dime operator, and I think he'd heard rumors of the multi-kilo deals my godfather and me had been putting together in New York. Anyway, I liked the guy, and as me and Anna were staying away from the corner, too, we teamed up to kill a little time, just riding around and going to the movies.

I met his friend Ricardo soon after, although I knew him already by reputation. Everybody in Little Havana knew Ricardo Morales. If Orlando Lamadrid was the neighborhood gorilla, Ricardo was the Man. One time he blew away some guy at the corner of Flagler and SW 7th Avenue with a submachine gun and silencer—it was the talk of the neighborhood. Just waited for the son of a bitch to come down the steps from his apartment, and cut loose on his ass in front of ten or twelve witnesses. Then he tossed the gun in his car and drove off. And right behind him went a green Plymouth with two guys in it, wearing suits and ties.

They followed him around a lot, those guys—I saw them. They looked like government issue, but nobody said nothing, nobody knew nothing. Ricardo had a lot of shoot-outs like that in Miami, but the cops never bothered him, and I never saw nothing about it in the newspapers. It was political. And that's what made him so powerful. Those suck-ass punks who hung around on the corner were all afraid of him. "Oh, shit," they'd say. "Here comes Ricardo."

He even looked like a cop. Strong. Stocky. Clean-shaven. Short black hair. He'd stand there in his Cuban shirt, with that goddamn 9mm. Browning in his waistband bulging it out, and they'd sidle up to him with a chicken-shit grin: "Wanna smoke, Ricardo? Wanna snort of coke, Ricardo?" Anything to keep him on your side.

He loved coke. One reason he was over at Orlando's house so much was because Orlando always gave him a spoon when he had some. "Here, Ricardo. Here's a little treat for you." And that son of a bitch would pull out his car key, stand in front of the mirror, and take two big snorts. Boom! Boom! Then wait a second and do it again. Jesus. Me and Orlando told him one time, "You know, Ricardo, you're a fucking savage." He'd be high as a dog—ready to kill anybody with that goddamn cannon of his.

After I got to know him better, he offered to give me one just like it. Fourteen shot. Nice weapon. But I didn't trust him, not the way Orlando did. "Screw you," I said. "Why would *I* want a piece like that? You probably blew somebody away with it anyhow." He laughed.

Ricardo was always into something. Second or third time we met, he told us about this guy he knew over in Miami Beach who was in the jewelry business and who ran around with about $40,000 worth of stuff in the trunk of his car. Ricardo wanted me to hotwire the car while they kept lookout, and take it some place quiet so we could take our time busting into it. I had mixed feelings about the deal, and in the end said no.

Another time, me and Anna were over at *his* house, and he suddenly pulls out an ounce of cocaine wrapped up in a plastic bag and gives it to Orlando.

"Here," he says. "I want you to move it for me. I paid three-fifty. We'll split whatever you make on it."

That rattled me. I figured Orlando had told him I'd moved X amount of kilos in New York, and the son of a bitch was trying to whet my appetite. But I didn't say a goddamn word. I just stood there and looked at it. I couldn't show I didn't trust him.

I couldn't walk out or nothing, although the stuff wasn't worth a damn anyway. It was all wet and shitty.

On the way home, I said to Orlando, "You know, you're a little open with this guy. You want to be careful."

"Listen," he said. "I know Ricardo thirteen years. He's my friend. I trust him with my life."

"Suit yourself. Only don't trust him with *my* life. Just leave me out of it, okay? Don't even talk to him about me."

"Ah, Georgie, you don't understand. You talk like he's a cop or something."

"Well, goddamn it, Orlando. He told us he worked for the CIA."

"So? He does what they want, and they leave him alone. What do they care if he deals a little dope? So what? They're going to lose a good man because he buys an ounce of coke? Shit. He's in tight with these people."

"Fine," I said. "But he still works for the government. And you don't. Maybe Ricardo can deal dope, but that don't mean *you* can."

Politics, though, was something else. I could sit and listen to Ricardo all night while he told us about the time the CIA parachuted him into the Congo, and about what was going on in Chile under Allende. He traveled a lot in Central and South America. At his house once, he showed us a bunch of passports he had in different names from different countries—he was full of that James Bond bullshit, and I ate it up. I admired the guy for what he stood for. Blow away Communists? Terrorists? Hey, I'm a hundred percent for you. And I told him so that night when I went over to Orlando's to hear what he had in mind.

"Okay," he says. "This is what's happening. There's these three or four guys who just got in, and they're here to make trouble. They want to hit a few big people on our side and make it look like some other group in the underground did it. I got solid information on that. So I been asked to take care of it—and quick. Before they make their move."

"That's it?"

"That's it," he says. "That's all I can tell you."

I loved it. "You know these people? I mean, you know what they look like?"

"I know them," he says. "But no names, okay?"

"Okay. So what have we got to do?"

"Well, I guess we'll have to take a run by and dust them off."

"Fantastic. And how are we going to go about this?"

"Oh, nothing fancy," he says. "We'll go look for them. Orlando keeps telling me you're a great wheelman, so you drive, and me and Orlando'll cut loose on their ass. First crack we get, we'll dump them right there."

"Fantastic. I'm ready."

"How about you, Orlando?" he says.

"You know me, Ricardo," he says. "Just show me where they're at."

"Okay. Then what about a weapon? You got a preference?"

"How about an Armalite?"

"I don't know," Ricardo says. "Depends what they got. If I can't get that, how about an M-16?"

"Sure."

"I'll bring something for you, too," he says, looking at me. "Just in case."

"Fine." And now I got butterflies. "When are we going to do this?"

"I'll be in touch," he says. "In a couple of days."

They were a long two days. If the hit had been in the line of business, I wouldn't have thought nothing of it, but this was political. If you're a Cuban in Miami, you're at war. You got to be on one side or the other, and I'd just been drafted. It's not every day you go out to shoot somebody you don't even know, and Anna saw the tension building up.

"What are you two so jumpy about?" she said.

"Nothing." I gave Orlando a warning look. "We're trying to get a deal together. We been idle a long time. You know how it is."

That satisfied her. When we heard the hit was set for Friday night and I told her we had to go out, she didn't bat an eye. She just asked me to drive her over to her sister's first.

I got to Orlando's house at about eight o'clock. He lived on SW 27th Lane, in a real dark neighborhood, and I stood outside for a minute wondering what they would say if I backed off now. There was no way I was going to do that, of course, but I'd broken a rule. I was sticking my neck out for no reason. I wasn't scared or nothing—I liked feeling keyed-up and ready to turn on a dime. But I was just indulging myself. It was unprofessional.

Orlando let me in, and we waited a few minutes, not saying much. When Ricardo arrived, he wasn't too talkative neither.

"Okay," he says. "Let's go."

On the street was a green 1970 Plymouth, like the one the two guys used when they followed him around. It could even have been the same car—two-door, no whitewalls, no extras.

"You ride in the back," he tells Orlando. "Your piece is on the floor. And use the gloves."

His own weapon was in front, propped up on the transmission hump. An M-16. Until now, I'd only seen pictures of them, but Orlando had obviously handled one before. I heard him working it as I got in behind the wheel.

"Hey," he says. "Silencers, too? Very nice."

"Sure," says Ricardo. "We're not going to make no noise." He hands me a pair of cotton gloves. "Look under your seat," he says. "And put these on when the time comes."

I'm not about to touch anything I don't have to, so I reach under the seat with the gloves in my hand and pull out some kind of machine pistol with a banana-shaped clip and a skeleton shoulder butt.

"Okay?" he says. "It's .30 caliber, and set to automatic. If you get the chance, just pull that lever on the side there and plug away at the mother-fuckers."

"Great," I says, and I push it back under. "Only one problem. How the hell do I do that when I'm driving?"

"Listen, you can't tell. They could shoot back. We could have a wreck. Who knows what can happen?"

That was just what I wanted to hear.

"And that reminds me," he says. "I brought along a couple of .45s as well. Just in case."

"Then let's get on with it," says Orlando.

"Wait a minute."

I already had my handkerchief out, and now I wind down the window with it and wipe off the outside door handle. If there's going to be a wreck, they may find my corpse in it, but they're not going to find any goddamn fingerprints. Then I start the car, still using the handkerchief, and put it in drive the same way.

"Okay," I says. "Now I'm ready." I leave the handkerchief in my lap, to wipe the wheel as I go. "Where to?"

"Make it over to Flagler," Ricardo says. "And when you get there, hang a left."

So we drive uptown on Flagler. Nobody's talking, and I'm trying to look casual, like we're out for a ride. I'm also staying in the middle of the street so nobody can look in and maybe see all that goddamn artillery.

The steering wheel bothers me. I can't keep wiping it all the time. That's just as suspicious as driving in gloves.

"Hang a right," says Ricardo, as we reach 32nd Avenue. And then, a block later, he says, "Now hang a left, and keep going steady."

Suddenly my heart is sounding noisy. We're in a tight little residential section now. Not much light on the street, and quiet. Nobody about.

Then he leans forward quickly to check out a house. It's just an ordinary, one-story house with a porch and a fence, but my balls wrinkle up to my chin. I hear Orlando's gun clink against something, so I guess he's feeling the tension too.

Now Ricardo sits back, and shakes his head. He don't say nothing, so I breathe out and keep on going.

At 37th Avenue, he tells me to hang a left, then a right a couple of blocks later, and we're heading uptown again on Flagler. Still not a word, except for the directions he's giving me.

"Take 52nd," he says.

I make the left up by the cemetery and carry on over to 4th Street, where we make a couple more turns and wind up on 53rd Avenue. It's another dark, quiet residential neighborhood, mostly one- or two-family homes with an occasional apartment building here and there. I keep looking at him out of the corner of my eye so he won't catch me by surprise, but sure enough, he does it again. He suddenly leans forward, and my heart jumps up.

"This is it," he says. "Keep on going."

It's just another one-story house, with a few steps up to a verandah along the front. There are lights on in the front room, and a car standing in the driveway.

"Okay," says Ricardo. "Go around and come back down the street behind the house. Go on for a couple of blocks, then come around on 53rd again. We'll make another pass. And this time we'll let the sons of bitches know we're here. Right, Orlando?"

"Right," he says, and starts winding down all the windows.

So I do like he tells me. Now it's begun, I've cooled right out. I put the gloves on and really scrub at that goddamn wheel with my handkerchief, remembering to put it in my pocket afterwards, so that if anything does go wrong, I won't leave nothing lying around.

At the last corner before turning back on 53rd, I wait to let another car go by, then ease around and move her up real steady. As we get near, it goes very quiet. Ricardo and Orlando cuddle their guns, and brace their feet against the car. Now here we are again . . . There's the house, just like it was before—and nothing happens.

"Shit," says Ricardo, as we roll on by.

"What's the matter?"

"Take the gloves off," he says. "We got to take a little ride."

This time, we come out on 8th Street, and he tells me to stop at a pay phone. As he gets out, I twist around to look at Orlando, but he just shakes his head. He's got nothing to say. So I watch

Ricardo. He gets through right away, talks fast for maybe fifteen, twenty seconds, then listens, butting in a couple of times, and winds up nodding his head a lot.

"Okay," he says, as he gets in beside me. "We'll give it another try. Hang a left, and put 'em on."

I go around again, and once more we're on 53rd, a few blocks below the house.

"Here we go," he says. "Last time, you went by a little fast. This time, I want you to go real slow. Take your foot off the gas, and just let her roll—okay?"

"Okay."

"Then take your piece and put it next to you."

The house is in the middle of the block. As we reach the corner, he says, "Okay. Slow down. You ready, Orlando?"

"Ready."

I see a guy standing at the window with the light behind him, and one out on the verandah by the door. Then they see us—I still got my lights on—and that's when Ricardo and Orlando cut loose on them.

Not much noise. Just squirts and chatter as the shells fly out. But them goddamn bullets are lashing that place apart. I hear them smacking into the walls and roof and banging through the car on the driveway. I hear the windows go where the guy was standing. I don't see him fall, but they're just pecking that house to pieces.

"Now hit it," Ricardo says, and I tramp on the gas—not burning tires or nothing, but hard enough to get us out of there fast. We're headed for 8th Street.

"Don't hit the intersection," he says. "Hang a left at 6th."

I see what he means. If we go barreling onto 8th, we could draw a lot of attention—that's U.S. 41, a main drag—but 6th is again a nice quiet residential street.

So I pushed it on down to about 48th Avenue, and then he says, "Okay. That's far enough. Ease off." And a block later he tells me to stop.

"You did good," he says. "Just leave everything in the car."

I don't know what to say. "That's it?"

"That's it. Catch yourselves a ride home."

I can't believe it. After what we just done together, he's going to dump us in the middle of no place? Me and Orlando get out without a word. I don't know about him, but my knees feel loose, like I just run five miles.

Ricardo slides over behind the wheel, and gives us a nod. "See you around," he says, and he drives off.

So me and Orlando started walking, and in the end walked all the way back to our own neighborhood. I didn't want no taxi or bus driver remembering later how he picked up two guys near the time and place of a big shooting. And I don't think we said more than ten words the whole way. In fact, I don't remember discussing what happened that night with Orlando or anybody. What was I going to say? Do you suppose we killed them? So some joker could overhear us?

There was nothing in the newspapers next day, or on the radio, and nothing in the days after that, which didn't surprise me. But there was no talk on the street either, like there always is after a shooting, and that *was* unusual. The only thing I ever heard was about a month later, when I run into a guy on the corner who always seemed to know a lot about Ricardo. I think he was one of his informers.

"Hey, Georgie," he says. "I hear Ricardo Morales had another one of his little escapades. Up by 50th Avenue somewhere. Shot the shit out of some house."

"You don't say."

"Yeah," he says. "Fucking guy never quits."

By that time, I was into something else, and it didn't bother me. Anna and me had other things to think about, like the money running out.

But then, that was about to turn around, too. Although I didn't know it, my godfather had just found himself a Venezuelan connection, and was getting in tight with Frank Matthews, the biggest goddamn dope dealer in the history of the world.

2

At the time of the shooting, which was in late September 1971, George Ramos was twenty years old. His girlfriend, Anna Gloria Pineiro Hernandez, was eighteen and going to Miami–Dade Junior College.

Unlike Anna, who was nine when she came to Miami with her father and sisters in 1962, leaving her mother behind in a Cuban prison, George had been born and bred in the United States. Though his parents came from Cuba, they had settled in Washington, D.C., years before the revolution.

His family lived there in a rambling old house presided over by his grandmother Carrie. Raised in New York City, she had gone to Havana at eighteen to marry a Cuban, by whom she had a daughter, Margarita, George's mother, and two sons, Uncles Francisco and José Daniel, but as the years went by, Carrie found the confines of a traditional Spanish marriage increasingly irksome. Reasserting her Yankee independence, which her husband found equally unendurable, she persuaded him at last to give her a divorce and returned with her three children to the United States, where she married an Irish short-order cook named Wilson Ziegler. They made their home in the middle of Washington's small Spanish-speaking community, and there they all lived together—grandparents, the two uncles, Margarita and her husband, and, eventually, George.

Before his first birthday, however, George's parents split up. His father's amorous eye had wandered once too often, and Margarita divorced him, preferring that to her brothers' solution, which was sudden widowhood. This left George fatherless at a critical moment in the life of a young Catholic, but a friend of his Uncle Francisco's now stepped into the breach.

"The kid's got no father," said Miguel Garcia-Montalvo. "Let *me* baptize him. I'll be his godfather."

The family agreed, though not without misgivings. Uncle Francisco was the wild one. Ten years later, he would go off to fight at the Bay of Pigs. And while his instincts were adventurous rather than criminal, as a young man he ran around in dubious company, none more so than George's new godfather. At nineteen, Miguel Garcia, Mikey, had already earned a reputation as a hell-raiser, and shown promise of a substantial police record.

Still, there was no doubting his fondness for young George, and soon after the baptism, he also provided him with a stepfather, in the person of Alberto Dominguez, a friend of his from childhood. Known in Cuba as El Artista, for his artistry at third base, Dominguez stopped off to see Garcia on his way to Rochester, New York, to join the farm club of the New York Yankees. He took one look at Margarita and never made it past Washington. They were married soon after.

Though Dominguez was rather less enchanted with the idea of a stepson, the family held together under the same roof until George was five. In 1956, however, Uncle Francisco went down to Miami with Miguel Garcia and came back starry-eyed.

"Hey!" he said. "I found paradise. Pretty town. Pretty weather. Lots of our people. We got to move there."

And move there they did, although not as one household. Margarita was now pregnant with George's half sister, and as her husband was still none too pleased to be raising somebody else's child, it was decided that George should in future live with his grandmother. This made everyone happy. Though Carrie had resigned herself to the idea of separate homes in Miami, now that her children had families of their own, she had not relished the prospect of parting with her grandson, nor he with her. And as it turned out, George's separation from his mother was purely nominal. Margarita and Carrie never lived more than a few minutes apart while he was growing up, and he slept over at his mother's house almost as often as he slept at home.

If not paradise, life in Miami was pretty good. They were not rich—everybody who could, including Carrie and Grandfather Wilson, went to work every day—but they had all they needed: an unassuming but comfortable home in a decent neighborhood; an old but serviceable car; a stereo set and, eventually, a color TV—the first on the block. When he had occasion to, Uncle Francisco would stand in as father for George, sternly denying him the liberties he had always allowed himself, and so, when he was around, did Miguel Garcia, although he construed his duties as godparent rather more indulgently.

George still remembers the two of them taking him out on Sundays when he was five or six to watch the planes come and go at the airport because Garcia would usually sit him on his knee behind the wheel and let him "drive." Indeed, except for this connection with his godfather, whose appearances in Miami became less frequent anyway as the law and other exigencies in a burglar's life made greater demands on his time, they were in most respects a fairly typical American family—honest, hard-working, respectable, and determined to do the best they could for their children.

In 1957, George was enrolled in Shenandoah Elementary School, where, as he puts it, he "won all the marbles." He was a good student and, as he grew older, an even better athlete, showing great promise as a quarterback and also in baseball, which delighted his Uncle José Daniel, the conservative one, who had played ball in Cuba with Chuck Connors. When he moved up to Shenandoah Junior High in 1965, George was good enough to make the football squad in his first year, and more than one high school coach made his way over to the house during that season with the idea of setting him up in the game as a career. But in 1966, in eighth grade, he dropped out.

The immediate cause was his grandmother Carrie, although no one was more distressed than she when he told her he was through with school. Since moving to Miami, she had worked in a meat-packing plant to supplement her husband's meager pay as a breakfast cook, but now her heart was giving her trouble.

"Listen, I'll finish school at night," George promised her, and he even meant it at the time. "Right now, let's worry about your health. I'm going to get a job."

His concern was entirely genuine, but not entirely disinterested. Physically, he had matured early. At fifteen, he was as tall, strong, and lustful as any of the eighteen- and nineteen-year-olds he hung around with on the corner after school. The only difference between them was that they had money in their pockets to finance their interest in girls, and he had none. Not that he was doing too badly without it. Lean and dark, with soulful brown eyes, he already looked like a junior edition of Omar Sharif. But he was also passionate on the related subject of cars, and determined to buy himself a suitable set of wheels. Accordingly, he went to work as a busboy in the Coronet Hotel in Miami Beach, where he averaged about $150 a week during the season.

Once he saw what money could do, he never did finish school. Rich people stayed at plush resorts, wore good clothes, and left half-eaten steaks on the table. They drove around in Cadillacs or Lincolns, had diamond rings, and could be induced to tip a busboy $10 without thinking anything of it. He liked that. He also liked to wheel and deal, as busboys must, and to defend his interests against all comers.

Having started out in a kosher hotel, George made it a rule never to work American-plan. At places like the Coronet and the Waldman, he served the same twenty-eight or thirty guests all week, which gave him plenty of time to impress them with his dedication to their comfort. The standard weekly tip was then $3 a couple. If he ever got less than $5, it was a considerable blow to his pride.

This did not always endear him to his colleagues. Part of his secret was to get in early and be prepared. If he knew he would need thirty cups, saucers, and spoons, for example, he lined them up in advance, so that no one at any of his tables need ever be kept waiting. But sooner or later, there was always at least one busboy who, partly from laziness, and partly to put one over on the hot-shot, would help himself to George's cups while his back was turned, and George naturally resented this. As he usually made his displeasure felt—on one occasion with a chair when the offender came back at him with a knife—George invariably earned a reputation for brawling, and never once managed to work a whole season through at any one hotel, either in Miami Beach or in the Catskills, to which he migrated in the summer.

Always a quick study, he had the measure of every seedy wrinkle in the hotel trade by the time he was seventeen. Now and again, he worked as a waiter, but on the whole preferred being a busboy. The job was easier, and the money almost as good—at least, the way *he* ran a station. By now he was making around $180 a week, and without resort to the petty cheating and thievery that went on in most dining rooms. He was not puritanical about it. He was simply clear in his mind that if he *were* to cross the line, it was not going to be for the few dollars he could make stealing food from the kitchen or pocketing a gold cigarette lighter left on a table. It would have to be for something big. Indeed, his whole attitude toward the hotel business had changed. There was nothing wrong with it, provided you owned the hotel.

Sam Cohen was responsible for that—the multimillionaire hotelier who owned several of the resort palaces strung along the ocean front. He took a liking to George, the whirlwind busboy, and often detained him at his table to talk football.

One morning, after chatting for a few minutes, he said: "Sit down and have a cup of coffee with me."

George stared. "I can't do that," he said.

Cohen leaned back in his chair and smiled. "Says who?"

That was when George saw the light. They talked for an hour about the Green Bay Packers and the state of the hotel trade, and when Cohen at last had to go, George walked him to the door and saw him off in his red Cadillac.

He now had a lot to think about. Besides age and experience, what set Sam Cohen apart, along with many of the people George waited on, was money and connections. They weren't any smarter than he was. Or more honest. The difference was money. That was what counted in this world. In the end, it all came down to the matter of hard cash. And he no longer had to mix with rich people in Miami Beach to see that. It was happening right under his nose in his own neighborhood.

In two or three years, starting from around 1965, Miami had become the principal port of entry for the marijuana trade. As importers found it more and more difficult to move really substantial loads over the Mexican border, they took to running them across the Gulf by boat and landing them in southern Florida, whose coastline was not only impossible to police but a mere 1,200 miles south of their richest market. Before long, George and his friends on the corner of SW 8th Street and 18th Avenue were counting the black Cadillacs with New York plates they saw go by, and measuring themselves against the guys inside, looking out in their $300 suits.

Until then, the only serious problem in Little Havana had been politics. Fed by the twin arteries of Flagler and 8th, it was a pleasant, quiet, averagely prosperous section of one- or two-story homes, neither old nor new but mostly well kept, and comfortably set about with shade trees and small palms. It was a subtropical suburb, owing its grid of respectable, grass-verged streets to its northern developers, and its green, white, and pink stucco to their Latin successors. The people who lived there were industrious, self-respecting, and knew at heart they had come to stay, so that within a few years they had re-created most of the circumstances they were used to.

By the late sixties, native Miamians were beginning to feel like tourists in their own city. The only signs in English to be seen in Little Havana were those put up by the Highways Department. Every day on Flagler or Calle Ocho, the old men sunned themselves on benches or played dominoes under the trees; the younger ones talked business or girls at street corners, sipping syrupy black coffee from tiny paper cups, while the women haggled and gossiped their way from *carnicería* to *frutería* to *especiería,* spending half their time shopping for food and the other half cooking it. Miami's Cuban community, growing larger with every plane or boat that put in from the south, had become a complete working transplant.

With the drug boom, however, the neighborhood changed. Once the nation's marijuana supply started to hit Miami first, a lot of it stuck, siphoned off by local dealers who now turned Little Havana into a wholesale distribution center, attracting buyers from all over the country. And not just buyers, but also the usual riffraff who always go where the hot money is.

It was a disturbing time for George. The first Cubans attracted into the drug business, people he knew, were making fortunes for themselves. In a matter of weeks sometimes, they would graduate from roach-trap apartments to $75,000 houses with swimming pools, and break out in a rash of silk shirts and diamond pinky rings. In his free time, he would hang around the bars and restaurants they patronized, contrasting their sudden wealth with his $180 a week, and seriously considering the possibility of a little dealing on his own. There was always a stray swinger at the hotel looking to make a connection. But, in the end, George always resisted the temptation. He had known people go down for five years for dealing a pound of marijuana and others cop the same for dealing 500 pounds. He had made up his mind that if they were ever to catch *him* with anything, it would be with a lot.

Meanwhile, the Miami police were doing little to win hearts and minds. Reacting predictably to the increase in drug trafficking, they came down hot and heavy on everyone they caught in periodic sweeps of the neighborhood. For dealer and bystander alike, it would be, "Freeze!" Then, "Up against the wall."

This happened to George. It not merely confirmed the normal teenage view of cops as the natural enemy but aggravated a real sense of injustice. Here he was, taking particular pains to stay out of trouble, and here *they* were, rousting him about, taking his name, and generally treating him like a common criminal. It need only happen a couple of times and next thing he knew he'd be as hot as a firecracker—without ever having earned an illegal penny to justify it.

But if still not ready to break the law, he was certainly willing to thwart it. As the corner of 8th Street and 18th Avenue was to the neighborhood, so the Yumuri Restaurant was to the corner—at the heart of the social and business life of the wise-guy fraternity. Then owned and run by an accommodating saloonkeeper who installed a pool table in the back room and seemed not to notice the card playing that went on there day and night, the Yumuri was headquarters for Herman Lamazares, one of the first big-shots to surface in the so-called Cuban Mafia. With his partner, Eugenio Repol, he ran a flourishing cocaine and marijuana business, shipping top-quality grass up to New York and elsewhere in loads of 2,000–3,000 pounds at a time.

Admiring their style, George often hung around the Yumuri, at some risk of bodily harm from Uncle Francisco, who still demanded that his nephew do as he told him, not do as he did. After repeated warnings, he caught George in the back room one day and cuffed him about severely. Deterred to the extent that he afterwards took good care to establish that his uncle was busy some place else before going there, George was watching Lamazares play cards one night when a lookout burst in from the bar to warn them of a raid.

As one man, players and kibitzers rose to their feet and fled through the back door, abandoning the money on the tables, samples of grass, foil-wrapped packets of cocaine, two guns, and George, who hated to be stampeded into anything by anybody, least of all by the cops. Without knowing quite why he did it, he gathered up the money, took one of the guns, and followed the others at a walk, breaking into a run only when the police started to batter through the door from the bar. They had not seen fit to cover the back of the building, however, and he escaped easily into the darkness. After stashing the money and the gun in a hollow tree near Shenandoah Junior High, he went home to his grandmother.

Next evening, he wrapped the gun and the money, some $1,800, in a plastic bag to keep them dry, returned the package to the tree, and went to look for Lamazares. But several days went by before he at last spotted him in his familiar cowboy hat and Pontiac Bonneville, and when George explained what he had done, they arranged to meet by the school that night.

Lamazares kept the appointment with Repol, who clapped George on the shoulder and gave him $100. As he had genuinely not expected this—George had taken the money, not in anticipation of reward or to curry favor, but as a gesture of solidarity against the common enemy—he was very pleased, but Lamazares shook his head and took it back.

"Wait a minute," he said. "This is no good. Kid goes home with $100? Could be trouble."

"No, listen," said George, in pain. "I work. It won't be no surprise. I make better than $150 a week."

"Yeah?" Lamazares gave him back the $100. Then he took the plastic bag from Repol, counted out another hundred, and added it to the first. "You're a good kid," he said. "Ever you need anything, you let me know."

The older guys on the corner treated George differently after that. In the next day or two, most of them came over to pat him on the shoulder and say, "I heard."

Uncle Francisco heard too. Instead of a pat on the shoulder, he hit George between the eyes so hard he was out for ten minutes.

It was not for this reason, however, that George turned down the offers he now started to get, including one from Lamazares, who asked him to run 500 pounds of marijuana up to New York. To be a mule—a courier—in the drug trade was like being a busboy in the hotel business. Neither offered the kind of future he now saw for himself. Waiting for it did not come easily, but he knew that opportunity lay just around the corner. The word around town was that Miguel Garcia had made it big up North.

George had seen nothing of him since the early summer of 1963, the federal government having interrupted his godfather's career with concurrent seven-year sentences for smuggling cocaine and marijuana into California. Now thirty-seven, Garcia had tried his hand with varying success at most forms of criminal enterprise. Starting out like his godson as a hotel busboy, he had risen through the ranks to room-service waiter, and then to burglar after helping himself to a $7,000 tip for delivering a drink to a guest careless enough to leave his billfold on the dresser while taking a shower.

This financed his relocation in New York, where he worked for a time as a freelance enforcer for Frank Costello. But Garcia soon realized there was more money to be made from servicing heads than breaking them, and eventually moved out West to catch the first tremulous flush of Haight-Ashbury's dawn. Convinced he had found his true métier at last, he then aimed for a more substantial class of customer in Beverly Hills, and became cocaine supplier-in-chief to the resident Italian colony.

Like them, Garcia found life good but boring. To relieve the monotony, he stole $100,000 worth of jewelry from Lana Turner and took it to a fence he knew in New York from his days with Costello. Offered $40,000, take it or leave it, he took it, but not before he had the pieces copied—with a view to passing the replicas off in Mexico as the real thing and, in effect, selling the haul twice.

Never one to let time hang heavy on his hands, Garcia kept in trim with a string of upstate burglaries while waiting for the fakes to be made, and was arrested twice. Having no previous convictions of any consequence, however, he made bail on each occasion and took off with the now finished copies for Mexico. There he met up with an old friend, Hector Duarte, who promptly killed a policeman. Arrested as an accessory to murder, Garcia bought himself a head start with the fake jewels, and wound up waist-deep in the Rio Grande, caught between the Mexican police on the bank behind him and federal agents waiting on the American side to arrest him, not for jewel theft, but for dope smuggling.

Sensibly surrendering to the U.S. authorities, he spent the next four years on a post-graduate criminal course on McNeil Island, then in Lewisburg and Allenwood, Pennsylvania, from which he emerged in 1967 with a wide circle of useful friends, including Nat Elder, soon to become one of Frank Matthews's most trusted lieutenants. Three years later, when George accidentally bumped into his godfather on the corner of 18th Avenue, Garcia looked older, wiser, and *rich.*

Indeed, they were both so changed they hardly recognized each other. George had been a boy of eleven the last time they had met, and Garcia a jaunty, black-haired young man of thirty. In the interval, George had grown up, and his godfather had become the living image of Al Capone—the same height and build, the same gray hair under a light fedora, the same long vicuña top-coat, and the same scar, from his left cheekbone to the corner of his mouth. The eyes had changed, too. An even paler green than George remembered, they were quite devoid of feeling, or even of interest in what they saw.

Miguel Garcia had done "hard time" in federal prison, and learned never to give his enemies a second chance. The convict who had opened his face with a knife during a yard brawl was first punished by having his buttocks cut off and then shot dead within days of his release. But there was no doubting the pleasure Garcia took in rediscovering his godson after eight years, and George realized that his moment had come. Not that his godfather seemed especially anxious to encourage him.

"Listen," he said. "What's the matter with you? You're working. Making good money. Drugs is a rough game. You don't need it."

George had heard all that from his uncles.

"*I'll* tell you what I don't need," he said. "I don't need nobody to tell me what I don't need. I stayed out because none of these people got anything to offer worth my while. But I'm going in when the time comes; you can make book on that."

"You're going to ruin your goddamn life, that's what you're going to do."

"Yeah? Well, first I'm going to ruin it with a nice home, and a halfway decent set of wheels, and maybe a couple of suits as good as yours, and then I'll worry about the rest later."

"Listen, your Uncle Francisco heard you talk like that, he'd put a dent in your ass. And mine, too."

"Come on, Miguel. What do you say?"

"I say you're crazy. You don't know what you're getting into. You want money? I'll give you money. It's worth it to me, just to keep your uncle off my back. How much you need? Fifteen thousand? Twenty? You figure it out and tell me."

"Jesus." George hardly hesitated. "You think I'm looking for a goddamn handout? Forget it. Don't give me nothing. I got hands. I just figured it would be good to go in with you, but you don't want me? Okay. Sooner or later, that offer's going to come around. And you better believe I'm going to take it."

His godfather wavered. "Fucking kids," he grumbled.

George waited expectantly.

"Well, if you're prone to do it," Garcia said, aiming a good-humored slap at his godson's head, "then I guess I got no choice. I got to play fucking nursemaid."

"Listen, I can take care of myself." George countered happily with a playful left jab. "And take care of you, too, if I have to."

That was in March 1970. Two months later, the Miami hotel season ended, and George went North as usual—not, as his family assumed, to find work in the Catskill resorts, but to seek his fortune in the drug trade.

3

My godfather had been making a hellatious amount of money. His two Chileans brought him about 10 kilos of cocaine every fifteen days. He paid them $4,000 a kilo—that's about 35 ounces. Then he'd cut the stuff one-on-one to make it 20 kilos, and move the whole load at $9,500 or $10,000 a crack. In other words, he'd lay out $40,000 to get back maybe $200,000, and, after paying expenses, show a profit of around $150,000. Every fifteen days.

Nice little business. And no trouble. His Chileans delivered in New York. He had a couple of wholesalers who took all he could get them. And he didn't even have to use his own money. Zack Robinson, a big black dealer in New York, was fronting the cash to pay off the Chileans. So, no doubt about it—Mikey was doing good.

He was living up at Riverdale, in the Bronx. 2400 Johnson Avenue. A blue building. Apartment 5K. And when I walked in, I just stopped and took a gulp of breath. I mean, my hands really shook, because this was what I'd come for.

He had a suit of Spanish armor in the hallway, and the red carpet was over my ankles. Beautiful. The living room was red, too. Red drapes at the window, lined in white, and pulled back with silk ropes, so you could see this fabulous view across the Hudson River. Big red sofa, curving around two walls, and covered in round cushions. Long oak table, Spanish-style, like the rest of the furniture. Fantastic stereo set. Exquisite paintings on the walls.

"This one is from Madison Avenue," he said. "Cost me $4,000. That one was $3,000. And you see them flowers? Fifty bucks. They come in every day and change them. Fifty bucks a crack."

"Man," I said, "you're living like Caesar."

And he was. Off to the side was the dining room, with a balcony, and a beautiful crystal chandelier over the table, and a French lace tablecloth and everything. Fabulous. So was the bedroom. His wife, Barbara—we always called her Barbara, but her real name was Raquel Maisonet—she made him buy a four-poster bed with like a canopy on top. And the bathrooms were all white marble with black in it. Big bathrooms, with dressing rooms leading off. Hers was pink and his was blue. All the towels and sheets had his initials on them, and so did the glass doors of the showers. Engraved right into the glass there, in a beautiful design. Exquisite taste, no doubt about it. He must have had $100,000 tied up in that place, not counting his clothes. That's what captured me—his wardrobe. There was a walk-in closet, about 15 feet long, with maybe thirty custom-made suits hanging there. Drawers full of shirts. Every color. Whatever you could dream of. And on the other side, his sports attire. His light sweaters, his hats—it was ultra-fantastic. You could not live any better.

Their daughter, Vicky, who was just a little kid and cute as hell, slept in the other bedroom with the Dominican maid. It was pink in there, too. I found out when I told my godfather I had no place to stay. He told the maid to go find herself a bed some place else for the next few nights so I could bunk in with Vicky, and that's what I did. The kid had taken a liking to me, and we had some good times together in there. I baby-sat with her when they went out.

During the day, I looked for an apartment. Mikey was giving me no more arguments about jumping the fence. He'd warned me, and I guess he figured I was old enough to know my mind. The first night I was there, he filled me in on what he wanted me to do.

"Look," he said. "You're new up here. Nobody knows you—and that's good. I got a lot of stuff spread around with people I can't trust like I trust you, okay? So here's what you're going to do. You're going to rent an apartment in a nice quiet neighborhood, and you're going to service my stash."

"Sure, Mikey. Anything you say."

"You'll work directly for me, understand? You'll get to know a few people, but don't tell nobody what you're doing. Don't ask no questions, and don't answer none. You see me out on the street, you walk right by me."

"Guess I can handle that," I said, and I was kind of disappointed. Didn't sound like much.

"Listen," he said. "You got a lot to learn. You're a young kid. Do this right, and you can make yourself a couple of hundred thousand dollars in no time."

I felt better right away. Three or four days later, I found the perfect place on 196th Street, right off Broadway and a few blocks down the hill from the subway at Dyckman Street. It was a two-bedroom apartment unfurnished, for $125 a month. I told the guy I was up in New York looking for a place big enough for me and my mother, who was going to join me later. So I went out, bought a bed, a TV set, a folding aluminum table, and a six-pack, and moved in.

That night, my godfather drove over with a suitcase full of the tools of his trade. We unpacked a gram scale, a couple of close-mesh strainers, some measuring spoons, plastic paddles, bowls and other little utensils, a roll of aluminum foil, a bunch of plastic bags, and a Sears bag-sealer—the kind you plug into the wall and use for bagging up stuff for the freezer. He set all this up on the folding table and unloaded a few cans of lactose into the closet.

"What's that for?" I said. "To mix it up with?"

"I'll show you tomorrow," he said. "Don't go out. I'll be over to pick you up sometime. I don't exactly know when."

So back he came next afternoon, and we drove over to 176th Street and St. Nicholas. There's a little park around in there some place, right next to a swimming pool, and that's where we meet Frank Gregory. Frank's working for my godfather. He's a Puerto Rican, and a noble guy. We get to know each other pretty good. Anyway, he points out this bearded creep sitting on a bench.

"Okay," Mikey says. He goes over to talk to the guy, who gives him a little brown paper bag, and takes off. Mikey comes back and hands me the bag.

"Frank will drive you," he says. "Take this home and stash it. Stay there. I'll see you later."

On the way back, I'm remembering what my godfather said about not asking questions, and Frank's just eyeing me, so it's a pretty quiet trip. I carry the stuff upstairs like it's an egg salad on rye, and lock myself in there with a half key of coke. 500 grams. And now I got nothing to do but wait.

He shows up just as the Mets are blowing their lead in the top of the ninth in a night game out at Shea, and I turn off the TV.

"Okay," he says. "I want to teach you how to fool with this stuff, because that's what you're going to be doing for me."

He cuts open the bag of coke and spills a little bit out on the table.

"Now let's say you don't know where the stuff is coming from," he says, "and you want to check it out. What do you do? You got your tongue, but that don't tell you much. You got your eye—the real stuff shines in the light. See that? If they stepped on it already, the shit they cut it with *don't* shine. But you still need more, so let me show you a couple of real easy tests you can try."

He takes a glass of water and drops in a pinch of the stuff.

"Now watch," he says. "The pure coke falls through. It dissolves, and the shit stays on top. Gives you an idea how much they hit it already."

"Looks pretty good to me," I says.

And he says, "Right. Here's another one. Put a bit in the palm of your hand and rub it. When it's moist, coke goes clear and gooey. Like that. The rest stays the way it is. So now you compare the clear stuff with the white specks in there with it, and you can more or less tell what percentage it's been cut to. Not exactly, of course, but it gives you an idea."

"Okay," I says. "It still looks good."

"Yeah. But here's a way to make sure."

He puts another pinch of the stuff on a piece of tinfoil and heats it from underneath with a match.

"Don't burn it," he tells me. "Just warm it gently, like this.

The coke'll fume right off and leave a stain, see? With pure coke, it's a very light yellow. So the darker the stain, the harder they've stepped on it. Simple, right? Believe me, there's a hell of a lot of people don't know."

"Well, *that's* a light yellow."

"Yeah, not bad," he says. "I seen better, but I figure we can hit this one-on-one. Make it a full kilo."

And he shows me how to do it. First, we empty out the coke on the table and spread it around with a piece of plastic. Then he gets me to pick out the rocks—lumps of solid cocaine—and put them aside in a bowl. Next, we weigh out an equal amount of lactose, 500 grams, sprinkle it on top of the spread-out cocaine, and now comes the mixing. We flip it over and over with the plastic paddles. Heap it up. Cut it up. Spread it out again. Then over and over, mixing it up good.

"Okay," he says. "Now take a couple of those big rocks and rub them through the strainer. Dust them over the mixture. And keep it low, so you don't lose none. That's pure stuff."

So I do that, stir again, dust the mixture with the other big rocks, and stir some more.

"Now just throw those little rocks back in there and spread them around even," he tells me. "Customers go crazy over rocks. They figure that's proof it's dynamite stuff."

And now we're finished. We bag the mixture up as two half kilos and seal them off with the bag-sealer. That's not just to keep the moisture out. It impresses the dealers, even those who ought to know better. They see a sealed bag and think it comes like that from South America. When they find out later the stuff's been cut, they figure the Indians did it. To them, Mikey's just the middle man, turning the stuff over as it comes, for a quick profit. And they don't care, anyway. There's enough money in this for everybody.

"Okay," he says. "Now you know what you got there? That's $10,000—to *us*. To the dealer? Forget it. Man, if he sells that stuff in ounces just the way it is, he can get $50,000 for it easy. But he's not going to. He's going to cut that shit another two, three times. He's going to make that one key into maybe four or five keys, and then he's going to sell it in $10 caps for $75, maybe $100 a gram. Now that's *money*. That's $300,000 at least. Maybe half a million."

"*Je*-sus."

"Yeah, well," he says. "His expenses are high. But you see what we're dealing with here. You see why we got to be a little careful."

I saw.

"So now you're looking after the stuff for me, I figure you'll need one of these," he said. He unzipped the hold-all he had with him and handed me a .38 automatic with a silencer screwed on the end. Beautiful. I always loved guns.

"Nobody's going to knock on that door except me or Frank or Barbara," he said. "If anybody else comes here, it's for one thing—to get what you're holding. If they get inside, they're going to dump you. So don't wait. Do what you got to do. Unless it's the cops, of course."

The idea didn't bother me one bit. I wasn't about to go out and shoot nobody. But someone comes around figuring to shoot *me*, or take my property, then he's a dead mother-fucker. That's all. I didn't see nothing wrong with that. That's what guns are for.

So the next night, Miguel comes around with Frank, and we drive up Bear Mountain way so I can shoot the gun and get the feel of it. And that's scary. You can't hardly hear nothing. Which is great, because if I ever have to use it in the hallway or the apartment, no noise can give me time to do a hundred things. I can hide the body in a closet. I can clean my fingerprints off everything, pack up my paraphernalia, and simply walk away.

Suddenly the gun's my best friend. After that, when I went to the door, I always had it with me. I also packed it on the street a couple of times—*without* the silencer. If you get caught with a gun in New York, well, that's not good news. But if it's got a silencer on it, then it's like goodbye for twenty years.

Anyway, for now the apartment's clean, and I got nothing to do. So most evenings I went over to Mikey's place to eat with them, and a couple of times Frank Gregory came by to pick me up for a ride around. He's a happy-go-lucky guy, about thirty years old, and I got to like him a lot. He lived up in the Bronx with his wife and three little girls, and although he had made big money with my godfather, he loved to gamble, so he was always broke. But he didn't talk about business much, and neither did Mikey. In fact, they both seemed to have a lot on their minds.

About a week later, Miguel came over to the apartment wearing a kilo of cocaine under his shirt.

"Take care of this," he says. "I want you to cut it like I showed you, and have it ready for Barbara when she comes by tomorrow."

"Check."

"Well, let me see you do the tests."

So I run through the tests, and it looks a lot like the half key we'd worked on before.

"Pretty good stuff," I says. "I figure we can hit this one-on-one like last time."

"Okay. Then hit it," he says. "I got to go."

I grew an inch right there. The big time, at last! Left alone with stuff worth maybe a million dollars by the time it hit the street—I was all excited. When Barbara stopped by next morning, she picked up four chubby half-kilo bags of the best-cut cocaine in all New York City.

A few hours later, Miguel showed up.

"I'm not staying," he says. "I just want to give you this."

He hands me a paper bag. It feels like money. He'd given me a couple of hundred a week so far, but that was just for expenses. I want to look inside, but he grins like he knows what's in my mind, so I just thank him and put it on the table.

"You did a good job," he says.

"Hey, I told you. I'm going to give you the best I got."

"Okay. I'll be back later, and we'll go for a ride."

The second that door closed, I looked in the bag, and my hands went cold. It was money all right. Oh, my God. Fifties. Hundreds. Enough to choke a horse. Oh, my God. This was what it was all about. I'd never seen so much. There was $5,000. I counted it three times to make sure. That was about the same as I'd put on my last tax return for a whole year's work as a busboy.

I must have played with that money for about two hours, seeing how it felt in my wallet, arranging it in piles, and getting the serial numbers in the right order. Then I hid it in the closet. But that didn't seem too safe, so I spent another half hour just moving it around the apartment. In the end, I took down the old-fashioned curtain pole at the window, rolled the bills up—except for $500 spending money—stuffed them inside, and screwed the pole back up again.

When my godfather comes around later, he knows how I got to be feeling. He cracks a smile, but he's not happy. As we're going out the door, he stops me.

"You got your piece with you?"

"No." And now I'm wondering what kind of a ride we're going to take.

"Get it," he says.

So I unscrew the silencer and stick the .38 in my waistband. The next surprise is, he's driving Frank Gregory's car, a '68 Riviera.

"Where's your LTD?" I ask him.

"Never mind," he says.

Okay. So I figure he'll tell me what he wants to tell me in his own good time. We get over onto Riverside Drive, heading downtown, and at about 96th Street, he jerks his head at a hotel there as we go by.

"They busted my Chilean," he says. "Right there. In that hotel."

"Your connection?"

"Right there."

Now that's serious. "Shit," I says. "So where does that leave us?"

He gives me a look. I'm not supposed to ask questions. "It leaves us out a connection," he says. "And out $250,000."

"No *shit.*" I should have known it was too good to last.

"And I know who did it to me," he says. "Umberto Rojas. You know him?"

"No."

"Well, remember the name. Because I'm going to feed that scumbag his ass when I catch him."

I knew how he felt. I was ready to hold the guy down while he did it. We drove around some more, and then stopped for a cup of Spanish coffee.

Now he starts to brighten up. "Don't worry," he says. "So I'll find another connection. We'll get back up there."

"I'm not worried."

"Right. I know a few people. And I still got a few kilos here and there. We're in good shape."

"Yeah, sure."

When he dropped me on 196th Street, I went straight upstairs and checked on the money.

Next morning, we both felt better. He came around early and said to stay in all day. He'd be back later with some stuff. Sure enough, that afternoon he showed up wearing a baseball cap and carrying three kilos in a black hold-all. He also left me six cans of lactose, which was enough, with the two I had left over from last time, to cut the three keys into six. Okay. $60,000 coming up. Not bad. We're still in there pitching. That night, he came back, all smiles, to collect the twelve half-kilo bags I had ready for him, and off he went.

Next day—nothing. Day after that—nothing. Not a word. I called the apartment, figuring Barbara might give me a hint of what's cooking—no answer. Third day—still nothing. They vanished. And now I *am* a little worried.

So is Frank Gregory. He comes around that night, wearing his piece. *With* the silencer.

"You heard from Mikey?" he says.

"No. Not in three days. And I checked the house."

"Yeah, me too."

"You know they busted his connection," I says. "You think he's caught?"

Frank shakes his head. "He's allowed a call. We'd a-heard. What else did he tell you?"

"What else? Well, he said he was out like a quarter of a million."

"Right. And did he tell you a hundred thousand of it wasn't his?"

"Oh, Jesus."

He says, "Zack Robinson fronted him the money. When they busted Mikey's Chilean, they got nine keys of coke, three keys of smack, *and* Zack's hundred thousand."

Now I know why he's carrying his piece. "Tell me about this guy Zack," I says. "Before we take a little run over there."

"Well, he's big. Got a lot of power. Owns a place called the Turntable down around 56th and Seventh Avenue."

"Then let's go."

"No, wait," he says. "We got to do this right. If Zack *does* have Mikey hid, he's got an army down there."

"So let's get some help."

"Good idea," he says. "Let's go find Willie Cox."

Willie's a black guy who dealt with my godfather a little bit, and in those days he owned an after-hours club with a gambling table up on Boston Road in the Bronx. He had a soft spot for Mikey, but that didn't matter. When it came to gunplay—"I'm here. I'm ready." So Frank drives us up there, and when he explains that my godfather's missing for three days and we think it's got something to do with the money he owes Zack, Willie just sticks a gun in his belt and follows us out to the Buick.

First we checked the bars Mikey used to hang out in. No. Nobody had seen him. And the more places we tried, the touchier it got. Maybe Zack iced him. What the hell for? He wants his money. Then he's been snatched. We don't know that for sure. Well, either way, we got to lock horns with this guy. Wait. We got a couple more places yet. Listen, if he's running round loose, he'd a-answered the phone. We're just wasting time.

When we reached Victor's Café at 71st and Columbus, I was ready to declare war on Zack, New York, and the federal government. But the first person I see on the sidewalk outside is Barbara. I jumped out of the car and grabbed her arm.

"Where the fuck is he?"

"Who? Mike?" she says. And then I see the son of a bitch through the window, sitting there calm as you like, eating his goddamn dinner.

"Oh, shit," says Willie. He's disappointed. And Frank starts to laugh.

So we go inside, and my godfather gives us the big hello. "Sit down," he says. "Pull up a chair. You guys eaten yet?"

"I hope you choke, goddammit," I says. "We been breaking our balls looking for you."

"Why? What's the matter?"

"Oh, Jesus."

Frank still thinks this is pretty funny. "Nothing," he says. "Forget it. Nothing's the matter."

So Mikey relaxes. "Me and Barbara took off for a couple of days with the kid," he says. "Felt like we needed a break."

"Yeah? Well, next time, give *us* a break," I says. "Tell us you're leaving. Here we are, ready to blow Zack Robinson away, and you're off on your fucking honeymoon."

"*Zack?*" he says, and he's not laughing.

"Yeah, Zack. I know the whole goddamn story now—about the money you owe him and everything. And you disappear on us. We don't know if you been killed or snatched or what."

"What the hell's going on here?" he says. "Zack's my friend. You talk to him about this?"

"Hell, no. I'm going to tell him what we're going to do? First time we see him, we're going to spill his brains for him."

I'm steaming. And I guess Miguel sees I really was worried about him, because he treats me warm, and in the end I calm down. Meanwhile, he's finished eating, so we drive up to their apartment, and now it turns into a party to celebrate he's still in one piece. He brings out the coke, and just to show there's no hard feelings, I take a snort—although I don't like drugs, and they don't do much for me. Then he's telling me all about Zack, and how tight they were, from their first deal two years before this, when Mikey gave him a load worth $77,000 on credit and got paid for it two days later.

"It's always been like that," he says. "I trust him and he trusts me. He knows I'm good for it."

"You could have told me that up front," I says. But it's okay. Now we understand each other. And after another couple of snorts, Willie says he's got to get back and mind the store.

So Frank and me dropped him off at his club and took a run back downtown. It was late, but we didn't feel like going to bed after all the excitement. I wanted to see what was happening in the Village, and we were cruising down Fifth Avenue when Frank suddenly stopped the car.

"There's that rat-fink Alexander," he says. "He owes us money."

Okay. Nothing wrong with mixing a little business and pleasure. I followed Frank over to hear what the guy had to say, and he's crawling.

"Man, you got to tell Mikey this ain't no rip-off or nothing. I just had a little trouble collecting the money. You know how these punks are. But I'll get it—you tell him, man. I just need a little time, but I'm good for it. He knows that."

And on and on he goes with the usual bullshit. Frank leans on him a little bit, but I'm not really listening. Until the guy says, "Hey, I hear Mikey's got troubles, too. That right? They say Zack Robinson put some money on his head."

So now I turn around and look at him, and Frank grabs him by the jacket.

"They?" he says. "What they? Who told you that?"

"I don't know, man. I'm just telling you what I hear around. Let go of me, man. I don't know who told me."

We got back in the car and drove uptown again. And when we told Miguel what we just heard, the man paused a minute. Who wouldn't? What the hell—this is not good news. No matter how much you trust a man, if you owe him $100,000 and somebody tells you the guy's put money on your head, you got to think twice. And it suddenly hit me. Whoever got the six keys we'd just moved, it sure as hell wasn't Zack Robinson.

"Well, I tell you what," Mikey says. "It's too late tonight. I got to figure this out before we take any steps. So go hit the sack, and be back here tomorrow. Around ten o'clock."

It was about 3 a.m. when Frank dropped me off at my apartment. I got into bed but stayed awake until it got light, and then I cleaned my gun. One way or another, it just had to be a bad day. I'd been sitting around ready and waiting for a couple of hours before Frank came back to pick me up, and he didn't look like he'd had much sleep either. We didn't say much on the way over.

Mikey was drinking coffee.

"So what's the strategy going to be?" I says.

"Well," he says, "I given it a lot of thought, and it still don't sound right to me. I'm pretty sure Zack wouldn't do that to me."

"You can't make book on 'pretty sure,' " I says.

"Right. So we got to clear this up. We can't take for granted that the rumor's true, and just go out and kill him. And we can't take for granted that it's *not* true, and just go about our business. So the only thing to do is confront this man. Right? Confront him as the man I know him to be. As the friend I consider him to be. And that's what I'm going to do. Tonight."

"What about us?" says Frank.

"You come along for the ride."

"With guns?"

"We got to be ready either way," he says. "You better get Willie as well."

So Frank goes off to check with Willie, and my godfather sits quiet for a minute. Then he says, "What do you think?"

"It's a decision of dignity," I says. "You consider this man your friend. You're doing it like you should. But since you ask me, why didn't you move those six keys to him?"

"I need the capital. I got other things planned. He'll get his money."

"Sure. You're not trying to rip him off, I know that," I says. "But does *he* know it? What would *you* do if somebody owed you a hundred thousand, and he's telling you he don't have the money, and then you hear he's moved six keys some place else? You'd dust him off—that's what you'd do."

"What makes you so sure Zack heard about it?" he says.

"What makes you so sure he didn't?"

"No," he says. "He wouldn't do that to me."

I didn't question the man no more.

That night, Frank and Willie picked me up in the Buick around seven, and we drove over to Mikey's place with the guns under the front seat. I wasn't scared. Scared wasn't going to help. But I did have a flutter inside. I don't care how brave you are—when you're going up against a guy who can kill you, it's not like going out for an ice-cream soda. You *got* to worry.

"Okay," Mikey says. "I'm going on ahead. I got to meet Barbara at Victor's Café. You pick me up there in about an hour, and we'll go on down to the Turntable and get this over with."

Shit. Another hour to kill. That's just what I *don't* need. I got a bad case of the butterflies now. I mean, this could be my last night out. So I figure it's best to keep on the move, feeling like that. And Frank's restless, too, so we go take a ride around Riverdale. None of us know what we're getting ourselves into here. This guy Zack is no pushover—I know that from what Mikey told me. He's not as big as Frank Matthews. Who *is?* But he's got a lot of guys working for him, and it don't take more than one bullet from one gun to put you on your ass.

At maybe twenty minutes of eight, we start on down the West Side Highway toward Victor's Café. Frank's driving; I'm next to him, and Willie's in the back. We're not hurrying. The traffic's light, and we got the radio tuned to WNEW, so nobody has to pretend he feels like talking.

Now we're coming down toward the 125th Street exit, and Frank pulls over into the left lane to pass somebody. We go on a bit farther, and I see this white Ford coming up alongside us, like he's going on by in the middle lane. And he does. Suddenly I hear it accelerate—whooo—and then: boom, boom, boom, boom.

The first bullet drills the goddamn windshield right in the corner. It goes under my arm and smacks through the seat into the back somewhere. I hear another one hit, and that son-of-a-bitching bullet must have gone straight through the car, because we never did find it. Then a tire blows out—all this in the same instant. The wheel kicks, and we slam into the goddamn wall. Frank fights it, hits the gas to go after the mother-fuckers, and we start to burn tires. Willie gets off a shot, but now the goddamn car's either lurching all over the road or dragging along the wall in a shower of sparks, and we got to stop.

Nobody says nothing. They don't have to. Now we know. There *is* a contract.

I waited for a gap in the traffic and got out to take a look at the damage. Although the body was a bit mashed up on Frank's side, the steering looked okay, and the motor was still running. But I couldn't get over that little hole in the windshield. How that mother missed me, I'll never understand.

"So what do we do now?" says Frank. "We got to warn Mikey."

"We jack the son of a bitch up and change the wheel," I says.

We got to Victor's about fifteen minutes late. Barbara was waiting for us on the sidewalk, and I just turned over inside.

"Where's Mike?"

"He's gone to Zack's," she says. "He'll meet you down there."

Frank hits his head, and now she sees the damage to the car.

"Oh, Jesus," she says. "What's the matter? What happened?" Then she looks at our faces and figures it out for herself.

"Go home," I says. "I'll call you."

Five minutes later, Frank parks about fifty feet away from the Turntable. There's a black guy standing outside.

"That's Billy Fair," Frank says. "Zack's lieutenant. He knows me."

"Son of a bitch don't know *me*," I says.

"Or me," says Willie.

"Okay. Then here's what we do. Me and Willie take a little walk. Frank stays in the car, and Willie hangs back in case of trouble. I'll come up around behind the bastard, and when you see me real close, Frank, you get out of the car and call his name. We'll see what he does. He goes for a gun or anything, I'll be right there."

I'm really wound up now, really focused on the moment. Not nervous, but like I'm on a hair trigger, ready to explode at a touch. And I like it. I like the feeling.

I get out of the car and walk up very casual. Willie follows me. I hear him. I hear everything. And when I'm about ten feet away, Frank calls out, "Hey, Billy."

Billy starts to turn, and that throws the switch. I pull the piece and jam it into his side.

"Don't even breathe."

"No problem, brother," he says. "No problem. I'm yours."

There's a flight of red-carpeted steps leading down into the joint, and it gets pretty dark toward the bottom.

"Okay, we're going down," I says. "Slow and easy. Try something funny, asshole, and you're dead."

Frank and Willie are with me now, but there's something wrong here. Something about this guy tells me he don't know nothing. If my people have started a war, when somebody calls my name on the street I'm not just going to turn around casually to see who it is.

"Hey, what's going on, man?" says Billy. "What are you doing?"

Frank hits his shoulder, and he stumbles down a couple of stairs.

"Walk, you cocksucker. The four you tried to put into us—that's what's going on."

At the bottom of the stairs, off to the side, there's a door to the office. Frank's been here before.

"Man, I don't know what you're talking about," says Billy.

I put the gun to his neck, and he shuts up. Frank and Willie each take a side of the door, and I knock, keeping well behind Billy. If there's any shooting, he gets it first.

The music's pretty loud, even out here, and I can't hear nothing inside. But then suddenly the door opens—and my godfather steps back, with three guns in his face.

"What the fuck?" he says. He's got a drink in his hand. Behind him, Zack's sitting at his desk with a bottle of whiskey. He also looks startled.

"Hey!" he says. "What the fuck's going on?"

So I let out my breath and put the piece away. "Walk on in, brother," I says to Billy Fair. "I guess we could all use a drink."

Mikey can't get over it. He looks from Willie to Frank to me. "Georgie, what the *hell* is this all about?"

"Well," I says. "It's a long story."

4

They never did find out for sure who had shot them up on the West Side Highway. It was certainly not Zack Robinson's people. He cared as little about the $100,000 debt as Miguel Garcia had supposed. They went looking for Alexander, thinking he might help them trace the rumor of a contract to its source—assuming there *was* one, other than Alexander himself—but the pusher had vanished as completely as the $5,000 he owed Garcia.

Frank Gregory believed the shooting and the rumor were unrelated. He had taken the Riviera from a man named Nelson Fraticelli, who owed him money from a drug deal. Gregory's theory was that some other, less accommodating creditor had coincidentally chosen that particular moment to close Fraticelli's account, thinking he was in the car.

Garcia inclined to the view that the story of a contract and the subsequent attack on George and the others were part of a power play by a rival black organization. He suspected that another group of dealers had tried to maneuver him into getting rid of Zack Robinson for them, thus avoiding the risk and possible odium of moving directly against such a powerful and well-liked brother. George also favored this theory, and heard later that somebody calling himself the "good Doctor" was responsible.

Robinson liked this explanation, too, although he slyly professed his amazement that anyone should have thought that Garcia was capable of getting rid of him. He pretended to believe rather that the incident had been staged by a rival *Cuban* group who wanted *him* to kill Garcia—and that was not impossible either.

Then Gregory ran into a former partner of Fraticelli's and discovered that *his* explanation was the right one. Fraticelli was in bad trouble with the Mob. He owed them big money and had been trying to get them off his back by bragging about the heavy protection he enjoyed from his black and Puerto Rican connections, who liked the quality of his stuff. As soon as he heard this, Gregory realized that the Mob's enforcers, on seeing him in the Buick with Cox and George, had probably assumed that *they* were the protection Fraticelli had been talking about, and let fly. As there was a real danger of this happening again, Gregory at once warned Garcia, who in turn passed word to the Mob through his friend Sonny Pinto that none of *his* people had any connection with Fraticelli or any interest in what happened to him.

After that, there was no more excitement, but Garcia was tired of New York, anyway. He gave George $15,000 as his end of the six-kilo deal, and told him he was leaving for Puerto Rico.

"The dope is finished," he said. "I ain't got nothing left. I could get stuff from a couple of people, but I want no part of these sons of bitches. We got to find a new hunting ground."

With nothing to stay for, George and Gregory decided to drive the Riviera down to Miami and wait for him there.

A good connection was now hard to find. Though Miami had become the cocaine capital of the world, the supplies available in southern Florida were already at wholesale prices. As a wholesaler himself, Garcia was looking for someone to replace his busted Chilean—a reliable South American source from whom he could buy in bulk—and for this he had to go farther south, in company with other would-be Cuban importers and a horde of middle-class American tourists hoping to finance their vacations, get their teeth fixed, or send their kids to private schools by means of a little cocaine smuggling on the side. For the professional dealer like Garcia, it was hard to say which represented the bigger nuisance: the rush of recruits into the Cuban Mafia or the romantic amateurs tracking up the Caribbean supply lines with their powerboats and homemade, false-bottom suitcases.

The U.S. market for cocaine, now said to be worth $8 billion a year, has always been a Cuban preserve. Before the revolution, the Cuban middle class regarded cocaine in much the same light as the American middle class regards Chivas Regal (except that

Cubans sometimes rub cocaine on their genitals in the belief that it enhances their sexual performance—one of the few claims never seriously advanced for scotch). Though it might be illegal, few Cubans considered the use of cocaine to be *criminal*. Nor could they be persuaded to treat cocaine traffickers any differently than Americans treated bootleggers in the twenties, or to begrudge the gringo market its share of the fun and profit. For Cuban dealers under Meyer Lansky and Fulgencio Batista, the rewards were great and the dangers remote.

Then, on New Year's Day 1959, the old order abruptly collapsed. Batista fell to Fidel Castro. The casinos closed, the Mob packed its bags, and its Cuban associates fled, joining the mass exodus of political refugees to Miami. Quick to present themselves as patriots, members of the old Cuban underworld now found a perfect cover in the new Cuban underground and for a time enjoyed as much protection from the authorities as they had previously received in Havana.

Committed to war by proxy against Castro's Cuba, the U.S. government empowered the CIA to train and equip a clandestine army of exiles for a seaborne invasion. While sponsoring this major impropriety, the CIA naturally saw little reason to cavil at minor ones, and perhaps jeopardize the Cubans' fragile sense of unity at a critical time. It therefore turned a blind eye to such peccadillos as cocaine smuggling, provided the business was done discreetly. If anybody got seriously out of line, the agency preferred to employ someone like Ricardo Morales, one of their own people, to take care of the problem, rather than mix justice with politics.

But in 1961 the rules were changed again. After the Bay of Pigs fiasco, armed attacks on Cuban targets could no longer be launched from the American mainland. The exiles had become an embarrassment, and officially at least, Washington withdrew its financial and military support. But no one supposed that the Cuban underground army, swollen by several thousand American-trained guerrilla fighters, would thereupon meekly disband and go about its lawful business. For one thing, it *had* no lawful business. And for another, the CIA had only bowed to pressure, not changed its mind. Castro was still in power, and the more militant exiles, not only in Miami but scattered around the rim of the Caribbean, were still determined to unseat him. All that was lacking was an alternative means of financing the war, and when the Cubans found one, their former paymasters managed to suppress their moral qualms. Cocaine had suddenly acquired a political significance.

George Ramos grew up in a community where any crime, from burglary and fraud to extortion and murder, could be justified if it helped "the cause." In such an atmosphere, cocaine dealing was almost a patriotic duty.

"A lot of Cuban immigrants had crime contacts from the old days—with the Italians, when Lansky was there. A lot of them knew what it was to make easy money. So they come to the U.S. in the sixties. Things are bad. They're stealing the milk off the doorsteps. Okay. So what is the best crime the Cubans got?

"With the CIA involvement and everything, a lot of Cubans went to South America, to set up bases there to hit Castro. What do they need? They need weapons. They need boats. Where is the best place to get weapons and boats? The United States. Do we got the money? No. How are we going to get the money? Simple. Look what we got here. Mountains of cocaine. They don't know the Italians, so they deal with their own people in Miami and New York. It's not for profit. It's patriotic. But it doesn't take long for the easy-money boys who couldn't care less about Castro to catch on: 'Hey! Look what's happening.' "

Before long, Cuban exile politics were tangled inextricably with illegal trafficking in drugs, and thus fatally compromised. Always prone to factionalism, the militants now split up into quarrelsome groups, each regarding itself as the true guardian of the flame, and the rest as opportunists or worse. In their frustration and anger, the zealots turned to rooting out heresy in their own ranks. A political argument between friends over the dinner table could end in mutual accusations of treason and sometimes in death.

The bombings and shootings multiplied, a trend that supporters of Castro were quick to encourage. United, 400,000 Cuban exiles, backed by American public opinion, presented a powerful threat to the revolutionary government in Havana. Dissolved in dissension and apparently committed to a life of crime, the Flagler Street commandos were no more than a minor annoyance. They were a bigger danger to those living in Little Havana. Though most of the exiles were soon more concerned with making a place for themselves than worrying much about politics, it was not safe to say so. A state of war existed, involving everybody. If you were not *for* the cause, you were against it.

The CIA had lost control. As the years passed, considerations of political expediency yielded to routine law-enforcement by federal, state, and local authorities. The Cuban underground, funded either by crime or by donations from law-abiding exiles nervous of appearing "soft" on Castro, was now a downright liability for which the CIA was still held publicly accountable. In its attempts to head off worse embarrassment, men like Ricardo Morales were kept very busy.

Though lethally anti-Castro, he was sometimes forced, like his employers, to work both sides of the fence to keep the situation stable. In 1968, this brought him up against Dr. Orlando Bosch, a pediatrician then in his early forties and one of the most fanatical leaders produced by the underground—a man whose hatred for Communism, whose ruthlessness and contempt for inaction matched his own.

Exiled in Miami with his wife and five children, Bosch had already launched his "freedom fighters" on several attacks against Cuban fishing boats and coastal villages, and had even organized an air raid by private planes on inland sugar factories. Though of doubtful strategic value, these exploits earned him a good deal of admiration and jealousy among his fellow exiles, and no real evidence of official displeasure until 1968, when Bosch opened fire with a bazooka on a Polish freighter in Miami harbor.

Thus challenged, Washington had no choice but to demonstrate its respect for international law, and fearing the whole Cuban cause would suffer, Morales turned him in. Bosch was tried, convicted, and sentenced to ten years' imprisonment.

But that was not the end of the story. Four years later, he was back in Miami on parole, as intransigent as ever, and determined now to clean up the corruption and apostasy he saw dishonoring the cause of Cuban liberation. Though he denied any connection with it, Bosch publicly endorsed the aims of Group Zero, a vigilante squad which had pledged itself to assassinate a round dozen exile leaders suspected of lining their pockets from political funds—among them, such well-known figures in Little Havana as José Elias de la Torriente.

Shortly before jumping parole in 1974 to carry on the war from Venezuela, Bosch was questioned by the Miami *News* about Torriente's death.

"Nobody will dare raise a false flag here any more, for fear of his life," he declared. "His slaying was a good lesson to the exile community, so that no one else will now come forth with phony theories to fool and rob the people."

In this, as in much else, Bosch overestimated the effectiveness of terrorism. More than a hundred Cubans died for "political" reasons in Miami in the next two years. The lure of easy money was too strong. As for Bosch himself, he carried on an increasingly destructive campaign against Cuban targets in the Caribbean until his arrest in 1976. On October 6 of that year, his group planted a bomb in the tail of a Cuban Airlines plane, which exploded on take-off from Barbados, killing all seventy-three people aboard. Three weeks later, he was picked up in Venezuela—on information supplied by Ricardo Morales.

But for George Ramos, as for most other young people who lived through the endless, sterile debate of their elders over fine shades of orthodoxy or the latest grandiose scheme for liberating the homeland, the example of Bosch had little force and no relevance. They had absorbed the community's hostility toward Castro as they had absorbed the Catholic religion, for the most part unthinkingly, but in neither case did they have much faith in the institutions that embodied it. Says Ramos:

"We got Brigada 2506. Alpha 66. We got this, we got that. No love lost between any of them. A lot of these guys have got balls, but there's also a lot of bullshit artists driving around in Cadillacs. They're not going to Cuba. Why should they? They own a $60,000 home. Got $200,000 in the bank. Go to Cuba for what? To get shot? Fuck them. There are too many jerks around to do it for us.

"Where do they get their money? One of their biggest rackets is making speeches. This is the year we're going to liberate Cuba, and all that shit. They take pictures of themselves in the Everglades, wearing uniforms, and the can goes around, and here's another $100,000 from the poor suckers, the fifty- and sixty-year-old Cubans whose only dream in life is to step on Cuban soil one more time before they die.

"On top of that, they got drug connections. And burglary rings, and fencing rings, and car-stealing rings, and protection rackets—all for the sake of the cause. Money for weapons. Money for Cadillacs. I'm not saying a lot of Cubans don't have balls and wouldn't go to Cuba to lock horns with Castro, but I *do* say they're being used."

They were used to such effect that by 1969, in testimony before a Congressional subcommittee, spokesmen for the Federal Bureau of Narcotics and Dangerous Drugs were referring to the groups then controlling the cocaine and much of the marijuana trade as the Cuban Mafia. But Cuban crime, whether politically motivated or not, was never organized in the same way as Italian crime. There were no "families," no criminal hierarchies with recognized jurisdiction in known areas. There was no "commission" to allocate rackets and territories among them or mediate disputes in the common interest.

There were plenty of Cuban gangs around, varying in size and formal structure, often based on blood relationships or common bonds of local sentiment, but they were just as happy to prey on one another as rip off the wider community. Whether singly or in groups, the Cuban criminal would grab for anything he thought he could hold, and it was in this atmosphere of unrestrained competition that the cocaine era got under way. The Lansky-trained gangsters, the CIA-trained guerrillas, and a wide assortment of untrained but money-hungry misfits from the Vietnam generation met head-on in the spirit of free enterprise and turned the Caribbean into a tank of embattled barracuda. In five years, seven hundred boats and their two thousand crew members vanished forever in the coastal waters of Colombia alone—silent witness to a level of piracy unknown since the days of Henry Morgan.

The traffic was unstoppable. Federal and state law-enforcement agencies, even with the help of the U.S. Navy, Air Force, and Coast Guard, could no more keep track of all the comings and goings in the Caribbean and Gulf of Mexico than the New York Police Department could watch every car in the city. Some 240,000 boats were registered in Florida alone. Cocaine, and marijuana, was also coming in by freighter, buried deep in crates of general cargo; by mail, and increasingly by tourist, hidden in vacation souvenirs, in plastic baggies taped to legs and armpits, and even in vaginas. Another good way was by private plane.

For twenty years, wartime flyers and off-duty airline pilots had made good money airlifting cigarettes, liquor, and other consumer goods over Latin American tariff walls. Now there was no need to fly back empty. Of the sixty small airfields south of Lake Okeechobee in southern Florida, most had no Customs for them to worry about, and some not even a tower.

In the Gulf states, the position was much the same. When a big shipment was expected, the ultra-cautious might perhaps bulldoze a special airstrip in some deserted area and light it with car headlamps while the plane came in and took off. Within weeks, the vegetation would grow back, leaving no trace of the landing, either on the ground or in airport records. As for the country's much vaunted radar defenses, one senior agent of the Drug Enforcement Administration reckoned he could fly 100,000 men into the southern United States without raising a blip on anybody's screen—and that any competent airline pilot could do the same.

By the mid-sixties, cocaine—the status drug; the jet-set, swinging, beautiful people's, pop stars', music and movie industry's, fashion and media, East Hampton, Aspen and Tahoe drug of choice; the intellectual and creative drug; the cool, chic, groovy black and white drug for people moving up from grass or down from speed—was pouring onto the American market in quantities large enough to support at least one dealer in every fair-sized town from coast to coast. And for all the federal and state governments could do to stop it, they might as soon have tried to dam the Mississippi with chicken wire.

And the price of a snort did not fall. It went up. The Cuban exiles, who sometimes like to call themselves the Jews of the Caribbean, may not set much store by collaboration in business, but those in the drug trade were as one in maintaining their profit margins, watching the price structure and supply as carefully as De Beers does for diamonds. And the Mob had nothing to say about it. The Italians had not been thrown out of the cocaine business, as some have supposed, in any titanic struggle for control of the vast profits to be made there; the Cubans, and their South American connections, had simply not allowed them to get into it.

The Mob had tried, of course. George Ramos had heard the stories, and seen it happen.

"The reputation of the Italians in South America is not the greatest. Many times, they went down there, bought cocaine for a good price—say, 10 keys—and said, 'Hey, let's not fool around. Next time, bring me 50 keys.' And when the connection came back with the 50 keys, they'd take the shipment and blow him away. Or scare the shit out of him, and short-change him on the price. Who needs that? Next thing you know, they got an Italian cutting the stuff over there. Then they got Italians cultivating it over there. Before you know what's happening, the Italians are running the whole goddamn thing. So why do business with people who move in on you like that? With the Cubans, the South Americans can do business with people who speak their own language, who pay a fair price and *don't* muscle in.

"So now who are the Cubans going to deal with? It's the same thing at the wholesale level. The Italians are Latins, sure, but it's a different story with them. You don't know what their intentions are. So we deal with our own people when we can, in Miami and New York. Or with the Puerto Ricans. We got a good relationship there because of the language, and anyway, Puerto Rico is a good stepping stone for us in the Caribbean.

"Then there's the blacks. That's the real market. The blacks use more dope than anybody, but you don't see Italian pushers no more in Harlem or Bed-Stuy. Not healthy. The blacks run the streets now, and look after their own. That's how guys like Frank Matthews got to be so big. He'll buy from Italians, sure, but when it comes to cocaine—and he *loves* cocaine—the Italians don't got the stuff. *We* got it. So the blacks deal with us. And guys like Frank and Zack Robinson—if he takes a liking to you, you can't beat a black as a business associate. Honest. Easygoing. Give his life for you. The blacks and Cubans who deal together generally get on well. When you hear different, it's usually from those who are out of it. They're jealous of the money being made."

With heroin, it was much the same story. A lot of the Mob's street-level business had already gone, either abandoned because the risks were disproportionate to the profit, or undermined by an ethnic mismatch between pusher and user. And although the Italians still held an entrenched position in the movement of bulk shipments, akin to the Cubans' grip on cocaine, they were being forced by circumstance to cede some of this wholesale business, too. They now needed the Cubans' supply routes.

The traditional ports of entry for European heroin—New York, Boston, Montreal, Philadelphia—were still in business, but since the French Connection busts in 1962, getting really big loads through had proved difficult and dangerous. The advantage of having only one customs checkpoint to pass and no middlemen to deal with had been largely offset by the risk of losing, not just the shipment, but the whole operation if a courier were arrested. Another, safer route to the East Coast markets was needed, and the Cubans had shown the way.

Starting in 1962, Mexico, Brazil, Bolivia, Uruguay, Ecuador,

Panama, Paraguay, Colombia, and Venezuela each acquired a small but amazingly influential Corsican colony—unremarkable-looking men of middle age mostly, with large, fleshy faces and eyes of Martian detachment. They were members of the Union Corse, an ancient secret society more closely knit than the Sicilian Mafia, more powerful everywhere except in the United States, and more deadly. In France, the Union had infiltrated every level of government, as well as the army, gendarmerie, the police, the customs, and intelligence services. In South America, as in Southeast Asia, the Corsicans now did the same—not in person, of course, but buying the people they needed, from local garrison commanders and harbor masters, to high court judges and government ministers. It was well worth their while to do this, and they could easily afford it, because the Union controlled the processing and supply of practically every gram of heroin that entered the United States from anywhere.

Their principal customers had always belonged to the Mob, and so the Italian populations of Central and South America were soon on the increase as well. Resident Mafia buyers like Thomas Buschetta, Giuseppe Catenia, Francisco Toscanino, and Carlo Zippo were now to be seen hobnobbing in Rio, Mexico City, Bogotá, and Asunción with resident Corsican sellers like André Condemine, Christian David, Michel Nicoli, Lucien Sarti, and Auguste Ricord, a former Gestapo agent and the granddaddy of them all. Before long, the ports of Buenos Aires and Montevideo were handling substantial bulk shipments of European heroin, and the only problem still remaining was how to run the stuff up to the Mob's established wholesale distributors in New York—men like Carmine Galante, Louis Cirillo, Carmine Tramunti, Joe Cordovano, and Vincent Papa.

The Cubans had the answer. By the end of the sixties, most of the narcotics consumed in the United States were coming in through southern Florida. And it was a heroin deal that got Miguel Garcia and George Ramos started again.

5

After we drove the Riviera down to Miami, Frank Gregory went on to San Juan, and I settled down to wait at my grandmother's. On top of the $20,000 I already had, my godfather had given me another $5,000 for moving expenses, so I wasn't hurting. And now I met Anna.

Or, I should say, I met her again. After they came here from Cuba in 1962, her family lived in my neighborhood for several years. Then they moved away when she was about twelve, and I didn't see her no more till one night I took a ride with a friend who was going to visit them. And Anna had *changed.*

It was September 1970 now—five years later—and she was doing wonders for a pair of blue hot pants. I mean, that girl was *built.* And I guess we both liked what we saw, because she stayed out on the porch with me while I did a little casual serenading, and my friend kept the family busy inside.

But this was a Spanish family—very protective—and I could see we had problems. Her father never let her go to parties or have dates. If she just wanted to go to the beach, she had to lie about it. She had to say she was going with her girlfriend's mother or something. Typical Cuban father. She was in her second year at junior high before he stopped taking her there every day and picking her up in the afternoons.

But by this time she was going to school in the mornings from seven until about midday and then taking a bus over to Coral Gables. She had a part-time job there, selling clothes in Maggie's Boutique. *And* buying them. Every store owner on the Miracle Mile knew Anna. She was a clothes freak.

Anyway, pretty soon I'm collecting her at the bus stop every morning, driving her down to the dock for a little serenade, then taking her off to school. At noon, I'd pick her up and run her over to the store. When she finished there, we'd go off some place and have another little serenade, then I'd take her home, and let her out half a block from the house. After that, we'd talk on the telephone for three, four hours every night.

Just as well I *wasn't* working. I went over to Puerto Rico for Vicky's birthday, and nothing much was happening, although my godfather hit the numbers for $20,000 while I was there. He used it to buy a piece of a jewelry store in Old San Juan. He said half his share of it would be mine—he'd front me the money—and every month he'd send me half of what he made from it. And he did. About $3,000 altogether over the next three or four months. And before I went back to Miami, he got Frank Gregory and me to take a run up to New York to collect $20,000 owing to him from a dealer in the Bronx named El Chino. At first the guy didn't want to know, but Frank and Willie Cox persuaded him. Those two lunatics shot up his house, and he paid.

I also made a couple of investments myself. I fronted $5,000 to a friend, a gambler, very good with cards, to set up a little casino in his apartment. He figured he could make maybe five, six hundred a day, and he was right. Once he got started, he kicked back $500 a week of what he owed me, plus two, three hundred for my trouble. And, around Christmas, I got a license and went into the painting business with another friend. Laid out $1,400, brought in a guy with a spray machine, and the three of us painted a hotel over on the corner of 5th Street and Ocean Drive in Miami Beach. $4,500 contract. Four or five days' work. Came out of it with $800 apiece, and ready for more. So I could wait. There was money coming in. I was getting serious with Anna now, and the weeks were going by.

Then one night—it must have been the end of February—I was standing on the corner, and I saw my godfather drive by, real slow. "Hey, Miguel!"

"Hey," he said. "Get in. I been looking for you."

Right away, I knew that nothing was going on. He was down.

He told me he had just blown into town and borrowed the car to come find me. "So how are you doing?"

"Fine," I said. "You know—ticking over. How about you? How are things in San Juan?"

"Slow," he said. "Very slow. I figure I can do better here."

"Yeah? What about the jewelry store?"

"Got rid of it."

"Uh-huh." There was a dent in the budget right off. "How's Barbara and the kid?"

"They're staying," he said, which wasn't what I had asked him. But something told me to leave it there. He said it like they had broken up.

"Then I guess you'll be moving into your mother's place," I said. "Out in Normandy Isle?"

"Right. She don't need all that room."

"Okay. So why don't you drop me off and get rid of the car? Then I'll come on over in mine and pick you up."

I had a 1966 Pontiac GTO at the time, and I knew where to go—1511 Biarritz Drive—because I'd left the Riviera there with his mother, Victoria Montalvo, when I got back from New York. So I drove over, and we went bar-hopping. My godfather was looking for a guy he'd known in the joint who had a contact with the Frenchmen. His name was Aladdino. For two days we checked out the bars around town. Nothing. Then just as Miguel was ready to give up, we ran into him in the Esquina de Tejas restaurant on the corner of 12th and Flagler.

"Hey! How are you doing?" Big reunion and everything. Only Aladdino had somebody with him, so we arranged to meet that night at the Flamingo, in the Dupont Plaza Hotel.

We got there around nine, but as we were going in, a guy grabbed my godfather by the arm.

"Hey, Miguelito," he said. "Wait a minute. You know who's upstairs? Umbertico."

My godfather went still.

"Who?" I said, and I'll never forget his face when he turned to me. The scar had gone white, like rope, and his eyes were dead.

"Umberto Rojas," he said. "That son of a bitch. What's he doing?"

"He's waiting for *me*," the guy said. "He thinks we got a deal cooking, but I been down here ten minutes already trying to figure out the best way to hit the bastard."

"Your troubles are over," Miguel said. "That scumbag cost me my connection. Did he ask about me?"

"Yeah. And I told him I hadn't seen you since last year in New York."

"Okay. Then come outside a minute."

My godfather showed him where we had parked the car.

"Here's what you do," he said. "He wants to deal? Okay. Go set up a meet. Find out where he's staying, and make it there. Then come back and tell us. We'll wait for you in the car."

"Sure."

"And listen. Make it good. Take your time. Get a few drinks down him, okay? And if you see Aladdino up there, don't say nothing. You never saw me."

As soon as he had gone, Miguel looked at me. "You in? This is the cocksucker I told you about. When my Chilean went down? This is the rat bastard that set up the bust."

"I guess so. Sure."

That wasn't good enough. "He *owes* you," he said. "You got twenty thousand, right? Without him, it could have been two *hundred* thousand."

"Okay," I said. "I'm *in*."

The guy came back about an hour later. "He's staying at the Airport Inn, up by 42nd Avenue there. He wanted to meet in his room, but I told him I don't talk business in hotel rooms. So he'll be outside, waiting by the pool."

"What time?" Miguel asked.

"In a couple of hours. Around twelve."

"Fine. Now go some place else and make yourself seen for the rest of the night. We got work to do."

I still had the pipe my godfather had given me in New York, but first we drove over to Victoria's house to fetch his—a .32. I didn't want to go running around over there with a gun on me because the Miami Beach police are very tacky. They snatch and stop you for no reason. And I wasn't about to use my own wheels on this deal either, so after we got back to my grandmother's place on 18th Avenue, I put both guns in a paper bag and left them there while we went to find another car.

A fat guy I knew—we called him El Gordo—used to work at Trail Dodge, at SW 8th and 32nd Avenue, and I remembered him telling me one time that the service department there was so busy they generally had to leave a couple of cars out on the street every night. After locking the doors, they hid the keys under the front fender, on top of the tire on the driver's side. So we drove over, my godfather picked himself a Plymouth, and we arranged to meet by the Holiday Inn on 42nd Avenue in about twenty minutes. Meantime, I was going to drive home, get the guns, park some place near the hotel, and start walking down 42nd toward the Airport Inn.

By the time I've done that, it's about ten minutes of twelve, and I'm strolling along with the guns in the paper bag, just inviting some cop in a cruiser to stop me and ask what I got in there. So where the hell is Miguel? I go two blocks, and figure the son of a bitch has stopped off for a drink some place. I go one more block, then I'm turning around and hightailing it back to the car. As I turn at the corner, there he is.

He slides over to let me drive, and I put on the pair of gloves I also brought with me.

The Airport Inn faces 42nd Avenue, but there's a service road behind it that runs right along by the airport fence. The swimming pool is back there, too, behind a wall with a front gate and a side gate, and as I roll slowly by, my godfather spots the guy sitting under the umbrella of a poolside table with a drink in his hand. Miguel grabs hold of the door, like he's going to charge in there like a bull, so I tell him to cool it, and we go around again.

This time I stop about fifty feet from the front gate, kill the lights, and leave the motor running.

"Okay," Miguel says. "You he don't know. You can walk right up to him. I'll go in the side gate and take him from behind."

He's gone before I say a word, and now I'm left with what I got to do. I keep telling myself how much this bastard has cost me. I'm inside the gate. I could be rich by now. So what the hell—let's get it over with. Miguel starts in from the other side.

The guy looks up, looks down again. He's not interested. He's wearing a tan suit. I got my hand on the pipe, but just before I pull it, something tells me, make sure your way out is clear. And as I look back over my shoulder I see a car coming by, and a quick glow of green on the side, like fluorescent letters. Holy Jesus.

"No, no," I says, and Miguel does an about-face, putting his piece away. Doesn't hesitate. He just turns around and walks back the way he came, with me right behind him.

The guy had looked up when I called out, and he's still looking at me as I go on by. And all I can think of is, you lucky son of a bitch.

"What the hell was that?" says Miguel, when I catch up with him by the car.

"You didn't see? Goddamn prowl car went by."

"Shit." He hits the roof with his fist, like a hammer. "Drive around front. If it's all clear, we'll give it another try."

By now I'm off the whole deal, but it's no use arguing. The mood he's in, if I don't go, he'll try it without me and do something stupid. So we drive around another lap, and the guy's gone.

"Tomorrow," I says. "We'll ice him tomorrow."

But next day we ran into Aladdino and didn't have time. Rojas blew town, and about a year later we heard he'd been killed in Spain.

By morning, my godfather had cooled off anyway. And when he heard what Aladdino had to say, it was strictly business before pleasure. Aladdino had been a burglar, and was always up to something, but he didn't deal in drugs.

"Hey, Miguelito," he says. "I got you this contact. A Frenchman. A real solid contact."

"Hey, Aladdino," says my godfather. "That's great, man. So what do you want for it?"

"Well, listen—you tell me. Narcotics is not my bag."

"Okay. You want I should cut you in, right?"

"Well, a little slice off the top maybe. I don't know. What's fair? A couple of thousand a kilo?"

Miguel pretends to think it over, but they both know he's going to do it. "Fine," he says. "If anything comes of it. Now what have you got?"

What Aladdino had got was a guy named Carlos who lived in an apartment building just over the George Washington Bridge from New York in Fort Lee, New Jersey. And what *we* had to do was check in with Carlos, who would know we were coming and take care of the rest. So I had the GTO tuned, put a couple of new belts on it, and two days later we were ringing his doorbell.

Carlos is comfortable. Not splashy rich, not drawing attention to himself, but the money is there. He's Cuban, in his thirties, dark, smooth, well dressed, and he greets Miguel like they're old friends. Hey, how *are* you? How was the trip? How's Aladdino? What will you drink? And la-di-da. Finally he gets down to cases.

"The guy you're going to meet," he says, "his name is Jean-Pierre. He's in tight with Ricord."

Now that meant something. When it came to heroin, Auguste Ricord was the biggest operator in South America. Other Frenchmen dealt in kilos, but Ricord dealt in tens and hundreds of kilos.

"You play it by the book with this guy," says Carlos, "and he can make you a lot of money."

Miguel's not too happy with that. "I *always* play by the book," he says. "Aladdino knows. If this guy does the same with us, then maybe we can make *him* a few dollars, too."

"Well, that's the name of the game," says Carlos. The guy's a diplomat. "But Jean-Pierre's got to be careful. He doesn't want you running around town before this deal goes down. *If* it goes down. We'll set up a meet for tomorrow, and you can spend the night here. If that suits you?"

It suited. Jean-Pierre showed up next morning at ten o'clock. He looked a little like Alain Delon, only older. He took my godfather into a corner, they talked for ten minutes, and then he left.

"We're in," Miguel tells me. "He's going to bring us a sample. He'll front us three keys of pure at $9,000 a key."

"He don't want no bread or nothing?"

"No, nothing. It's a little expensive, but it's *here*—and no money up front."

"How about that? Looks like Aladdino did it for us."

"Pulled one right out of his lamp," he says, "If it's pure, we can cut that stuff, make it six, and drop them at $15,000 a key without no trouble at all."

I made that a profit of $60,000 plus. And so far, all it had cost was a few tankfuls of gas.

"Sounds like a winner. Where we going to do it?"

Not in Carlos's apartment, he soon made *that* clear. The minute Jean-Pierre delivered the stuff, we had to haul ass with it.

"Okay. How about Zack Robinson?" I says.

"No." And Miguel's down my throat. "For now, I don't want nobody to know I'm in New York. Not Zack. Not nobody. Got that?"

"Okay, okay." It didn't seem right to me, but I figured he knew what he was doing.

Jean-Pierre came back with the sample around five that afternoon, and we ran it over to some apartment house in Brooklyn. I didn't like riding around in a car with a Florida tag—the narcs are not dumb—but renting one would have been risky, too. We just had to sweat it out for twenty-four hours, until the deal went down.

Most of them seemed to go by while I waited outside in the car for Miguel. When he came back, he was all excited.

"Dynamite stuff," he said. "We're in business. The shit is fantastic."

We took delivery from Jean-Pierre next day at 2 p.m. Three sealed plastic packs in a Pan Am flight bag.

"You want to weigh it?" he says.

"Weigh it?" Miguel sounded shocked, like the idea never occurred to him. "Why? Is it short?"

Jean-Pierre smiles, and shakes his head. "You want to test it? Make sure it's like the sample?"

"That's not the way I do business," says Miguel. "There's something wrong, you'll hear from me."

Up to now, he hadn't laid out a cent, so he could afford to play big-shot, but he was making his point. Both sides were on trial, not just him. He was thinking about the future.

So, with our Florida tag and the three keys of European pure, I drove very carefully back over the bridge and down to the hotel we'd found that morning in the West Forties, near Tenth Avenue. It was a flophouse, but quiet. Miguel had already paid three days' rent on Room 210, so while I guarded the stash, he went off on his own to rustle up a few things. Two hours later, he came back with a suitcase full of cans of dextrose, a gram scale, another Sears bag-sealer, and the rest of the paraphernalia we needed.

By eight o'clock that night, we had ourselves twelve fat little half-kilo bags. And now he left me again to go check on the buyer, to make sure he'd got all the money together. Ninety thousand cash is a lot of scratch to come up with in a day. He was back around nine. I had everything packed up, ready to leave.

"Okay," he said. "Let's take a little drive."

We crossed over the Brooklyn Bridge, hit Fulton and Flatbush Avenue, and finally headed east on Atlantic. Then he told me to make a few turns and I soon lost track of where we were. It could have been around St. Marks Place or Prospect Place, near Brower Park. Anyway, we stopped at another tenement, and he went inside, leaving the stuff with me in the car. I locked the doors and kept my piece handy, just under the seat.

Ten minutes later, he comes out with a couple of white guys, which is unusual in this neighborhood. One of them is carrying an attaché case. Miguel gives me a nod, so I wind down the window and pass out our grocery bag with the six keys. The two guys check it out. If they make a dumb move, they'll never know what hit them. But then they hand my godfather the attaché case, and he gets in the car.

"So what do you know?" he says. "We're in the money. Let's get out of here."

"Yes, *sir,*" I says. "Next stop, Miami."

"You kidding? Next stop, Howard Johnson's Motor Lodge. We got something to celebrate."

"Oh, shit," I says.

I knew what was coming. One of us was going to have to look after the money, and it didn't take a genius to figure out who. For safety, we checked into a double room, and sure enough, as soon as he had cleaned up, he helped himself to a wad of bills from the attaché case and left me alone with the color TV.

Hours later, he came back very drunk.

"Tomorrow," he said, "you're gonna buy yourself some clothes. We're stepping out."

"Oh, yeah? Like tonight, you mean?"

"Yeah. No. Not like tonight." He opened up the attaché case and tossed about two thousand onto the bed. "Get yourself a couple of suits. We're back on top, and you gotta look sharp. Because tomorrow night I got us two seats for the Ali–Frazier fight."

God knows what he'd paid for them, but it was worth it. Hell, there was as much action around the ring as inside it. I never saw so many decked-out dudes. As the green changed hands in those first dozen rows, they twinkled with diamonds like sun on the sea. There was one big black guy in a long white mink coat. I didn't know him then, but I was going to. It was Frank Matthews.

We got back to our room pretty late.

"Can't top that," said Miguel. "We'll get our ass out of here in the morning."

That was good news. Me and Anna had been talking about moving in together, and I didn't want to be away too long. "What about the Frenchman?" I said.

"He's paid. I took a run over there while you were shopping out Leighton's men's store. You got room in the trunk for all those fucking boxes?"

"So I bought a couple of suits, like you told me."

"Yeah. Look, I got something for you." And he gave me a shoe box full of money.

"What the hell's this?"

"That's like $30,000," he said. "Give or take a thousand for your fucking suits."

"You mean, you're giving me this?" We'd had a few drinks, and I had to make sure.

"That's your end of the deal, right?"

"Oh, shit," I said. "I never expected nothing like that. Hey, thanks, Miguel."

"No, you earned it," he said. "All that waiting around and everything? Hell, no—it's yours. And that ain't nothing, not with the connection we got ourselves now."

I put the money in my suitcase, along with the things I'd bought Anna. There was a set of towels with her initials on them, and these two angels, male and female, made out of white china. They were in a beautiful French frame, and the back was padded with pink velvet. Paid $100 for it. It was one of a pair—the set cost $300—but the other got broke in the store.

So I locked the suitcase and stretched out on the bed, thinking what I would do with the money.

"Can I ask you something?" I said. "Why didn't we sell that shit to Zack Robinson?"

My godfather never liked to be questioned, and he gave me the eye. "You're getting a little smart for your pants yet."

"Smart? No. Curious? Yes. You sell him the six keys—same price and everything—and then he can turn around and make money on them, same as these other people. I don't get it."

"Who asked you? I got my reasons."

"Okay." I had to respect that. "Then why don't we pay something back to Zack out of this money we got here?"

"You want to give him your thirty thousand?"

"Hell, no. Not all of it."

"What, then? Is ten thousand going to make a difference? You want we should owe him ninety grand instead of a hundred?"

"No. If it was up to me," I said, "I'd give him thirty, and keep fifteen back for each of us."

"That's bad business. Thirty don't mean nothing to Zack. Seventy thousand, a hundred thousand—it's all the same to him. But we can use this money. So just shut up about it."

"Okay. I just don't like to owe the guy, that's all."

"I'll take care of Zack, don't worry about it. Jean-Pierre comes through once, he'll come through again. Nice clean deal. No problems either way. That's how these Frenchmen like to do business."

It still didn't seem right to me, but I'm going to quarrel with a guy who just gave me $30,000? Next morning, we left for Miami.

After that, Anna kept me busy for a while, making up for lost time. She wasn't too crazy about my godfather even then. When he stopped by to pick me up, it was always, "Oh, leave her behind," and I couldn't tell her what we were into. So when he came by a few nights later and said I had to go, well, that just lit her fuse. And when I told her later on that I was going to have to give her a break for a few days, I had business to attend to, she went up like a goddamn skyrocket. I was lucky to get out of there with my ass in one piece.

But my godfather was setting up the next deal. He'd been told that the Frenchman was weighing in with another three kilos, this time through his associates in Miami.

"Got a buyer?" I said, and Miguel just looked at me.

Next day, we drove out to the airport to meet Henry Morgan. "Who's Henry Morgan?" I asked him.

"He's the buyer." Miguel always gave out information like it was gold nuggets. "Black guy from Detroit."

So I guess I expected another one of those skinny, jive-ass dudes in silver lamé pants like I'd seen at the fight, because I really wasn't ready for this strong, light-skinned, good-looking guy who came off that Delta flight dressed like a Wall Street banker. Henry

Morgan was big-time—no doubt about it. As sure of himself as a middleweight champ. And right behind him came his bodyguard, Johnny.

We drove them over to Victoria Montalvo's house, where my godfather now had a separate little apartment at the back. Then we sat around a while talking the usual bullshit, until Henry said: "So all right, Mikey. What am I doing here?"

"Well, I'll tell you," he said. "You just flew in to buy six kilos of horse."

"Fantastic. How much?"

"Fifteen a crack," Miguel said.

"Sounds like we might have a deal. Just the six? I can use all you got."

"For right now, six is it. But there's more on the way."

"Okay. Then let's get this show on the road."

After a quiet little conversation with Johnny in the corner, Henry said he had to make a call to Detroit. So we took him to a pay phone down the street and waited in the car while he talked to his people. It didn't take long.

"I got it in gear," he said. "You want to find me a place to stay? Then you can take Johnny back to the airport."

I liked this man. And I guess he took a shine to me, too, because when we got him a room in the Sands, at 35th and Biscayne, he said I should share it with him. Now there was more to it than that, of course. With his bodyguard gone, it wasn't smart for a guy like him to stay by himself. And with a deal going down, it wouldn't have been smart for us to let him. But we just hit it off right away, and I got to know him pretty well while we waited to hear from Johnny, now back in Detroit.

Henry was also in the music business, as a legitimate promoter, and you couldn't want for a better cover than that, not when you're paying off half the narcs in town as well. He had also figured out a way of protecting his people from the other half.

"You know, Georgie," he said, "cops in this country don't usually hassle people with money, so you know what I did? I bought all my main men brand-new Lincoln Mark IIIs. That's tax-deductible. And there ain't nobody going to bother them now."

I told him I didn't think they would, anyway. Henry was also a Black Panther, *and* a black belt in karate.

So, after a night on the town, we jumped in the car next morning and went to Sambo's for breakfast. That's when the hurricane hit. Hurricane Anna. She was going by in the bus when she spotted my car. So she got off, and came in there at about seventy-five miles an hour.

"*This* is how busy you are?" And she looks at Henry like he's a flu germ.

"We still got to eat," I says, trying to warn her by my tone of voice. "This is Henry. Henry, meet Anna."

He stands up, but now to her he's suddenly invisible. "If you got time to eat, you got time to call me," she says.

"Yeah, well. Why don't you join us? Have some breakfast."

"Shove your breakfast," she says, and Henry sits down again, eyes open wide.

"Whew!" he says.

She won't eat nothing, or even take a cup of coffee. She just stands there, tapping her foot and breathing hard, but we're about finished anyway.

"Look," I says. "I'm tied up. Me and Henry got things to do. I'll drop you off downtown."

"Don't do me any favors," she says, and comes along anyway. Henry tries to be nice to her, but she don't want to know. She's still bent all out of shape.

"Listen, I'm going to call you this afternoon," I tell her as she gets out, and *slam* goes that door.

Henry watches her go, shaking his head. "Wow!" he says, and he flips his fingers like he just burned them. "Man, you got yourself a hell of a Cuban spitfire there. Shit! What did you *do* to that woman?"

"Would you believe—nothing?"

"Shit," he says. "You got to get me one of them."

But we didn't have time. When we got back to the hotel, there was a message from Johnny saying he was coming in at four. So now we had to find Miguel. I called Victoria Montalvo, and she said he was over at Barbarito's. I should have known. My godfather, who was hung up on voodoo, spent a lot of time with Barbarito Arrechea in his pet shop on 12th Avenue and Flagler. Barbarito was a *palero*, a high priest—not the Spanish-style voodoo they call *santería*, but the real heavy Haitian kind. *Santería* is based on the Catholic saints and the Virgin, but Barbarito messed with the spirits of the dead. That's what he sold his birds and animals for—for blood sacrifice.

I don't believe in it myself. I'm a Catholic, although I don't go to Mass. I believe in God and the devil, and for me that's enough to explain the things that happened later. But Miguel? He couldn't move without consulting the spirits and going through the rituals. Nearly all the Cubans I know in the drug business do the same. In fact, a hell of a lot of Spanish people believe in voodoo—and most of those who don't are generally afraid of it. It's a very big thing in Miami, and guys like Barbarito have a lot of power.

When me and Henry got over there, Miguel had just had a little ceremony performed on him, and as we left, Barbarito gave him some weed and flowers to put in the tub next time he took a bath. The whole scene really grabbed Henry. As we drove on over to the airport, he couldn't stop talking about it, and I had to promise to take him back to see Barbarito next day.

Johnny came off the plane carrying a green suitcase. He threw it in the back of the car, and we went to Victoria's house. As soon as we got inside, Henry opened it up, and the goddamn thing was stuffed full of money.

"Oh, shit," I said. "How much you got there?"

And Johnny said, "$125,000."

So I sat down beside it.

"You want to stash that, or take it with you?" my godfather wanted to know.

"Better we keep an eye on it," Henry said. "When are you going to make the buy?"

"Well, I got to go see these people now over at the Sheraton Four Ambassadors. So why don't you drop me off and go back to the Sands? I'll contact you there when I got everything set up."

"Okay," he said. "Then the money goes with us."

So Johnny carried the suitcase back to the car, and off we went again. It made me nervous, riding around with it like that. I figured Johnny was probably packing a pipe, but if somebody tried to take that money away, I wanted to have something to say about it, too. So we stopped first at my grandmother's. I brought down a .38 Smith & Wesson Police Special I kept in my room there, and shoved it under the seat.

After we dropped Miguel off, we didn't hear from him again until about ten o'clock that night. He came over to the Sands and said, "Tomorrow. We got a meeting set for two o'clock tomorrow."

Henry just shrugged, but I could tell my godfather wasn't happy. He didn't say nothing about it, but I could read him well enough now to know things weren't going smooth.

Next morning, I took Henry over to Barbarito, who did a number on his ass, and we were back at the hotel by two. But we needn't have hurried. Came six o'clock, with no word, and Henry started getting restless.

"Georgie," he said, "this don't look too promising. No news is bad news. Looks like I better send Johnny home."

"Hell no. Not yet." The idea of all that money flying back to Detroit was very hard to take. "You know Mikey. Give him time. Could be the shipment's delayed."

So we gave him time. Around nine o'clock, he showed up, shaking his head.

"Man, these people are sticky," he said. "Now they say they want to see the money first, and all that shit."

Right then, I knew the deal had gone bad. No reason why Jean-Pierre should trust us the first time and not the second. That's not how it's done. When you deal with the Frenchmen, they trust you all the way—until you give them a reason to change their mind. Then they kill you.

Henry looked at me, and then at my godfather. "I don't like it, Mikey," he said. "Could be a rip-off."

"Ain't no way they're going to get the chance," he said. "I don't know these people, but I know who they work for. And the connection's good. The best. It's worth a last try. I fixed another meet tomorrow at the Sheraton."

He knew—better than me—that he was wasting his time, but he just couldn't face it.

Henry thought for a minute. "Okay, Mikey. Whatever you say. But I feel kind of naked. Can you lend me a piece?"

"Sure," I said. "I got one you can have. You stay here."

I went and got the .38 automatic I'd brought down from New York. Henry also knew the deal was dead. He was staying on another day because he liked us.

That night, we all went out to a nightclub called the Penthouse—all except me. I stayed in the car with the money.

There it was. $125,000 in a green suitcase on the seat beside me. There *they* were, settling in upstairs for the next few hours to get stoned. And there *I* was—about twenty minutes from Miami International Airport. I had a lot to think about.

Next day, it was the same story. My godfather came back and said they wouldn't move before they saw the money.

"Hell," I said. "We're going to have to put an end to this." It was getting to be embarrassing.

"Georgie's right." Henry had had enough. "Goddamn, Mikey, these people are punks, or what's the matter with them? They gonna deal or ain't they gonna deal? I don't have time for this shit."

There was nothing my godfather could say to the man. "I guess you're right," he said. "We better call it quits. I don't like the atmosphere here."

That night, we drove them back out to the airport. I was sorry that Henry had to go, and heartbroken to see all that money leave, but there were no hard feelings. That kind of thing happens all the time in this business.

A few days later, Miguel left, too.

"Things are just not working out," he said. "I got to move around and see. You stay here. I'll be in touch. You got enough money?"

"I'll make out," I said.

And I did, although I didn't hear from him again for a whole year.

In April, Anna left home. We found a little apartment on Coral Way, and moved in together.

In August, we took a run up to New York to see if Frank Gregory or Zack Robinson knew where Miguel was at, but no, they hadn't heard nothing.

In September, I teamed up with Orlando Lamadrid, and we played a few games with Ricardo Morales. Or maybe the other way around.

And in October, though I didn't know about it until several months later, my godfather found himself a Venezuelan connection, and started to deal with Frank Matthews.

6

On March 23, 1971, Auguste Joseph Ricord, also known as Mr. André, was arrested at the Paris-Nice Motel Restaurant in Asunción, Paraguay, just as he was attempting to slip away to Argentina. Though he had never set foot on American soil, he had been indicted by a federal grand jury a week earlier on charges of conspiring to smuggle narcotics into the United States. He was said to have supplied the American market with fifteen *tons* of heroin in the previous five years—perhaps half the total consumed there.

Born in Marseilles of Corsican parents in 1911, Ricord was convicted of extortion at the age of sixteen and branched out into pimping at eighteen. After the fall of France in 1940, he collaborated with the Gestapo in shaking down Paris nightclubs to such effect that in 1945 he was able to flee the country with $100,000. Though sentenced to death *in absentia* for collaboration and robbery, Ricord became a naturalized citizen of Argentina, and South America's leading criminal. He not only dominated the heroin trade but kept up with his earlier interests. At the time of his arrest, he was also wanted on procuring charges in Buenos Aires and in Venezuela, where he owned a nightclub in partnership with Henri Antoine Charrières, better known as Papillon.

Eventually extradited to the United States, Ricord was brought to trial in New York at the end of 1972 and sentenced to twenty years' imprisonment.

Though the ring was temporarily broken, many of Ricord's principal lieutenants remained at large for a year or more after his arrest, among them Christian Jacques David. Also known as Le Beau Serge and Jean-Pierre, David was about forty in March 1971, and some thought he looked a little like Alain Delon. He, too, was wanted in France, where he faced execution for the murder of the Paris police commissioner investigating the assassination of Mehdi

Ben Barka in 1965. And while it is not certain that David was the Jean-Pierre to whom Miguel Garcia and George Ramos were introduced in New York, *their* Jean-Pierre had also been described as "tight with Ricord." Ricord's arrest at the same time as they were trying to set up the second deal in Miami may well explain, therefore, why it stalled and fell through.

A lot of other deals collapsed as well. It was the beginning of a heroin shortage that would turn to famine within a year. But there was no shortage of candidates measuring themselves for Ricord's shoes. As always, everywhere down the line, whenever a dealer dropped out, a dozen stood ready to take his place—the economics of the business saw to that.

In 1971, the Corsicans were buying raw opium in Turkey at around $25 for 10 kilos. Transported to their clandestine laboratories in Marseilles, these 10 kilos were turned into one kilo of high-grade heroin hydrochloride worth perhaps $5,000 f.o.b. At the American border, the price doubled. On the New York wholesale market, it doubled again to $20,000, at least for large shipments, and sharply more for smaller buys. At the peak of the famine in 1972, European pure was fetching no less than $785 a *gram* in Boston, netting those wholesalers who had any, and who were prepared to take the trouble and risks of making multiple small-volume sales, nearly $800,000 a kilo.

As a wholesale price, this was altogether exceptional, and it fell again heavily as supplies improved. But, at street level, a kilo of pure that started out in Marseilles at $5,000 was routinely grossing that much and more.

A street "bag"—a single dose—contains perhaps 100 milligrams of powder, of which only 10 percent at the very most is pure heroin. The other 90 percent is usually dextrose, lactose, starch, powdered milk, quinine, Epsom salts, or mannite (a mild Italian laxative). In other words, one kilo of pure is theoretically enough to produce 100,000 bags, although some wastage is inevitable in handling, cutting, and bagging. At $10 a bag to the user, that placed the final value of the original kilo in 1971 at around $1 million. By mid-1972, the average heroin content of a street bag had fallen to 2 or 3 percent, and the price had gone to $15 in many places.

This was a normal free-market response to a shortage deliberately engineered by police action. The Harrison Narcotic Act of 1914 had committed the federal government to a policy of treating drug misuse and addiction not as a medical but as a criminal problem, thereby bringing about the very situation it had sought to avoid. Five years later, the Volstead Act achieved a similar result with alcohol, but drinkers, being more numerous and therefore more politically influential than users of other drugs, managed to secure the repeal of Prohibition before the machinery of law-enforcement either broke down or was entirely corrupted.

The evil effects of a prohibition on narcotics and other potentially dangerous drugs were slower to appear. Addiction became a social rather than a personal problem only because there was no legal way for a drug user to support his habit. A criminal network therefore came into being to supply him with illegal drugs, and he in turn was often forced into crime in order to pay for them, the price being dictated, not by the cost of the product, but by its scarcity and the risks involved in handling it.

Even so, as a social problem, drug misuse was easily contained for almost fifty years by conventional police methods. As the number of criminal users and criminal dealers increased, so did the size, budgets, and expertise of the government agencies charged with resisting the trend. By the sixties, the investment in repression, both intellectual and financial, had become so great that even though the policy had clearly failed, few were disposed to question the wisdom of it, let alone change their minds.

The sickly flowering of an underground drug culture meant simply that the battle had been lost. The casualty lists were there for all to see in the runaway figures, not just for drug offenses, but for muggings, burglaries, holdups—and police corruption. Public safety now required a reexamination of first principles, but no one in public office was brave enough to say so. Though some federal, state, and local funds were voted—too little and too late—for counseling and rehabilitation, Washington's bankrupt answer to a flood tide of crime on the streets was more, much more, of the same: President Nixon's War on Drugs.

It was to be fought on two fronts. Overseas, diplomatic and economic pressure would be brought to bear on foreign governments to close down the labs operated by producers of illegal drugs, to interrupt their supply lines and deny them sanctuary. At home, a major offensive would be launched against the comparative handful of national distributors controlling the narcotics trade, with a view to choking off the flow before it reached the streets. If each prong of this attack achieved its objective, the White House claimed, then a solution to the drug problem would be in sight. For if there were no drugs, then quite obviously there could be no problem.

The results were not slow in coming. Nixon was now running for a second term. The diplomatic campaign produced an undertaking from the Turkish government in 1971 to halt the legal cultivation of *Papaver somniferum*, the opium poppy, in return for $35 million in aid to its farmers. This was a sharp setback for the Corsicans, though their stockpiles were high and the ban only temporary. Turkish opium was the preferred variety because of its high morphine content—a consistent 10–15 percent.

An even harder blow was delivered by the French police. In the preceding twenty years, they had managed to find and close only six heroin laboratories in Marseilles. In fourteen months from the end of 1971, they now closed six more.

Though the chemistry of converting morphine to heroin is simple, and new labs soon took their place, the loss of production, the capital costs, and the general inconvenience to the Corsicans were considerable. An average rate of production for a heroin lab is about 100 kilos a month, so that only five or six were needed to supply the entire U.S. market, then taking between 5,000 and 7,000 kilos a year. The temporary loss of even one laboratory, therefore, meant a temporary cut of 20 percent in the number of bags on American streets (or a 20 percent drop in their strength).

The number of intercepts and arrests in France also rose dramatically after the passage of stricter drug laws on December 31, 1970. In 1971, 755 kilos of heroin and morphine base were seized there, and 2,592 people arrested. In the previous year, the comparable totals had been 325 kilos and 57 arrests.

In Southeast Asia, a combined diplomatic and military assault with the United Nations and the governments of Thailand and Laos began to make an impression on the Golden Triangle, the remote, mountainous region on the borders of those two countries with Burma, which was then producing about a thousand tons of opium a year—some 70 percent of the world's supply. Luckily for Washington, and unluckily for the Thais, most of this was consumed in the area. There were an estimated 300,000 addicts in Thailand, thousands more in Laos, and probably tens of thousands among the Meo, Lahu, Akha, and Yao hill tribesmen who grew opium poppies as their only cash crop. But there *was* a surplus, and the Corsicans, together with some of the more enterprising American mobsters, like Santo Trafficante, Jr., from Florida, and the Chinese Triad societies, were already channeling it onto the world market. It was quite clear that, as the supply of Turkish opium tapered away, arrangements were well in hand to make up the deficit with exports from the Golden Triangle—while the CIA looked studiously off in another direction.

During the sixties, the Agency had helped the trade along more positively—to the extent of allowing shipments to be flown around Asia by Air America. Preoccupied with the difficulties of suppressing Communist insurgents in this wild and inaccessible region, the CIA was not about to alienate the Communists' natural enemies, the local warlords and their armies of former Chinese Nationalist troops, even if they *were* supporting themselves on the profits of opium trafficking. It was not until drug addiction became a serious problem among American servicemen in Vietnam that the CIA assumed an entirely neutral role—neither helping nor hindering the business arrangements of its dubious allies.

Spurred on by Washington's concern over crime on the streets, the Bureau of Narcotics and Dangerous Drugs set up a joint task force with the Thai National Police in 1971 to harry the supply routes leading south from the Golden Triangle. Before long, caravans of illegal opium were being intercepted, carrying loads that made seizures in the United States and Europe seem trivial, loads of four or five *tons.* Still more ominously, quantities of locally produced heroin also came to light.

Brown heroin (discolored in processing) was also being produced in Mexico and probably in Ecuador—enough to supply 10–15 percent of the American market, and no doubt more if the need arose. Under pressure from Washington, the Mexican government instructed its Federal Judicial Police to work in closer harmony with American agents on Mexican soil. Similar arangements were soon in force throughout most of Latin America, although the emphasis here was mainly on catching the Corsicans and the Mob's buying agents.

Ricord was one of the first, and certainly not the last, to go. Though drug-dealing was not an offense in Paraguay, American arm-twisting not only secured his arrest there but, in a parody of due process, brought about his extradition by means that led Ricord's defense counsel to complain that his client had been literally shanghaied by American agents. The court's sympathy seemed muted, however, even when counsel went on to describe the former Gestapo agent as the victim of an official conspiracy and "a man who loves children and animals."

Though his complaint was well-founded, this was the era of Watergate. Almost any measure could be justified if it worked. Several other wanted men in South America also woke up suddenly to find themselves in American hands. Some claimed to have been tapped on the head and carried across national frontiers in a mailbag; others, that they were smuggled out to the United States in the bellies of U.S. Army transport aircraft. Still others never woke up at all, and were simply found dead in mysterious circumstances. So far as the White House was concerned, a policy of hot pursuit and no sanctuary was just as appropriate in this war as in any other.

But Brazil was not Cambodia. As Ricord was coming to trial in New York, the Brazilians were induced by more peaceful means to expel six leading Corsican drug suppliers into the waiting arms of French and American agents. Among the six were Claude André Pastou, also wanted in France in connection with the Ben Barka assassination; Michel Nicoli, wanted in the U.S. for pioneering the South American connection with Lucien Sarti, and Le Beau Serge, Christian David, also known as Jean-Pierre. Facing execution in France, David elected instead to plead guilty to drug charges in New York, where he was sentenced to twenty years' imprisonment without parole.

Before long, the Corsican establishment in Latin America was wilting visibly under fire. François Rossi, its kingpin in Buenos Aires, was arrested in Barcelona. Lucien Sarti was killed in a gun battle with the Mexican police. André Gaetan Condemine was missing, believed dead, in France. Carlo Zippo was picked up in Naples. Giuseppe Catenia, late of Palermo, Sicily, was expelled from Mexico and taken off an Air France plane at Houston, Texas. On paper, it looked like a rout.

On the overseas front, after one year of war, the Bureau of Narcotics and Dangerous Drugs was able to report that the cooperation of foreign governments had led to the seizure abroad of 120,670 pounds of illegal drugs destined for the American market. Had they reached the streets, the Bureau claimed, they would have fetched a cool $892,931,440.

It had also done pretty well on the home front. In the same twelve months ending June 30, 1972, seizures *inside* the United States totaled 49,265 pounds—including about two and a half tons of heroin—worth $676,590,347 on the street. But here it had to share some of the glory not only with state and local police authorities but with other federal agencies as well, including U.S. Customs, the Office of Narcotics Intelligence, and the Office of Drug Abuse Law Enforcement.

ODALE was President Nixon's own creation, his chosen instrument for pressing home the war against the home-grown drug dealer. In the first half of 1972, ODALE task forces went to work in thirty-four cities and made one thousand arrests. As the new agency was set up by Egil Krogh, G. Gordon Liddy, and Attorney General John Mitchell, some have suggested that ODALE was simply a front for the White House plumbers. Others, notably Edward Jay Epstein in *Agency of Fear,* now see it as a cloak for a Nixon attempt to found an American Gestapo. But no matter how dubious its ancestry, ODALE *did* employ many able and conscientious men in the field who *did* make a dent in the drug trade—men like Andrew Maloney, New York regional director, and Special Attorney William Callahan, who later coordinated the federal government's all-out assault on Frank Matthews.

Indeed, as the stinking corruption of the drug scene began slowly to poison the whole fabric of American city life, it fired a strong sense of mission in many of those who had gone into law enforcement with a sense of vocation rather than simply to make a living. As government servants, it was not their business to question or interpret the law. Their duty was to apprehend and convict those who broke it.

Not always trusting their colleagues or even the agencies that employed them, they improvised a lot and cut bureaucratic corners. They often worked on their cases off-duty, following up leads, playing their hunches, and sometimes putting in hundreds of hours of unpaid overtime on surveillance and stakeouts, just for the satisfaction of nailing their man. For them, the war had become personal.

As it was easy for officers of this sort to recognize one another, they tended to deal directly among themselves, instead of always going through official channels. If Bill Warner, a BNDD agent in Miami, saw a connection, for example, between a case he was on and another in New York, he would probably call Gerard Miller, then supervisor of Group 12, New York Joint Task Force. They belonged to an unofficial freemasonry of agents who liked to get things done. At its core were veterans, like Miller, of the old Federal Bureau of Narcotics, survivors of an agency that had been asked to police the world with 270 men. Those who remained were now the professional elite of the BNDD. They were also close friends. Besides lending the bureaucratic machinery of justice a certain flexibility, they quickened its responses, which helped even up the odds when taking on the key importers and distributors of illegal drugs.

A city policeman, if he is so inclined, may try to earn promotion by busting ten pushers a week, catching them bags in hand. At the neighborhood level, undercover cops will try to make buys from dealers in ounces and bundles, while at city-wide level the narcotics squad will try to catch the local wholesalers in their cutting and bagging mills. In each case, if they are lucky, they will seize not only the criminal but the physical evidence they need to get a conviction in court.

But at regional and national levels the men responsible for supplying the whole city network with drugs will probably never even see the loads they send in, or the money that comes back from them until it is properly laundered. In practice, the chance of catching an importer or major distributor within a mile of any incriminating physical evidence is so remote that federal agents and prosecutors must generally concentrate instead on trying to build a case against him of *conspiracy* to break the drug laws—a case that will probably depend on evidence of a documentary and circumstantial nature, and, above all, on witnesses who can testify from their own knowledge as to the defendant's guilty involvement with the narcotics trade, preferably as co-conspirators.

Conspiracy cases, however, are notoriously difficult and expensive to put together. They generally rest on a mosaic of evidence that has to be assembled piece by piece from many different sources. For this reason, they are hard to try in court. Juries always dislike them—partly because they are seldom easy to follow, and very often because the witnesses the juries are asked to believe have worse criminal records than the men they are asked to convict. If much of the government's evidence has been "bought" in return for clemency, then the suspicion of tainted testimony may well cloud the proceedings to the extent of leaving a doubt in the jury's mind even when the case was thought to be ironclad. There have been very few conspiracy trials in which even the most sanguine of federal prosecutors were ready to make book on the outcome.

And credibility is only a secondary problem. A much harder one is finding witnesses in the first place. Given the mortality rate among informers, they are not likely to come forward of their own accord. They have to be coerced.

A neighborhood dealer facing certain conviction on a fifteen-year rap may be offered a minor sentence on a minor charge on condition that he agrees to testify against his wholesaler. His wholesaler, booked on the strength of that testimony, is then offered the same deal if he will give the prosecutor *his* connection, who may be a known associate of the government's real quarry. Now the associate in turn is worked on with the idea of widening the range of possible witnesses at his level, and so on, until the prosecutor feels he has enough people in the net who have more to lose by *not* testifying, and who will together spin a strong enough web of evidence in court to snare the top man himself. *Then* he can worry about keeping them all alive long enough to face a jury who may not believe them anyway.

By definition, law enforcement means that the initiative rests always with the criminal. *He* decides when, where, and how to commit a crime; then the police have to find out who did it. *He* decides when, where, and how to hide; then the police must try to catch him. Even with advance notice of a crime, the police still usually have to wait for it to happen before making an arrest; they are always coming from behind (except in a police state). But in going after the big-time professional criminal on conspiracy charges, the courthouse squads of the U.S. Attorneys most heavily involved with narcotics cases—notably those in the Eastern and Southern Districts of New York—could, and did, even up the odds by employing the enormous, wide-ranging powers of the federal grand jury system.

Once a federal prosecutor has convened a panel of twenty-three citizens to decide if there is evidence enough to detain a fellow citizen for trial, he can subpoena anybody to appear before it, without explanation. He can subpoena their private papers, financial records, letters—anything he wants. There are no rules of evidence, so anything goes: rumor, conjecture, hearsay—even the results of illegal wiretaps and searches. He can ask any questions he likes any way he likes; a witness is not entitled to have a lawyer present, and has no right to remain silent. If the protection of the Fifth Amendment is invoked, the federal attorney can grant the witness limited immunity from prosecution and ask the question again. If it remains unanswered, the witness can be sent to prison without trial for eighteen months. If he lies and this can be proved, he may be tried and imprisoned for longer terms on charges of criminal perjury.

As a weapon of war against drug dealers, a federal grand jury subpoena could be as deadly as a bullet. A small-time pusher in fear for his life if he testified against his connection might perhaps stick it out on the witness stand and give nothing away. But if the federal attorney smiled and put an arm around the pusher's shoulders as they left the sealed courtroom, well, what was his connection supposed to think?

As soon as the juggernaut of a grand jury started to roll, a skillful government attorney could bulldoze a path right up to his quarry's front door, and the Organized Crime Control Act, 1970, encouraged him to do just that. It gave the Justice Department almost unlimited powers to empanel special investigative grand juries with a life of up to three years, in effect authorizing U.S. Attorneys to set out on prolonged fishing expeditions with all the resources of the federal government behind them. Working with the BNDD and ODALE, they still had to put a case together that would hold up in court, and this still meant persuading witnesses to testify against their former associates, but now, besides the carrot of clemency, they also carried a very big stick.

The only serious limitation on their attack was the Justice Department's budget. Investigations of this sort are very expensive, making huge demands on manpower and equipment over long periods. Just to keep a prime suspect under continuous moving surveillance for twenty-four hours without him suspecting could easily involve as many as forty men and a dozen cars. But the war on drugs was also part of a war on Democrats, and funds could usually be found.

A former White House official remembers President Nixon summoning the regional directors of ODALE and their senior attorneys to Washington for a conference in the election-year summer of 1972. As he chatted with them informally before the meeting began, Nixon asked William Callahan, "What's happening in New York?"

"Well, Mr. President," said Callahan, taken slightly aback by the size of the question, "our intelligence reports show that the big dealers believe this is just a political gimmick. They say the heat will come off as soon as the election is over."

At this, the White House aide recalls, Nixon stepped back and punched his palm with his fist. "Goddammit," he said. "I'll show those sons of bitches. I'll ram this gimmick up their ass."

On July 27, 1972, he asked Congress to vote another $135.2 million in supplemental funds.

As on the overseas front, there was no resisting an assault of this weight. Once an enemy stronghold had been identified, it was usually only a matter of time before its defenses were brought down by an elite corps of highly motivated policemen and government attorneys using the grand jury system as a siege weapon and backed to the hilt with almost all the money and political heft it could use.

In New York, Louis Cirillo was one of the first to go. Along with twenty-two of his associates, he was indicted by a federal grand jury in January 1972 on charges of importing and wholesaling about one-sixth of all the heroin used in the United States each year. Agents dug up over $1 million in cash buried in the back yard and basement of his home on Randall Avenue in the Bronx—a useful nest egg for a man who described himself as a bagelmaker. He was later convicted and sentenced to twenty-five years' imprisonment on the testimony of Roger Preiss, one of Cirillo's smugglers, whom the U.S. Attorney for the Southern District of New York had persuaded to "cooperate."

In February, it was Vincent C. Papa's turn. He was picked up, also in the Bronx, with a green suitcase on the back seat of his car. It contained $968,550. For his inability to explain this, he was awarded five years in prison on income tax charges—another line of attack that proved so useful that the Internal Revenue Service set up a special unit to check on the tax returns of people suspected of dealing in narcotics.

And so the war went on. Those who thought it could be won by breaking up the smuggling and distribution rings, by keeping narcotics from reaching the streets, watched the dealers go down and supplies dwindle, and saw in this the final vindication of the hard-nosed approach to the drug problem.

But the number of addicts did not go down. It went up. Though its figures have been challenged by Edward Jay Epstein (too high) and George Richardson (too low), the Justice Department's 1972 estimate of the number of heroin users in the country was 600,000, and rising—a twelvefold increase in ten years. In New York, the Mayor's Narcotics Control Council put the total of users in the city at 316,000, and rising—most sharply in the fifteen- to forty-four-year-old age group, of whom forty-four in every one thousand were said to be addicted to hard drugs.

The problem of street crime did not improve, either. It got worse. At the height of the famine, a typical junkie needed about $200 a week to support his habit. If he was out of work or broke—as most of them usually are—he had to steal for it, adding to an already uncontrollable epidemic of mugging, shoplifting, bag-snatching, prostitution, break-ins, and stick-ups an extra edge of viciousness or desperation lent by the fear that, even with the money, a fix might be hard to find.

In short, the closer President Nixon came to achieving the hard-liners' ultimate goal of shutting off the supply of illegal drugs altogether, the more dangerous it was to go out on the streets.

Victory in his war could come only from total suppression—no drugs, therefore no addicts, therefore no problem—but that was unattainable. His partial victory, bought by a major diversion of government resources into law enforcement, merely turned the screw on the user, and opened up gaps in the largely Italian monopoly of drug distribution that Frank Matthews and his colleagues in the Black Mafia were only too happy to fill.

7

A few months after our little adventure with Ricardo Morales, Orlando came over to the house, all excited.

"Hey," he said. "Your godfather wants to see you. And he is doing *good*."

It was about time. We were now in the middle of March 1972. A whole damn year had gone by.

"Yeah, I ran into him at the Yumuri," Orlando said. "And I told him we're partners."

I didn't say nothing. Let him dream.

"You told Miguel where I'm living?" I said.

"Right. He's coming over tonight, around seven."

Anna and me had rented another apartment, away from the old neighborhood. Back in August, there'd been a double murder on our corner, at 18th Avenue and SW 8th Street. Two guys I knew had ripped off their partner in a drug deal, so he played dumb and asked them to meet him, like he didn't know. Soon as they got there, he pulled out a 9mm. Browning and chopped them to pieces. Then he jumped in his car, drove off like a maniac, and killed an old man crossing 8th Street, a few blocks downtown.

Well, naturally that brought down a hellatious amount of heat, and those bastards weren't even from our neighborhood. Our corner had the best Cuban car dealer in Miami. It had the best Cuban bakery—Los Pinos Nuevos. Had the Yumuri, the only Latin restaurant open twenty-four hours a day. It was a real classy corner. Almost everybody made money there. It had room for fences, for thieves, for dope—you could move anything around there. But after that double killing, the corner died, too. It was like a ghost town. And that was when me and Anna took off.

Anyway, as it got near seven, I sent her about her business and told Orlando to get lost, thinking Miguel would want to talk to me alone, but he showed up with two guys. So right away I knew things wouldn't be the same as last time. He had partners. One was Ricky Acosta. I wasn't worried about him. He's an easygoing guy who'd done time with my godfather. But the other one was José Martinez. He'd dealt with Miguel back in the sixties, and we'd visited him once or twice when we were running around town looking to make a connection last time.

So we sat down and kicked things around over a couple of drinks, and Orlando was right. Miguel *was* back on top. I could tell from his clothes and the way he talked. He was living at his mother's house—and having it rebuilt, from what he said—but not a word about Barbara or Vicky. I was sorry they'd broken up. Barbara wasn't pretty or nothing, but she was class, strictly Fifth Avenue, and had more balls than most men. We used to call her the "Enforcer"—La Bacana, the big-shot.

"Listen," he said, when we got through with the bullshit. "I want you to do something for me."

"Yeah, what's that?"

He looked kind of uncomfortable. "Well, would you be interested in taking some stuff up to New York?"

Now that was a blow, compared with what I had done with him before, but I figured we had to start somewhere. These guys had been with him when he got going again, so it wasn't like they were cutting me out. In fact, Miguel was trying to cut me in.

"Okay. What have you got?"

"You want to take five keys up for me? Five keys of coke?"

"Sure," I said, showing him it was okay. "Why not?"

That relieved his mind. "Well, listen, I got a car you can use. It's clean. It's cool. I figure you can put the stuff in the spare tire or something."

"Uh-uh. No good. You can have an accident. The car can get stolen. A hundred things can happen to you on the road. No thanks."

"Well, you can't catch a plane," he said. "They're hot as hell now, with all these goddamn hijacks and shit. How about the train?"

"No, I'll do it the conservative way," I said. "I'll take the bus."

"The *bus?*" But I could see he was relieved. "That's a bitch. That's thirty hours."

"I got patience," I said. "I just sat out twelve months."

So that was settled. And now he asked me if I'd paint his mother's house while I waited for the load to come through—just me, no helpers. He didn't want nobody snooping around out there.

"Sure," I said. "And that reminds me. If I'm going to run some stuff for you, I want to move. The neighbors are a little nosey. Throw me five hundred so I can rent a new pad."

Anna wasn't too pleased that Miguel was back, but she had her eye on this nice new apartment out in Coral Gables, and I figured that moving would keep her happy. So he pulled out a roll of hundreds as big as both fists and counted off five. Then he told me to meet him at his mother's place in the morning, and they left.

I hadn't seen Victoria Montalvo's house on Biarritz Drive in almost a year, and next day I nearly drove by it. The money Miguel had spent on that place. It had a new roof, which cost him $15,000, and they were just finishing a new porch, for another $5,000. Inside, it was the same story. He had fixed up his own apartment like the old one in Riverdale, only the bedroom was better. It had a blue carpet, ankle-deep, and another canopy bed, but the ceiling was draped with striped silk, blue and white, like a tent, with a crystal chandelier hanging down in the middle. And out back he had built his own little voodoo shrine.

So I asked the old lady what color she wanted the house. It needed a paint job sure enough, but all the preparation had been done.

"White," she said. "And look, I seen houses that sparkle when the sun hits them. You know how to do that?"

"Sure," I said. "No problem. You throw the glitter stuff on while the paint is still wet. Just leave it to me."

As I was getting started, my godfather showed up. He stood and watched me work for a while.

"Listen, I know this ain't easy," he said.

"Painting the house? It's a snip."

"I mean, carrying the stuff. Not after what we've been through."

"I don't mind doing it for *you,*" I said.

"Right. I know that. This thing started over in Venezuela in October, and they were with me at the time. I got to give them a fair shake."

"Sure. Who's complaining?"

"I just want you to understand," he said. "I want you to play along, because I got a feeling things'll change."

"You better believe it."

"Martinez? Well, I owe him something. Ricky you don't got to worry about."

"*I'm* not the one who's got to worry," I said.

Two days later, I was just finishing the house, when the old lady came out.

"Your godfather called," she said. "As soon as you're done here, he wants to see you over at Raquel's place."

Raquel Dumois was José Martinez's mother. She was a voodoo queen. Ya-Llocha, which means "mother of saints." And I guess a pretty good one, because I know for a fact my godfather paid her $21,000 in one year to make him a saint in her religion. She called it Yorubi Lucumi, but it was *santería*—half Catholic, half voodoo.

Anyway, she lived in a dump behind the city courthouse, around 14th Street and 14th Avenue. It was raining when I got there, indoors as well. They had pans and bowls all through the house to catch the drips coming through the ceiling. Plink, plonk. The place stank. There were piles of dirty rags in the corners.

Miguel was tearing into Martinez about some guy who had put them in bad with Henry Morgan by undercutting their kilo price for cocaine. And Martinez was trying to talk Miguel out of having the guy killed.

"You got a phone yet?" my godfather suddenly said to me.

"Jesus," I said. "We only moved in yesterday."

Anna hadn't wasted much time. I gave her the $500, and twelve hours later we were living at 131 Menores, Coral Gables.

"All right. Well, go home and stay there. I'll be in touch. I don't know when exactly."

I felt like asking him why he couldn't have got Victoria to tell me that, instead of dragging me down from Normandy Isle, but he was mad enough already, so I let it pass.

The next afternoon, Martinez came by and told me to be at Raquel's house at about eleven. So I took a shower, had something to eat, and around 10:30 hopped in my car and went over there. My godfather had quite a reception committee waiting. Raquel. Her boyfriend, who was another *santero*. Martinez. His brother Pedro. And Martinez's girlfriend Isabelle, who was a spiritualist. They looked at me as I came in like I had my fly undone.

"Look," Miguel said. "I want you to have a little number done on you, okay? It's for your own good."

"What kind of a number?"

"Just a blessing," Raquel said. "To cleanse you of evil spirits."

"No shit."

I wondered what would happen if I told her to forget it. My godfather wouldn't help me out. He really believed in this stuff, probably more than she did. Looking at their faces, I knew if I didn't go along with this game, there'd be no game to go along with.

So they took my clothes off, and sat me in a chair. Then Raquel made white streaks on my forehead and shoulders and foot with some chalk. When that was done, she went through a whole routine with a big feather, mumbling and chanting things, and after that, it was Isabelle's turn. She puffed at a big cigar and blew smoke over me, talking and mumbling at the same time—these dingbats were getting all carried away with this bullshit. Finally, Raquel turned around to my godfather and said, "He's a son of Yemaya, Virgin of Regla. And he's clean."

Great. I got out of the chair, thinking it was all over, but no. Now they stuck my ass in a big wooden tub, and before I could say anything, she poured this shit all over me. Mostly water, but there was something in it that smelled funny. And that *really* pissed me off. I'd just taken a shower and put perfume on, and now they were pouring this garbage over me.

"All right," she said to my godfather. "He's ready."

I was ready to open her head. She handed me a towel, and as I dried myself off, she started in with the instructions.

"Don't take a bath or a shower for two days," she said. "You mustn't wash it off your body. That's your protection. And don't go with a woman."

"What?" I said. Shit. I was going to be away for a while, and Anna was hopping mad already.

"No sex for two days. That's very important. And wear white. Dress in white as much as you can."

Then she hung some beads around my neck, and that was it. I got dressed, tried to comb some of the shit out of my hair, and went across the street with Martinez to the house he lived in with Isabelle. The load was hidden in a linen basket, under their dirty clothes—10 half-kilo packages in a grocery bag. He said I was to take it to an address at 48th Street and Park in West New York, and he would meet me there in two days.

I put the bag in the trunk of my car, and as I was getting ready to drive off, my godfather came out to say goodbye. It was the first chance I'd had to talk to him alone since I finished the old lady's house.

"So who are we going to move this stuff to when I get it up there?" I asked him.

"José knows what to do," he said, and then he saw my face. "I want you to go see Zack Robinson and offer him a choice of deals. He can have the five keys for $35,000, and take twenty thousand off the hundred we owe him. Or you can move the stuff elsewhere, and give him twenty when you done it. It's up to Zack, okay?"

"Hell, he'll take the stuff for sure," I said. "That way, he can make himself a heavy piece of change as well."

"Right. But do it like I told you. He's got to know that twenty is the limit this time."

"Check." Knowing we were going to start paying the guy back

at last put me in a better mood. But not for long. When I got home, Orlando was waiting there with Anna, and I didn't mind, because I could see another storm brewing. I told him about the voodoo, and that made him very happy.

"Man," he said, "you're one of us now. This is good. You'll see."

But all I could see was Anna getting pink and twitchy the longer I stalled. So I told them I had an eight o'clock bus to catch in the morning, and Orlando said he'd come by at about 7:15 to run us over to the depot. Then he left, and after I'd packed the five keys into a small suitcase with a few things I needed, me and Anna went to bed.

First, I tried to stay away from her on my side, and when that didn't work, I pretended to be asleep. But there was no way she was going to let me get away with that, so I got up for a glass of water. I tried to make it last, but after a couple of minutes she called me back to bed, and we went through the whole routine again.

"What the hell's the matter with you?" she said.

"Nothing. I got things on my mind, that's all."

"So have I," she said. "Come here."

"No, listen—I can't. No sex."

"What?"

So then I told her what Raquel Dumois had said, and Anna blew a fuse. She cussed and swore and bawled me out, so the whole street could hear. She worked herself up until she hated everybody. Even Feo, her Pekinese, went and hid in the closet.

"Take it easy," I told her. "Just play along until this thing straightens out. Will you do that for me?"

"Will I *shit.* Next thing you know, they'll tell you to divorce me."

"We're not married," I said. "Come on, honey. You know why I got to do this. If I can hang in there, I'll get it all. So play along and let's see what happens, okay? We need the money."

"I don't want it," she said. "This is dirty money. Drug money? Voodoo? I don't want it. I don't want nothing."

And she spent what was left of the night on *her* side of the bed. I got up at 6:30, feeling like hell, and we drove over with Orlando to the bus depot. Though Anna had cooled off by now, she didn't say much, even when she kissed me goodbye. She waited while I found a seat near the back of the bus and put my suitcase up on the rack, then she waved once and walked away to the car.

Things didn't get better. The bus made its first stop upstate at Orlando, and I got off to use the washroom. I couldn't shower because I was going to meet Martinez, and if the smell was gone, he would know, but I figured I could take a wash at least. So I carried the suitcase in there with me—no way I was going to leave it on the bus—and stood over it while I splashed water in my face.

Using the sink next to me was a skinny little black guy, who wasn't afraid of nobody. All of a sudden, he jumped back like something bit him.

"Man, what you doing, splashing me?"

"Hey, I'm sorry," I said. "Didn't mean to do that. These sinks are kind of small."

"Sorry?" he said, getting all bent out of shape. "What you mean, sorry? Goddamn, I'll whip your ass. *Then* you'll be sorry."

"Oh, shit," I said. I couldn't just knock him on the side of the head. There were five keys of coke between my legs, and maybe a cop outside. So I gave him the eye, and reached for a towel to dry myself. "I'm telling you I'm sorry, man. What more do you want?"

"I want to whip your ass, you mother-fucker," he said. "That's what I want."

As I picked up the suitcase to leave, the son of a bitch pushed me, but I kept on going.

Twenty hours later, I ran into the next problem. Trailways was on strike between Washington and New York, so we all had to get off and hang around the bus station for a couple of hours, waiting for a Greyhound to pick us up for the rest of the trip. Naturally, with a strike on, there were cops all over the place with nothing to do but nose around, and I began to wonder if Raquel

Dumois had got her words straight. Next time, if there *was* a next time, I'd try to get by *without* a blessing. But nothing happened, and when we finally reached the Port Authority Terminal in New York, I switched buses again, onto an Orange and Black, and got off on the Jersey side a couple of blocks away from 48th and Park.

Martinez opened the door of the apartment.

"Well, I see you made it okay," he said. "How was the trip? No trouble?"

"Well, we met a couple of evil spirits on the way," I said. "And what the hell's all this?" The place was full of kids running about.

"Oh, they're Portomeno's," he said. "He lives here with his wife. They're good people. I know them from Cuba."

"Yeah? Well, I got no lock on this bag. I don't want none of these good people getting their little paws in here, you know what I mean?"

So after we shooed the kids out of the bedroom, he stashed the ten bags in *his* suitcase, locked it, and hid it on the top shelf of the closet.

"Good," he said. "Now you can take a shower."

"So *that's* it," I said. "I wondered why everybody kept moving away from me on the bus."

We both knew this wasn't the start of a beautiful friendship. He had probably seen a threat in me all along, but now he began to give up the game without a fight. Around eight, I was ready to go see Zack, but Martinez had settled in for the night.

"You're not coming?" I said.

"What for? You know what to say. You can handle it."

"Okay." He had tried to make it sound like he was giving me a break, and that was really stupid. If anything went wrong, he'd get the blame. If it didn't—and what the hell could go wrong?—then I'd get the credit.

"There's a car downstairs you can use," he said, changing channels. The jerk had come all the way up here just to watch TV. "The keys are on the table."

So I drove through the tunnel and parked near Mother's, Zack's new place at 23rd Street and Ninth Avenue. It was another of his small, dark night spots—just a bar, really, with live acts—and when I told the barmaid I wanted to see him, she signaled the bouncer. He was a big guy. I'm not small, but if I'd had to put the gun to *his* head instead of Billy Fair's that time, I would have had to stand on a chair.

"I'm looking for Zack," I said. "Tell him it's Mikey's godson."

So he went off in the back some place, and right away there was Zack, waving me over like I was the best thing he'd seen since sliced bread.

"Hey, how are you, Georgie?" he said. "You're looking good, man. Where's Mikey? He in town?"

"No, not this trip. He's in Miami. But he sent me up to talk a little business with you."

"Yeah? That's good. Let's go sit in my office. You know, I don't blame the guy, staying down there. I could use a little of that Florida sunshine myself. It's been cold as a son of a bitch up here."

"Then pay us a visit, why don't you?"

"You know, I might just do that." He poured two belts of scotch. "I already told Mikey, the next time you're in New York, the both of you, maybe we'll sail my boat down there. I got a big Chris-Craft. Forty-seven foot. Plenty big enough for the three of us. And maybe for a couple of broads, too."

"Each?" I said, and he laughed.

"Now I know you're Mikey's godson. That's the horniest son of a bitch I ever did see."

"Yeah, well. He likes his little comforts. We know a couple of places down there could warm a corpse."

"That I could use," Zack said. "You hear what happened?"

"Yeah, I heard you were sick, you know? I heard you were in the hospital."

"Yeah, I was sick. I'll show you." He stood up behind his desk, pulled his shirt out and undid it, holding it away from his body.

"Holy Jesus," I said. The guy looked like an old gravy strainer. "Who the hell did that?"

"Count them," he said.

So I did. "I make it ten. Jesus."

"You missed one," he said. "How about up by the neck here—see that?"

"Eleven. Jesus. The son of a bitch really had it in for you."

"Yeah. I'm suing the government," he said. "The bastard. You know what he did? This agent sees me getting out of the car, so he pulls his pipe and says, 'Freeze.' So I freeze. You think I'm stupid? I start to tell him, 'Hey, man, be cool. I'm not carrying nothing,' and the son of a bitch cuts loose on me. Hits me about five times, and down I go. I'm telling myself, Christ! The bastard just killed me—and what's he doing? He's reloading his piece, that's what he's doing. He's fumbling with it because his hands are all shaky, and I'm just lying there watching him. I can't figure out what he's got in mind. Now I'm starting to hurt. Finally he gets through and comes over to see what's happening. I try to ask him what he done that for, and goddammit if he don't start plugging away at me again. So I just shut my eyes. Next thing I know, I'm in the hospital."

"Jesus," I said. "You got nine lives."

"Well, I got eight now. And I'm suing the bastards. I got my lawyer on it. They got no right going around killing people like that. They got laws in this country."

But he was really proud of those holes, and I had to admire them again before we got down to business. I offered him the choice of five kilos at $11,000 each for $35,000 cash plus $20,000 off the bill, or a straight $20,000 cash repayment, and naturally he settled for the coke, like I knew he would.

"Okay," I said. "So how are we going to work this now?"

"Well, not around here," he said. "I got to be careful, after what happened. All this excitement ain't good for my health. Let's make it uptown, where the heat ain't around so much. You know where 86th and Madison is?"

"Sure."

"Okay, well, that's a good corner. Let's go check it out."

So I followed Zack uptown in his gold Toronado, and like he

said, it looked like a good corner—busy, but not busy enough to attract any flies. We arranged to meet there at nine o'clock the next night, and I drove back to Jersey. Martinez was still watching television, with Portomeno and some other guy. It turned out I was using this other guy's car, so after I told them we were all set for tomorrow, he drove me over to the Tunnel Motel for the night.

The following afternoon, Martinez and me set up shop in the apartment and cut three of the kilos into five. Then around eight o'clock I loaded the ten half-kilo packages we had made into a plastic shopping bag from the No Name boutique in Coral Gables, and got ready to go.

"We know who we're dealing with," Martinez said. "You don't need me to ride shotgun, right?"

"Right," I said. "I don't need you."

It was raining like hell. I got soaked, just crossing the sidewalk. The car didn't want to start either, but I finally made it go and headed for the Lincoln Tunnel, driving slow and easy because the wipers couldn't hardly keep up with the downpour. I paid the toll, and I hadn't gone more than a few yards past the booth when the son of a bitch stalled on me.

I hit the starter. Nothing. Hit it again. Still nothing. Oh, shit. And I got a honker behind me. He's trying to blow me away with his horn. There are the cops, not fifty feet away, watching the traffic. And here am I, in a car that won't go, with five keys of coke in a Florida shopping bag. Just perfect. So I give that mother a real long burst, cussing it out like a lunatic. No good. If I go on like this, I'm going to flood it. Now one of the cops is getting out of the car. Okay. I can't refuse his help, so I'll ask for a wrecker right off. I'll get him to help me push the goddamn thing out of the way, and hope he don't get too nosey while I'm waiting for the wrecker. One more try before I get out to meet him. Come on, you bastard—and it starts. Coughs. Stutters. But I catch it with the gas pedal and damn near gun its guts out. The cop shakes his head and runs back out of the rain.

I was ten minutes early at 86th Street and Madison, but Zack had been even earlier. As I pulled into a parking space behind his Toronado, he was already getting out—with a girl. They climbed into the back of my car, fussing about the weather.

"Shit," he said. "Look at that." There were big wet spots on his leather coat. "That's going to leave rings."

"No, it'll dry," I said. "Don't worry about it. You want to take the stuff now?"

"No. Follow me. Drop her off with it where she tells you to, and then we'll go to my place and I'll get you the money. You sure that won't stain?"

"Positive. I guarantee it. I got a jacket like that. Same kind of leather."

He ran back to his car, and I followed him across to Park Avenue, and then up to around 96th Street, where the girl told me to stop. Zack waited till he saw her get out with the shopping bag, and then we went up to the Bronx somewhere. I didn't know that part of town, and what with the rain and everything, I soon got lost.

It was a pretty rough neighborhood, and the apartment building he lived in wasn't about to get written up in *House and Garden* either. Zack liked to live among his people. But it was nice inside. Not plush, but comfortable. He undid about six locks, then sat me down and went to a closet. I couldn't see what he had in there exactly, but he came back with seven rolls of $100 bills done up in rubber bands.

"Five thousand in each," he said. "And seven times five is $35,000. Okay?"

"Man, it's a pleasure doing business with you," I said. "But how the fuck do I get out of here?"

"No problem. I'll lead you out on the Major Deegan Expressway, then take the Third Avenue Bridge."

We hadn't gone more than a few blocks before he signaled with his brake lights and double-parked outside a beat-up-looking row of stores. Now what? I trusted Zack as much as I trusted anybody, but I was lost in the Bronx with $35,000 in a brown paper bag, and not even packing a toothpick. I pulled in behind him, and wound down the window as he walked back.

"What's wrong?" I said, looking around.

"Wrong? Nothing. You want an ice cream?"

Turned out the man was a freak for mint chocolate chip.

Martinez must have been listening by the front door, because he opened it the second I rang the bell.

"You got the money?" he said, and I just handed him the bag as I went on through.

"It's all here? You count it?"

I couldn't talk to him. If I'd opened my mouth, it would have been to tell him to go fuck himself. The stupid scumbag just didn't know how it was when you dealt with big people. They're not out to cheat you, not if it's going to cost them a good connection. What's the point? In any case, we still owed Zack a little matter of $80,000. I'm going to count his money in case he's short a couple of dollars? Martinez was a small-minded punk.

"Okay," he said. "I got to call Florida."

I figured he was going to check with my godfather and make it sound like he'd pulled off the deal himself, but no, he didn't even have the sense to do that. He called Raquel Dumois.

"That you, Momma?" he said, all excited. "Listen, we got the money for the house."

I couldn't listen to any more of that. I went into the kitchen to get a beer. A few minutes later, he came in there after me and handed over the paper bag with the money.

"Okay. Here's what you do," he said. "I want you to take this back to Miami for me. And be careful. If you lose it, I'll kill you."

He meant it as a joke, but after all that had happened, I wasn't laughing.

"I'm just kidding," he said. "Take three thousand out for yourself, and hold the rest at your place until you hear from Miguel. How will you go?"

"Same way I came," I said. "By bus."

I spent the night at the Skyline Motel over in Manhattan and caught the Greyhound next morning. Thirty hours later, I was back in Miami with Anna.

The storm had blown over. After a little serenading and mending fences, we were as good as new. Except she kept saying she wished my godfather would break a leg. And I have to admit I was a little buggy with him myself. We had a phone now, and he called up a couple of days after I got back and told me to bring $20,000 over to Raquel's place. Martinez was going to buy her a new house. Well, okay. They could use one. But *I'd* done all the work. It was me that bought them the goddamn house. They got twenty. Miguel got twelve. I got three. But, so . . . Patience. Martinez was burying himself.

Then I fell in love. Me and Anna were out driving in our little Corvair, and suddenly I saw this 1967 Corvette for $2,800 cash. No question about it; we were meant for each other. I had to have that car. So we drove on over to 21st Avenue, just off Flagler. Since around Christmas, Miguel had been shacking up there with a call girl named Ana Baños, and I figured that was where he would be.

"I need some money to buy a car," I said.

"Sure." He knew how I felt. "Take my keys. There's a hold-all downstairs in the trunk."

So I brought the bag up and put it on the table.

"Open it," he said. "Tell me what I got in there."

I counted out a bit over $18,000.

"Okay," he said. "Take what you need."

Miguel was like that. He didn't even want to see what I took. For all he knew, I wanted to buy a Rolls-Royce. And if I had, he wouldn't have cared. As long as the money was coming in, he never worried. That did a lot for me. It did something for Anna, too, because a few days later, when he called to say, "Come on over to Raquel's house, and be ready to leave," she didn't hardly say a word. We went there together by cab.

This time, there were no surprises—maybe because Anna was with me, or maybe the blessing I got was good for two trips.

"José is up in New York with some stuff," my godfather said. "I want you to take him a few things."

"Sure. Like what?"

"Like this suitcase."

Inside was a new Sears bag-sealer, a gallon can of acetone, a little bottle of citric acid, sealed up tight, and some other bits and pieces.

"What's this for?"

"We're going to try cutting the stuff a new way. If we got time."

"Okay. Where do I take it? Same place?"

I was ready to leave, but my godfather looked at Raquel. "Hold it," he said. "First we got to figure out how you're going to go."

I started to tell him that was my business, but I could see from his expression that he didn't think so. And it was his ball game. Like I'd told Anna, it didn't hurt me to have a little patience and put up with this voodoo bullshit. I wouldn't do nothing that looked risky, or liable to draw attention to me, but otherwise it could have been dangerous *not* to play along. If I didn't, and something went wrong with the operation, then *I'd* be the jinx.

Raquel Dumois took him into a corner, squatted down, and threw a handful of seashells on the floor. Then she whispered to him, gathered up the shells, and threw them out again. They did this a few times, and then he said: "How do you want to go up there?"

"Airplane," I said. "I've had it with the bus. I got nothing here they can make a federal case out of."

More shell-throwing. More whispering.

"Okay," he said. "Looks good. I'll drive you out to the airport."

"Fine. You want to fill me in on this? Anything special we got to do this time?"

"I'm coming up myself," he said. "I'll see you there tomorrow."

"It's not Zack, then?"

"No, it's not Zack."

I found out who it was next day. After I delivered the suitcase to Martinez at 48th Street and Park, we met up with two other guys I never saw before, named José Medina and Pedro Diaz. They were my godfather's Venezuelan connection, although I didn't know it at the time. The four of us ate together that night in a diner near the Tunnel Motel, where we all had rooms, and in the morning we took a cab back to the apartment. As we pulled up outside, I saw my godfather and two black guys getting out of a brand-new, blue-gray Cadillac with Georgia tags.

"That's him," Martinez said. "That's the man."

"Who?" I said, but he was already climbing out of the cab with the suitcase full of stuff and didn't hear me.

So I followed them upstairs, and they all sat around for a while, bullshitting. I didn't pay much attention. When people in the drug business get together over a deal, they always talk a lot—it's a whole big social ritual they go through—and it bores the shit out of me. But I have to say the two black guys made quite an impression on me, especially the boss.

Now, with Zack, you could tell at a glance he was rich, and nobody to monkey around with. Same thing with Henry Morgan, although he was quieter, more like a young executive. But this guy, you looked at him and you could feel his power. It came off like warmth from a stove. He stood about five feet ten, and weighed maybe 180 pounds. A strong man. Big neck and shoulders. Not good-looking—in fact, he was ugly—but the charm was there. Easy. Sure of himself. You could see it never crossed his mind that people wouldn't do like he told them. Looking at him, you didn't see a rich black guy. His color didn't register. What you saw was a millionaire.

The other one was not a guy to tangle with, either. He came across like a high-class bodyguard, only more than that. He joined in the bullshit like an equal, but nobody made a move in that room he didn't know about. Not hostile or nothing. He was a very friendly guy. But every time I reached for my can of beer, I found he was looking at me.

"Why don't you take delivery over here?" I heard Miguel say to them. "It's quieter. Better than New York."

"Don't make no difference to me, Mikey," the millionaire said. "We'll do it any way you want. Around seven, maybe?"

"Okay. We'll be ready."

"Fine. Then I guess that about wraps it up. Just have somebody watch out for a black T-bird with a white top."

"You hear the man, Georgie?" my godfather said.

"I hear him."

"That's my godson," he told them. "You'll be seeing him a lot."

The guy gave me a nod and a smile. "You keep bringing me those big rocks, Georgie," he said, "and you can come see me just as often as you like."

"Man," I said, "you keep coming through with the money, and I'll keep coming through with the stuff." I didn't want him to get any wrong ideas about me.

"Who was that?" I asked my godfather, when he came back up from seeing them off.

"That was Frank Matthews," he said.

8

In the late summer of 1969, Detective Joseph Kowalski of the New York Police Department noticed some unusual comings and goings in the apartment house he lived in, at 130 Clarkson Avenue, Brooklyn. To begin with, he paid little attention to the men he saw entering and leaving the building with suitcases or carrying paper bags, but after a while it occurred to him that he was seeing them far too often.

As time went by, Detective Kowalski also started to take an interest in the cars they drove. Clarkson was a respectable residential street in a low- to middle-income neighborhood, but on occasion it looked like a parking lot at a Cadillac dealers' convention.

Out of professional curiosity, he made a note of their license-plate numbers. Many of these were from out of state, but working in the Intelligence Division, he found it easy enough to check up on them. Without much surprise, he discovered that several of the cars were registered to known or suspected drug dealers, and in his spare time he took to keeping a detailed log of their appearances on the street.

Weeks stretched into months, and Detective Kowalski managed to identify a few of the more regular visitors. Among them were Gattis "Bud" Hinton, originally from Durham, North Carolina; William "Mickey" Beckwith, a native son of Brooklyn; John "Pop" Darby, from Philadelphia; John Wesley Carter, a Baltimore dealer better known as Brother Carter or Bighead Brother; and Nathaniel Elder, from Atlanta. And Kowalski now knew who it was they came to see. He lived on the fourth floor with his common-law wife and their three kids, and his name was Frank Matthews.

On May 18, 1971, Detective Kowalski submitted a detailed report of his findings, confident he had done enough to warrant an official investigation. Had he worked in Brooklyn, his confidence might have been misplaced, because Matthews had bought a lot of local protection, but Kowalski commuted to Police Headquarters in Manhattan every day. Far from being buried, his report was turned over to the newly formed New York Joint Task Force, where it was seized upon by Gerard Miller, supervisor of Group 12, who saw in it the makings of a case that could put the Task Force on the map.

The puzzling thing was that although Frank Matthews was clearly a major distributor of illegal drugs—the toll records of his telephone at 130 Clarkson showed him to be in regular contact with dealers in twenty-one states—nobody in law enforcement had ever heard of him. Not, at any rate, in connection with narcotics. He had only once been convicted of a crime, and then at the age of sixteen. In October 1960, Frank Matthews had been arrested for stealing chickens.

Born in Durham, North Carolina, on February 13, 1944, Matthews was raised by his aunt, Marzella Steele Webb, who took him in when his mother died in 1948. He was not much of a scholar and dropped out of school after a year in junior high, but he was already a capable organizer with mesmeric powers of leadership. At fourteen, his first act as an independent businessman was to recruit a gang of eight- and nine-year-old kids to raid local chicken coops, and they loved him for it. Indeed, the attachments formed then were so strong, and Matthews's feeling for the neighborhood he grew up in so sentimental, that afterwards he would always try to surround himself with "home boys," who in turn always looked to him for help when in trouble.

After serving a year in Raleigh for assaulting the owner of the chickens he stole, Matthews exchanged the poultry business for the trade of barber, and Durham for Philadelphia. There the traditional connection between barbershops and gambling led to his arrest in 1963 on a numbers charge, but his employers evidently enjoyed some influence in law-enforcement circles, for it was never pressed. Moving on to New York, Matthews now found work as a numbers runner in Bedford-Stuyvesant and by 1965 was operating as a collector-enforcer out of a barbershop on Tompkins Avenue. He had made his mark so quickly in the policy business that it came as no surprise when once again, after an arrest for gambling at the end of 1966, the charges somehow never came to trial.

But he wasn't satisfied. At twenty-two, Frank Matthews had learned that all problems would melt in the solvent of money. Money was warm and romantic. Money made you beautiful and wise. Money meant respect and admiration and limitless supplies of cocaine. *Enough* money could buy you anything, but how much was enough? With a piece of a policy bank, he could reasonably expect to clear about $100,000 a year after covering his overhead. But there were eighteen-year-old punks making that much and more just by turning over a load of narcotics.

The Mob's monopoly of the drug business had become very shaky. In black and Spanish-speaking neighborhoods, the distribution system was being taken over by the people who lived there. They were no longer content to remain in the pay of Mob importers and wholesalers; many of them were now customers, looking to their former employers, not just for supplies, but for working capital and management expertise as well. They were also beginning to organize themselves, much as the Italian street gangs had done in the twenties, with the object of ratifying one another's territorial claims and spheres of interest and eliminating competition of the sort that benefited nobody but the customer.

The first tentative steps toward forming a black Mafia had been taken in the early sixties under the auspices of Leon Aiken, in his day the king of Harlem. One of the first really big black distributors to coexist with the Mob, Aiken had made a vast fortune from narcotics and converted much of it into valuable tracts of real estate in New York, Chicago, and Los Angeles. He also diversified, like his Italian exemplars, into all kinds of legitimate businesses, from fish-and-chip joints to neighborhood dry cleaners, using them not only to launder his drug money and provide him with an honest front for the IRS but also as a springboard into New

York's social and political life. As a successful black businessman in the early years of the civil rights movement, Aiken was much in demand among the liberal establishment until 1966, when he was sent down for twenty-five years.

The wealth and power he had enjoyed through running a tight, orderly operation naturally inspired other black dealers to follow his lead. They were not slow to see the advantages of a good working relationship with the Mob, although it took them a little longer to appreciate the benefits of mutual cooperation. One of the first to respond was Leroy "Nicky" Barnes. Twenty years younger than Aiken, who was fifty-five when he went down, Barnes had started out as a pusher on territory run by the Lucchese family in Harlem, and gone into business for himself, with Mob approval, in 1964. Within a year, he had fifty people on his payroll, but then he got careless. Caught with $500,000 worth of heroin, he was sent to Greenhaven to bone up on technique.

There he fell in with Joey Gallo, who had reasons of his own for objecting to Mob domination, and together they dreamed up the idea of organizing the black gangs into a national syndicate along Mafia lines. The project was eventually vetoed at a conclave in New York, not because black mobsters objected in principle to the idea of organizing themselves—to some extent they had already done so—but because they disliked the idea of racial integration. They were going to do their own thing in their own way.

In practice, this meant that while they avoided the risk of being used by a Mob dissident like Gallo for his own ends, they were also committing themselves to an era of gang strife like that among the Italians forty years earlier, and with every prospect of the same result: the emergence of a national hierarchy among the top dozen or so surviving bosses, a tightening of gang discipline, and for the rank and file a heightened sense of personal identity through membership in the group. But, in the meantime, a seat on the Black Mafia's highly informal commission belonged to anybody who could hold on to it.

Though disappointed, Nicky Barnes held on to his (with the

help of the Bonanno family), as did "Hollywood" Harold Munger, who not only sold narcotics all the way down to street level but also serviced wholesale outlets in other Eastern cities; Willie "Goldfinger" Terrell, who made a bid for brand loyalty by packaging his product in a twist of yellow paper; Zack Robinson; and Elvin Lee Bynum, "Big El," who was set up in business by Leon Aiken himself.

But there was still room at the top for someone like Frank Matthews, a man who knew the moves, who knew he could stake out a piece of the Brooklyn market and use it as a base for an out-of-town network. The practical requirements were a good connection with an IBM—in 1967, nobody could get very far without an Italian Business Man behind him—and enough working capital to finance at least the first shipment. The Mob's standard terms of business were 30 percent down and the balance on delivery—in cash. Only the very biggest of its black customers were allowed credit, and then only on punitive terms.

Following precedent, Frank Matthews approached the Mob for supplies and finance, and was refused both. Its narcotics coordinating committee, consisting then of two Jewish and two Italian representatives, was more interested in stabilizing the market than in stirring up another round of guerrilla warfare among its customers. Although Matthews knew people in both the Bonanno and Gambino families, they declined to help. They were already selling all the horse they could land and saw no point in cutting him in when it would just make life tougher for everybody.

Set back on his heels, Matthews angrily changed tack. The Italians might have an import monopoly on heroin—for the moment—but they had no such control over cocaine, or over the Cubans who brought it in. Among his many contacts in the policy business was "Spanish Raymond" Marquez, who introduced him to Rolando Gonzalez, then the biggest Cuban dealer in New York.

He was only just in time. Gonzalez had been tipped off that police and federal agents were about to move in and he was packing his bags, mainly with money, to leave for Venezuela. Liquidating the last of his Manhattan inventory, he sold Matthews a kilo of 50 percent pure for $20,000—no bargain at the going rate, but good enough for the breakthrough. Inside a year, Matthews had built an organization around him, mainly of "home boys," with dealer connections in a dozen Eastern and Southern cities, while Gonzalez, working out of Caracas, shipped him bigger and bigger loads at better and better prices.

And not just Gonzalez. And not just cocaine. Matthews was already too big to ignore. His contacts in the Gambino family had soon changed their minds about selling him heroin, partly to head him off from attempting to deal directly with the Corsicans, and partly with the idea of retaining some sort of influence over his cavalier business methods, but both hopes were vain. To keep his empire on the move, he would buy from almost anyone at almost any price, knowing full well that profit margins in the drug trade were so extortionate that it was virtually impossible to *lose* money.

Nobody was encouraged to *over*charge him exactly, but he was less greedy and inflexible than most big distributors. Matthews was always ready to pay premium prices for what he wanted and to buy at any level, from multi-kilo shipments of pure all the way down to bundles of 3 percent street bags if that was the best he could find.

The Mob flourished in narcotics because it bought cheap and sold dear. Matthews flourished because he bought and sold at the best prices he could get. In consequence, his profits were now higher, now lower, but there were profits *all* the time because he always had something to sell. The drug trade soon learned that if Frank Matthews was dry, everybody was dry.

On July 15, 1968, he signed a lease on apartment 3D, 925 Prospect Place, Brooklyn. This was the Ponderosa, one of Matthews's two main narcotics mills in Brooklyn. The other—the O.K. Corral—was at 101 East 56th Street, on the first floor of a modest, three-story brick apartment building owned by his friend and lieutenant, Mickey Beckwith. Other mills would come and go in rented houses and apartments in Queens or Brooklyn as the need arose, but these two were the permanent inner citadels of Matthews's New York operation. Fortified with steel and concrete and guarded by men with rifles, shotguns, and automatic weapons, they were reception points for most of the cocaine and heroin he handled, and his main production centers for cutting, bagging, and bundling narcotics for sale on the street. Every day, the mill-workers would be brought in by car or truck to work a regular, eight-hour, $100 shift, and then be driven home again.

Thomas Lee Morehead saw how the system worked from the inside. He was a home boy, one of Matthews's original gang of chicken thieves, who followed his leader into drug dealing, although only as a small-time pusher. Down on his luck, he came looking for Matthews in Brooklyn, and was given a standing invitation to work as often as he liked as a heroin bagger in the Ponderosa.

Taking advantage of the offer whenever he ran short of money, Morehead worked at the mill on and off for a year. Trusted implicitly by the other home boys, he met most of Matthews's key men, including Scarvey McCargo, who ran things in New Haven, Connecticut, and Donald Conner, who managed the business in Queens. He also got to know some of Matthews's more important customers, among them Charles "Swayzie" Cameron and Donald "Keno" James, two of the biggest bundle dealers in New York.

Matthews's customers generally obeyed his orders as readily as any man on his payroll. It was Swayzie Cameron, for instance, who showed Morehead the proper way to seal a glassine bag of heroin with Scotch tape. But Morehead did more than just package about 150 kilos of horse during his part-time employment at the Ponderosa; he also delivered his handiwork, boxed in bundles of twenty-five bags, to dealers who met him by prearrangement on street corners all over Brooklyn. Orders awaiting delivery were left out for him in a trash can in the basement of 925 Prospect.

While working there, he saw Matthews himself only once, on November 11, 1969. Morehead was not to forget the date, for the occasion gave him both a severe fright and a striking demonstration of Matthews's power in Brooklyn. Morehead arrived on Prospect Place that day in company with Beckwith, but it was some time before anybody answered the door. They were then greeted with the news that a millworker named Stanley Harrison had been found dead from an overdose in the Ponderosa's bathtub.

Minutes later, Donald Conner and Scarvey McCargo arrived, and together they decided to ask Matthews what to do. He told them to call the police! And, to Morehead's astonishment, Beckwith duly telephoned the local precinct to invite the cops around to one of the most important heroin mills in Brooklyn.

Conner then told Morehead to clean the place up. With the help of another millworker, he stuffed one army duffel bag full of money, and a second with three kilos of heroin and a large quantity of cutting materials. Everything else, all the bags, tapes, boxes, implements, utensils, cutting tables, and other paraphernalia, was left exactly as it was. Running thankfully downstairs with the duffel bags, Morehead met the police on their way up. They stood aside politely to let him pass.

He dumped the load in the trunk of his Riviera, drove around the corner, and parked a few blocks away on New York Avenue. Then he walked back to the apartment just in time to hear Matthews, who had meanwhile joined his men, telling the police that of course it was his place. He lived somewhere else, but kept it for his friends.

McCargo then took Morehead with him to fetch Harrison's wife, Rosalind. The police were still there when they returned with her, and as soon as she saw the body, she broke down, screaming and railing hysterically at Matthews, whom she obviously held responsible for the manner of her husband's death. No one listening to her could have doubted for a moment what Matthews's business was or what the apartment was used for.

"What am I going to *do?*" she sobbed, knocking over a lamp in her agitation. "Where am I going to get the money to bury him?"

The broken lamp seemed to annoy Matthews more than anything. He cursed at her and then at the police, telling them to get the hell out of there, that he would take care of it.

And they did—as readily as everybody else on his payroll carried out his orders.

It was another two years before Matthews became the subject of an official police investigation, and another four years before anyone knew officially that the Ponderosa was leased in his name, let alone what went on there.

It was no mystery to William "Babe" Cameron, however. Cameron was a veteran moonshiner who, after injuring his leg while trying to run a roadblock, had turned to the less energetic business of dealing narcotics in Durham, where he had known Matthews as a kid. His connection was a wholesaler named Pete Thorp in Jersey City, who took him over to the Ponderosa one day to meet Beckwith and make a buy.

While Thorp negotiated the deal, Cameron waited in a comfortably furnished room with wall-to-wall carpeting, a well-stocked bar, and a king-sized bed, on which the resident millworkers both slept and entertained their girlfriends. To the left of the hallway, as he went in, he had noticed a cutting room, with seven or eight people at work under Beckwith's supervision, but Cameron was not allowed to buy at mill prices. He had to pay Thorp $4,500 for one-eighth of a kilo, which his girl carried out for him in the front of her dress.

Back in Durham, Cameron ran into Matthews himself a few days later.

"Hey, Babe, how's it going? I hear you been doing pretty good for yourself."

"Ain't complaining, Pee Wee," said Cameron. "It's coming along real nice."

"Well, that's what I heard. Man, you go on like this, you'll take over this town."

Cameron laughed. "That a promise, Frank? You going to give it to me?"

"Sure. Why not? Next time you want to make a buy, you call me, you hear? I got to take care of my friends."

"Okay. But what about Pete?"

"He's a friend, too," Matthews said. "But you might as well get it straight from the horse."

On his next trip to New York, Cameron met Matthews in his apartment at 130 Clarkson. He gave him $12,000 for three-eighths of a kilo, but Matthews was in no hurry to close the deal. After a few drinks, he asked Cameron if he would like to go for a ride.

Thinking they were now going to get the stuff, Cameron agreed, and they drove off together in a black T-bird with a white top. But Matthews had other ideas. He stopped outside a tenement building, went in, and eventually returned, not with heroin, but with a shopping bag half full of money. Dumping it casually in Cameron's lap, he drove on to the next stop, where he collected a second bag of money. And so on, at the third, fourth, fifth, and sixth stops, until Cameron could hardly move his feet without spilling money on the floor.

Still not tired of his game, Matthews then stowed the bags in the trunk and drove Cameron to Philadelphia to make another series of collections. By the time they got back to Clarkson Avenue, there was more money in the car than both of them could carry up in one trip.

"Now what do we got to do?" Cameron asked, as Matthews dropped several hundred thousand dollars on his living-room floor. "Count it?"

Matthews hesitated. "Shit," he said. "Ain't nobody going to shortchange *me*. We'll just put it in the closet."

Cameron helped him gather up the bags again, and they carried them through to a small bedroom next to the kitchen. Cradling his load, he waited while Matthews fumbled for his keys and unlocked the clothes closet. As the door opened, the bags slid through Cameron's arms. He stared and stared helplessly at a wall of money. The closet was stacked to bursting with bundles of bills from floor to eye level.

"Je-sus *Christ,*" he said. The lesson had been learned.

Matthews locked the money away and took Cameron back to the living room, where they snorted a little coke.

"Don't mess with nobody else," said Matthews. "I'm the biggest. Just don't go spending your money with nobody else because all you'll get is a bunch of junk."

"Yeah, but what do I do if you're dry?" It was Cameron's last flicker of independence.

"Listen," he said. "When I ain't got nothing, ain't nobody else got nothing. You hear me? So don't you try to buy no drugs from nobody else if I ain't got none, because all they'll do is take your money. I'm the biggest man you'll ever see."

On his next trip to Brooklyn, Cameron was taken around to the O.K. Corral and kitted out with two cases of mannite, 15 pounds of quinine, two boxes of glassine bags, and all the other paraphernalia required by an accredited dealer in the Matthews organization. Now in the big time, he drove back home with all this and a full kilo of horse, for, true to his promise, Matthews had given him Durham.

With this kind of horsepower behind him, Cameron's business took wing; he was soon employing twenty people. And it would probably have continued to prosper, like all of Matthews's franchises, but for an unfortunate accident. After taking delivery of a consignment of brown heroin, a variant he had not handled before, Cameron called Matthews for instructions and was told to cut it ten times. This he did, but one of his customers immediately died of an overdose. Aggrieved, Cameron reported this to Matthews, who, after investigating the complaint, called back to say there had been an error in the shipping department. The mill had sent him "croak dope"—heroin requiring not a ten- but a minimum fourteen-to-one cut. He was sorry about that.

So was Babe Cameron. He was subsequently arrested and charged with murder (although the case was later dismissed).

Matthews had naturally chosen a home boy to service his home town, but in other cities, and with other dealers, his recruiting methods were a little different. Actual violence was rarely necessary, however. He would just descend on a town by Lincoln or Cadillac like Jove in his chariot and give local distributors the benefit of his advice.

In most cases, a suitable candidate for a Matthews dealership would be set up in advance by one of several legmen he employed to identify market opportunities for him, and it was almost always an agreeable experience. Among those who got the Matthews treatment was Norman Lee Coleman, a dealer from Baltimore.

To soften him up, he was first given free samples of high-grade merchandise, and then invited on an expense-paid junket to Atlantic City with Bighead Brother Carter, Matthews's Baltimore distributor, and two other senior executives, one of them named Emerson Dorsey. After two days of wine, women, coke, and gambling, they were joined at the hotel by Matthews himself, who drove down from New York in a gold Lincoln Mark III. When Dorsey greeted his boss with the news that they had spent all their money, Matthews sent him downstairs to bring up a sackful from the car, and the magic worked once again. Coleman placed orders for cocaine and heroin and went home exhausted but mightily impressed.

Nor was he disappointed by the quality of the goods that Matthews supplied through Carter. His price for cocaine was then $1,500 an ounce, but Coleman found he could cut this ten times at least to make enough for thirty or forty bundles of twenty-five bags each. At $5 a bag and up, that meant a profit of 300 to 400 percent, and his net income rose to around $20,000 a month. In contrast, the coke he had been buying from other sources for about the same price would take only a five or a six cut at most.

But Matthews's drive to corner the Baltimore market was always breaking down on Bighead Brother's limited span of attention. Between 1968 and 1969, Carter moved up from a 1962 Chevrolet and a project apartment to a brand-new Cadillac convertible and a house on Ferndale, but then his ambition faltered. In an effort to spur him on, Matthews set up Purcell Wylie, one of

Carter's own lieutenants, in competition with him, but that did not last long. In January 1971, Wylie's attaché case activated a magnetometer at the security checkpoint at La Guardia Airport, and two quarter-kilo bags of pure heroin were found inside.

Coming at the problem another way, Matthews now started to squeeze John Edward "Liddy" Jones, who controlled the other big narcotics network in the city. At the wholesale level, Jones and Carter were not in competition. Jones bought most of his drugs from Matthews, through Carter, and the rest from Korea Henderson, an independent wholesaler in Harlem. But, at the street level, the two were intensely competitive, particularly Jones, who always needed to be reassured that he was the biggest in Baltimore, as indeed he was. At its peak, his organization employed about seventy-five people, including eighteen baggers, thirty-five bundle dealers, and at least two hit men.

By threatening Jones's supplies, Matthews forced him into an uneasy partnership with Carter, the idea being that the energetic Liddy would keep the indolent Bighead Brother on his toes, but Jones never gave up trying to bypass Carter and deal with Matthews direct. In July 1972, he flew with his new manager, Reece Whiting, to Las Vegas, where Matthews had booked a suite of rooms at the Sands Hotel to entertain his major dealers at the Ali–Quarry fight.

Whiting had heard that Carter, facing prosecution on a state narcotics charge, was cooperating with the government, and Jones wanted Matthews to hear this at first hand—which took a certain amount of gall, because Jones himself at that time was cooperating with the Baltimore Narcotics Strike Force to save his *own* skin. But Matthews refused to listen. He had done business with Carter for years, he said, and knew he could be trusted.

Jones persisted. He was uneasy about dealing with Carter in view of what Whiting had heard. In future, he wanted to deal only with Matthews, he said, and offered him then and there a $50,000 down payment for his next package.

It was street money—creased, dirty, and in small denominations.

Matthews glanced at it indifferently, and told Jones he only took money in big, clean bills (which was not quite true; few of his dealers were properly equipped to launder their take). Jones closed the bag and left. An hour later, he came back, having somehow changed the $50,000 into $100 bills. Matthews smiled at him lazily.

"Man," he said, "I got five times that much with me just to lose at the tables. Now just you give that loose change to Brother Carter, and he'll take care of you like always."

Jones at that time was moving about 5,000 bundles of twenty-five bags each every month, and grossing around $6 million a year, but he was in no position to argue. Through Carter, Matthews now controlled at least 80 percent of the narcotics trade in Baltimore.

It was the same story in Cincinnati, Ohio. In 1969, the two big wholesalers there were James Perry Cravens, who was Matthews's man, and Dickie Diamond, also known (to a few) by his real name of Alexander Randolph, and as Mr. Wiggles. A protégé of Leon Aiken and, through him, a close associate of Big El Bynum, Diamond renamed himself after a successful jewel robbery early in his career, but turned to the richer pasture of narcotics in 1964, when he was twenty-seven. Within five years, he and Cravens were meeting regularly to compare notes and agree on uniform strengths for the drugs they sold, so as to avoid wasteful competition.

Diamond was then "copping" from Bynum, but his packages were of variable quality and not always on time. Early in 1970, he decided to try Matthews, who readily agreed to sell him a half kilo of horse for $15,000. Diamond went to his New York apartment at 265 Hawthorn Street, Brooklyn, to get the money, which he kept, wrapped like meat, in the freezer compartment of his refrigerator, and delivered it to Matthews in the Lincoln Lounge on Rochester Street.

"Go home and lay," Matthews told him. "Someone will ring your bell three times. When they do, go up on the hundred block of Hawthorn Street, and somebody will be up there who you know."

That somebody was Mickey Beckwith, whom Diamond had known for years. But to his surprise and consternation, when they met as arranged, Beckwith produced a package from under his coat and handed it to him on the street. Jumping hastily back into his car, Diamond drove off by a circuitous route to his second Brooklyn apartment, on St. Marks Place, which he used as his stash.

Two weeks later, he was back in New York to buy some more, though complaining bitterly to Matthews about Beckwith's unprofessional conduct.

"He's got to be crazy, hitting me with a package on the street like that. Supposing a cop was watching me."

"Okay." Matthews rarely seemed worried by problems of that sort in Brooklyn. "So how do you *want* to be serviced?"

"I got a beautiful system," said Diamond. "Where I live is a garage, and down in the garage, by one of my parking spaces, I got a pile of sand. I will get Mickey a key to my garage, and any time I give him the money, I want the dope hidden underneath the sand. Then ring my doorbell, and I'll come down, or get one of my workers to go down and get it."

"That's beautiful," said Matthews. "Give me the key. I'll see Mickey gets it."

From then on, that was how it was done, with the cash usually changing hands in Brownee's bar on St. Marks Place, just off Nostrand Avenue. Matthews was a close friend of the then owner, Vinny Moore, and hung out there a lot with his lieutenants and with visiting dealers like Diamond, who found it a useful place to do business, as it was only five doors down from his stash.

"You come into Brownee's through a little passage, and there's a bar, seating about ten people, and a dining area to the left, with a bathroom, and then a transaction kitchen in the back. It wasn't used for food. The guy that owned the bar, Vinny—well, he's a little shady himself, so he let a lot of activity go down in there. Because it's a hustle bar—drugs and numbers. Basically, that's what it was, the crowd that hung in there. As long as you're picking up your tab and spending your money, he didn't care what went on—as long as you put a little cover on. The kitchen is where certain guys were hanging around and spending good money so that they could go in there and transact their confidential business.

"Let's say someone would come in from Virginia, or Ohio, or down South, I would tell them to go to Brownee's. They'd be sitting there like a normal customer. I'd come in, meet them, get the money, and then I'd tell Skip [Diamond's lieutenant] or whoever is working for me to go in there and hit them in Brownee's. He'd go to the stash box, come back with a package, and give it to who I say give it to."

Used by practically everybody of any consequence in the Matthews organization, Brownee's at that time was a kind of national commodity exchange for narcotics, a place where import agents, brokers, and distributors met with wholesalers and some of the bigger retailers to fix prices and deliveries and even to deal in options and futures.

Most of them worked behind some kind of legitimate front. Diamond's was the music business. He owned a concert promotion agency called Capital City Attractions in Jersey City, and his own reasonably successful record label, Sound of Soul. He was also the representative of Motown Records Inc. in Alabama, and had a chain of record stores through the South.

As a promoter, Diamond worked with top groups like the Jackson Five, Sly and the Family Stone, the Moments, and the Delfonics.

"I would buy them for thirty days. I guarantee them three thousand a night. In return, I would take them on a tour, like Trenton, next stop would be Baltimore, next would be Washington, then Richmond, Norfolk, Scranton, Fayetteville, Durham, Raleigh, Winston-Salem, Greensboro, Columbia—I worked them straight down the line."

He would also deal a little dope here and there, and launder the money in with his box-office receipts.

Diamond's record company served a similar purpose. In 1971 he wrote, produced, manufactured, and distributed a record on his

Sound of Soul label called "Where the Peace Go?" Sung by Larry Sanders, it won a lot of air time and proved a popular jukebox selection across the country. As he went from city to city, wearing his record distributor's hat, he would collect the drug money owing to him, falsify the sales figures of his records to account for it, and change the street bills at the nearest bank into clean fifties and hundreds or buy certified checks made out to himself.

He also found the record business a good way of involving bus companies, airlines, and even the U.S. Post Office in his narcotics-distribution system. If a customer with a record store in Winston, or the manager in one of his own stores in, say, Mobile, ordered an eighth of heroin, Diamond would take a box of a hundred singles, remove twenty-five, pack the dope between the rest of the records, and send it off without a qualm by any convenient carrier.

Frank Matthews greatly admired Diamond's front, and several times offered to buy it, although he already had an interest in the record business through Bobby Nesbitt, his chosen instrument for rolling up the drug trade in Washington, D.C.

Nesbitt had his own recording studio; his own label, Monica Records; and, on the same block, an after-hours club called the Celebrity, an uninhibited little dive with a downstairs lounge for those who liked to snort cocaine, and an upstairs crap game for those who preferred to lose their shirts. He had once been a customer of El Bynum's, but by 1971 Matthews had won him over entirely, not only because his merchandise was better but also because he had financed Nesbitt's musical career.

As a goodwill investment, it paid off handsomely. Business in Washington was so good that in August 1971 a four-man cutting and bagging crew had to be flown down from New York to cope with the surge in demand. One of them was Norman Harris, a home boy from Durham.

He and another man moved into a house in a quiet suburban neighborhood about fifteen minutes away from Dulles Airport and, while more permanent arrangements were being made, worked an eight-hour day, five-day week cutting heroin and cocaine flown in a kilo at a time by courier. After about a month, when the new local mill was ready to go into production, Harris was asked to move on to Miami, with two suitcases containing between 1,500 and 2,000 "halves" (22,500–30,000 street bags). He declined, feeling the risks were too great for the $500 payment he was offered, but his co-worker was less fussy. He flew down with the merchandise to await further instructions at the Playboy Motel in Miami, the next town on Matthews's shopping list.

And so it went on. Through 1969, 1970, and 1971, Matthews rolled up the narcotics business in city after city, state after state. Where no effective dealership existed, he started one. Where one *did* exist, he took it over, making the sort of offer that dealers had no *wish* to refuse. Nothing like Frank Matthews had ever happened to them before. Nothing quite like Frank Matthews had ever happened in *crime* before, which was why law-enforcement agencies were generally so slow to latch on to him. Though flamboyant, aggressive, and impossible to overlook in person, what with his pink leather suits and Superfly floor-length mink coats, he made very little noise when it came to business. People *liked* to deal with him. He made them rich.

Through Nat Elder, he took over Atlanta as his headquarters for the South and Southwest. He bought a house there, sunk millions into local real estate, and commuted back and forth from New York about once a week. Through Gattis Hinton and Scarvey McCargo, he fanned out through the Northeast, mopping up the industrial towns of Connecticut first, and then reaching into the rest of New England through wholesale connections with entrenched distributors in cities like Boston and Providence. Through Mickey Beckwith, and in person, he serviced other major wholesale outlets in Detroit, Cleveland, Chicago, and on to Los Angeles, buying and selling, wheeling and dealing, moving dope and taking his enormous profits.

There was rarely any trouble of the sort to attract attention. Matthews usually preferred to buy what he wanted, and if that failed, then to eliminate obstacles quietly. He was not looking to build a reputation as a heavy; he was already too big for people to mess with. Nor was he out to dethrone local kings and proclaim himself emperor. Outside of the territories he controlled directly, he liked to form alliances, to avoid the heat, danger, and expense of open war, and instead reap the benefits of mutual trade. By October 1971, he had the national distribution of narcotics well enough organized to hold a business convention in Atlanta.

They came from all parts of the country, from New York, New Jersey, New England, Pennsylvania, Ohio, Illinois, from the South, from the West—over forty of the biggest dope dealers in the United States, men whose millions of dollars of purchasing power controlled a market worth billions. As an event, it probably eclipsed in significance the Italian Mob's interrupted summit meeting at Apalachin, New York, in 1957. Most people had known about the Mafia before that, but Matthews's Atlanta conference was the first positive proof that a *Black* Mafia existed—and it was *not* interrupted.

The main business of the meeting was to discuss ways and means of breaking the Mob's stranglehold on heroin imports. It had to be done peacefully, so as not to upset existing supply arrangements—indeed, with a view to augmenting rather than replacing them—but the need for an independent source was critical. It would not only remove a serious brake on expansion and keep the Mob in line on price, but provide a margin of safety in the event of an IBM going down the tubes, which they were doing with some frequency as the War on Drugs warmed up.

After several days of discussion, the general feeling was that more business had to be done directly with the Corsicans, perhaps through the Cubans, and maybe on a cooperative basis, with Matthews and some of the other big distributors getting together to place bulk orders to ensure preferential treatment. Meanwhile, they would try to eke out their supplies by pushing cocaine, in which connection Matthews was delighted to announce that he had large quantities of dynamite coke available for immediate delivery (thanks to his old friend Rolando Gonzalez, and his new friend Miguel Garcia).

In one way, Nixon's War on Drugs was making things easier for him by creaming off his competitors and thus creating a vacuum he was only too happy to fill, but at the same time it was also making life harder, because the higher he went, the more he had to have of what, in 1971, was a shrinking volume of imports. The level of demand he had to meet was quite frightening, particularly in New York, where almost half the nation's addicts were concentrated. Just one of the street rings he supplied, the "Dutch Schultz" organization in Bedford-Stuyvesant, bought enough to have kept any ordinary wholesaler in Cadillacs. In twelve months, it took about a hundred kilos from Matthews at prices ranging up to $26,500 a kilo—and by the end of that year the rate of consumption had risen to five kilos a week.

At that point, the ring was grossing around $45,000 a day from the bulk sale of 17,500 bags a day, enough for perhaps ten thousand retail customers. In the same twelve-month period, Ray "Dutch Schultz" Daniels and his partner Donald "Keno" James had expanded their payroll from about forty people serving a Brooklyn/Queens clientele to more than 150 baggers, pushers, street lieutenants, and enforcers operating in all five boroughs.

James regularly took delivery of five-kilo or larger packages from Matthews himself and often made cash payments to him of up to $250,000 at a time, but when he could, he preferred to deal with Beckwith. Matthews's methods frankly terrified him.

"One time I took a cab and met Frank in Brooklyn and he gave me a package of like five keys, wrapped up. He offered to drive me back. During the ride, he was driving extremely fast. We ran across a couple of traffic lights and I became frightened. He was driving a green convertible Cadillac, and scared the shit out of me. I said, 'Maybe I ought to take a cab,' because I had the five keys on me and any minute the cops are going to stop us. He just laughed."

James devised with Ray Daniels a system of quality control that other dealers soon copied. Instead of messing with complicated chemical tests to check the strength of the bags they sold, they would take a sample along to a "shooting gallery," an apartment or vacant store where addicts would gather in relative safety to shoot up, and there give it to a junkie lacking the price of a fix. If he died, they knew they could cut it some more.

By the spring of 1972, however, users were more likely to be struck by lightning than die of an overdose. The average strength of a street bag was down in some areas to 3 percent heroin or less, and some addicts were involuntarily detoxifying themselves. This, of course, was a result of Matthews's trying to stretch the available supply by cutting harder at the distributor level; in a matter of months, the whole thrust of his operation had changed from expansion to procurement.

The Mob was still his principal source, although it strongly disapproved of his reckless business methods and would have preferred to kill him. Nobody did so, because nobody could say for sure what the effect of this would be on their second most important racket after gambling. Black sensitivities were involved. Sooner than risk winning the war but losing the game, therefore, the Mob played along, hoping to moderate his more exotic ambitions. As a result, Matthews now had several IBMs. Besides his Gambino connection, which worked through the Midwood Lounge in Brooklyn, he was also well enough in with the Lucchese family to have Anthony "Tony Ducks" Corallo as an investor in C. I. Carpet Service Inc., one of his front corporations.

Then, too, he had acquired a financial adviser and general counselor in the person of Don Andrews.

Andrews's job was to plug Matthews into the network of influence and patronage that screened the Mob from public view, and help cope with the daily avalanche of street money that threatened to bury Matthews and his lieutenants now that they had run out of closet space.

There were other Italian links as well. Through 1971, Matthews worked closely with Big El Bynum, whose white partner, Joseph Cordovano, had an important Corsican connection. Set up in the drug trade by Leon Aiken, Bynum had been the biggest black dealer around until Matthews came along, diversifying, like his mentor, into shylocking, hijacking, and numbers, and a dozen legitimate businesses as well, including a parking garage, a gypsy cab company, a wholesale record distributor, a meat company, several bars, a men's clothing store, and the Bed-Stuy Tobacco and Candy Company.

Like Matthews, Bynum enjoyed a lot of protection. They shared Dickie Diamond as a fixer, to corrupt police officers in Brooklyn and Queens, and, through contacts in the District Attorneys' offices in those boroughs, to short-circuit criminal charges brought against them and their men. And for really serious problems, Bynum could always turn for a serious solution to his crown prince, Black Buster Watson, who liked telling people he had trained Floyd Patterson when he was heavyweight champ. Since then, Watson had become a heavy himself. Under Bynum's wing, he controlled a group that had taken over the goodwill and stock in trade of Murder, Inc.

Between them, Matthews and Bynum probably accounted for the distribution of about one-third of all the heroin entering the country. Theirs was the kind of purchasing power that the Corsicans simply could not ignore, and some of the deals they put together were astounding. In the summer of 1971, Matthews took delivery of 75 kilos—his half of a joint order—at Bynum's house at 623 East 37th Street, Brooklyn. Five weeks later, they shared another 100 kilos. That winter, there were further huge shipments of 112 kilos and 152 kilos.

Some loads went astray, of course. In January 1972, Matthews went down to Miami with David "Rev" Bates, one of his Philadelphia distributors, to supervise the final stage in the long haul from Marseilles of a mammoth consignment of 175 kilos of pure, costing a cool $1,750,000. Matthews himself would have grossed a profit of at least $2.5 million on this one deal, and by the time the heroin reached the street, cut perhaps thirty to one, it would have fetched in those dry times about $150 million. But agents of the BNDD, acting on a tip, moved in as the first three couriers were leaving by air for New York, and Matthews went home empty-handed. It was the biggest shipment the government had ever seized, but by no means the biggest that Matthews and Bynum had ever organized.

In 1971, Bynum's Corsican friends found some limpet mines of the type used by frogmen in World War II to attack ships in port. Dropped by night outside an enemy harbor, the frogmen would slip through the antisubmarine defenses, clamp the mines by means of built-in magnets to the steel hulls of the vessels selected, swim back to the mother ship, and be long gone before delay fuses exploded the charges. Now, some thirty years later, and faced with the not dissimilar problem of getting past the U.S. Customs harbor defenses, the Corsicans were about to employ the same technique—after steaming the charges out of the mines and replacing them with hermetically sealed packs of heroin.

That done, they had merely to consult the shipping tables to identify vessels sailing from Marseilles or Barcelona or Genoa to Brooklyn, send down skin divers after dark to attach the mines to their hulls, advise the customer in New York, and let nature take its course. When the ships docked, Matthews and Bynum would simply have their own divers go down at night to detach the heroin mines, swim back with them to Pier 3, drop them into the trunk of a waiting Cadillac, and America's addicts could breathe again. A few mines might drop off in mid-Atlantic, but the Corsicans were confident they could deliver about 400 kilos in this fashion—*if* Matthews and Bynum could find the money.

A few weeks later, one of Bynum's dealers, an old and trusted friend, drove over to Bynum's house on East 37th Street to make a down payment on a package. He parked as usual around the corner and walked down the street, stopping every few yards for a word with people who worked for Bynum or Matthews. Indeed, he had never before seen so many of their men on the block at one time.

They were all around the house as well—some of them with what he was ready to swear were shotguns under their coats. He rang the bell. Two men opened the door and closed it quickly behind him. They were carrying M-16s.

"What's going on?" the dealer asked them. "Where's El?"

"In there with Frank," said one of the guards, pointing his gun at the living-room door.

The dealer knocked and went inside.

Matthews and Bynum were knee-deep in money. Bundled up in rubber bands, it was stacked in broad parallel rows, like green brick walls, three or four feet high, from one side of the room to the other, with aisles between them to help make the counting easier. They had furnished the living room with $4 million in cash.

9

About a week after I brought the money down to Miami from the deal we did with Frank, I was out riding with my godfather and Ana Baños one night, and he said to me, "I got a big problem."

"Yeah?" I said. "What's that?"

"It's Martinez. Frankie don't want to see him no more."

"That right?" I made sure he didn't see me smile. "Why? What did he do?"

"Well, he took the package down, right? After you went up and told him the T-bird was on the street?"

"Right."

"Yeah. Well, Frank tells him to get in the car. He don't want it to look like a drop. He wants it to look like he's just picking somebody up, okay? 'No, no, no,' says José. 'Here—take it.' And he throws the goddamn package through the window and runs."

"Oh, Jesus," I said. Martinez was just handing me the whole thing on a plate.

"So naturally Frank's madder than hell. 'What's the matter with the guy?' he says to me. 'He's scared to get in the car with me? He thinks I'm a cop or something? Shit. I don't like nervous people,' he says. 'You keep him away from me, Mikey.' "

"So what are you going to do?" I said, and he cracked a smile.

"Well, there ain't much I *can* do, is there?"

"No, I guess not," I said, and I was smiling right back at him.

"Stop at the next pay phone," he said. "I got to call Raquel Dumois."

So I found him a phone, and he came back to the car a few minutes later with a face like bad news.

"We better get over there," he said. "Sounds like there's trouble."

So long as it involved Martinez, that was all right with me, and sure enough, the first thing the old lady said when we got to her house was, "Oh, oh—my son called me. Things are bad. They have problems. You got to help him."

"What kind of problems?" my godfather asked her. "They been arrested or what?"

"No, no. It's just that they can't do what they were supposed to do."

Miguel looked at her, and then at me. Now he was ready to cut somebody's heart out. I tried to look sympathetic, but Martinez had screwed up again.

"Okay," he said. "We got to go."

He grabbed the phone and called his mother to tell her to start packing his bag. Then we dropped Ana Baños off at her house to pack, because she was coming with us, and I drove him over to Normandy Isle.

"What the hell's going on?" I said, seeing he had cooled off a bit.

"Nothing," he said. "I sent the son of a bitch over to Santo Domingo to move some stuff into Haiti. And he's still sitting there."

"You mean, he crapped out?"

He didn't answer. As he got out of the car, he told me to make three reservations on the ten o'clock flight to Puerto Rico.

They drove over to my place around eight. Orlando was there, and I left him to bullshit with my godfather while I got dressed. Then Anna came home while I was still in the bedroom, and caught them raiding the icebox. None of us had eaten yet. But Ana Baños was kind of embarrassed—it was the first time they had met—and she started complimenting Anna on her fried chicken. "Mmm, delicious," she said. "You got to give me the recipe." So Anna looked at them. "That's Feo's," she said. "What are you doing, eating my dog's chicken?" After that, they kind of lost their appetites, but it was true. She used to sit on the floor and feed that damn dog strawberry ice cream with a spoon.

Anyway, she drove out to the airport with Orlando to see us off, and we checked in at La Concha Hotel in San Juan around one in the morning. I still wasn't asking any questions, because things were going my way. I didn't even say nothing next morning when we caught a Pan Am flight to Santo Domingo, and my godfather told the airline clerk his name was Marcello Cabot. You don't need a passport to travel to the Dominican Republic or Haiti; a birth certificate is enough. It was the first time I'd seen him use phony papers.

We got there in time for lunch, and Martinez met us upstairs at the El Embajador Hotel. He looked flustered, and my godfather's face didn't help steady his nerves.

"So what the hell happened?"

Martinez gave him a chicken-shit grin. "Well, you see, Mikey, we tried renting a car to get the stuff over the border, but you don't know what a hassle that is. You got to get a permit days before. And when we went to check the roads across, they got guards everywhere. It don't look good, Mikey."

"You mean you ain't done nothing—that what you telling me?"

"Well, like I said, Mikey, you got to get a permit and everything."

"Then why the fuck didn't you? And stash the stuff in the door panels? Shit, the Haitians, they're not going to give you a hard time. You came here to do something, right? Shit."

It was lucky for Martinez my godfather had already gotten mad about this in Miami, and couldn't work himself up a second time. But he was still pissed off enough to turn the guy white.

"Well, it's not my fault, Mikey," he said, going all limp and feathery. "Things just didn't work out the way we figured. And I thought you ought to know."

"So? What do you want to do? Throw six keys down the toilet? Shit. You got to find a way. This has put us back a week. What about the goddamn boat?"

"We'll make it, Mikey."

"Yeah? How? Are the Venezuelans still here?"

"Sure, they're here. So's the Doctor."

"Okay." My godfather tested the bed, and snooped around the room looking for something else to complain about. "Then get some booze sent up and tell them we're going to have a meet."

"I think they're out with their women, Mikey," said Martinez, like he was apologizing for that, too.

"Shit. I hope you sons of bitches are enjoying your fucking vacation."

That night, we all had dinner together in the hotel—everybody except the Doctor. As the women were there, it was just a social evening to start with. Miguel wasn't happy, but he made an effort to be pleasant with Medina and Diaz, the two Venezuelans I'd met in New York. They worked for the Doctor, Albino Perez, a Peruvian and a real hump, who was my godfather's new connection.

I hit it off good with Diaz right away. He was a short, bald, happy-go-lucky guy of about forty who knew his way around. A ballsy guy—different from José Medina, who was small, thin, and shifty-looking. Anybody stared him straight in the eye and his knees would buckle. But he'd been raised with the Indians, and that gave him the inside track when it came to buying cocaine up in the mountains.

After dinner, we caught the Platters, who were playing the hotel nightclub, but then the women got lost, and we went upstairs to talk to the Doctor. Diaz and Medina showed the guy a lot of respect, but to me he was just another goddamn Indian. He knew we needed him, so he came on very aloof and superior. When the others broke out some coke and started snorting it, he watched them like they was monkeys with a handful of nuts he'd thrown them. My godfather didn't care. He probably didn't even notice, but *I* did. And when I didn't join in, the Doctor and me kept giving each other the eye.

Finally, Miguel got things going by making Martinez explain again how he'd screwed up, and I just lay back there and listened while the guy buried himself. Then they started to discuss other ways of getting the stuff across, like carrying it over after dark. But that was no good. Nobody knew the country. And, anyway, what would they do on the other side with no car and no entry papers? The next idea was to charter a boat. And that was no good either. Then you got the coast guard and navy to worry about.

I took my godfather off in a corner, and said, "Don't ponder the thought no more. False-bottom suitcases. We'll catch a plane and just walk it in. Forget all this bullshit. It's the only way."

So he turned around and told the others that was how we had to do it.

"Okay," said Pedro Diaz. "You can have the suitcases *we* used. And I'm sorry we can't go with you."

Venezuela and Haiti were talking about restoring diplomatic relations, but they hadn't yet, which was why they'd brought the stuff to Santo Domingo in the first place.

"No sweat," said Miguel. "This is our part of it anyway."

"They can have *two* of the suitcases," the Doctor said. "The other is no good."

"Shit, that's right," said Pedro. "I had a little trouble with one of them in Curaçao. The lining came unglued. The customs guy saw a bit of cloth sticking up, and I nearly came unglued myself."

"Is no problem," said the Doctor. "We'll take that one. Tomorrow I will make another."

So that was settled, and now everybody but me and the Doctor got wired to the teeth. I finally left them to it around five in the morning, and slept until noon.

When I got downstairs, there was no one around except Ana Baños. To fill in time, we took a ride downtown to pick up a few souvenirs of Santo Domingo, and got back to the hotel at about three. The Doctor was just finishing a beautiful job on the third suitcase. He had made a false bottom from fairly heavy board, and it fitted perfectly, leaving a secret compartment about half an inch deep—enough to take two kilos flattened out in plastic bags. The only way anyone could tell the case had been touched was by measuring the depth of it very carefully, inside and out. And if a customs agent was suspicious enough to do that, we were dead anyway.

All we had to do now was get rid of the smell of glue on all three of them, because he had touched up the others as well. The girls had sprinkled perfume on them, but it wasn't enough. We were going to have to wait until the glue dried right out.

"Okay," my godfather said. "No point taking chances. We'll go tomorrow."

"What about the boat?" I said.

"We'll make it. Just about. If nobody fouls up."

Martinez cleared his throat. "Ah, we owe the hotel about $2,000," he said.

Miguel looked at him a long time. "So?"

"Ah—well, you see—I don't have it. I didn't bring enough with me."

My godfather took out his billfold, still looking at Martinez like he never saw him before, then counted what he had.

"How much you got, Georgie?"

"Two, three hundred."

"Shit." He looked ready to kill Martinez now, but he couldn't say much with the others there. "Why the hell didn't you tell the old lady you needed more money?"

"You don't got enough?" he said, and Miguel turned his back on him.

"*Now* what the hell are we going to do?" I said. "Anna can't come. She's not an American citizen. Orlando's on bail. My grandmother's too old. How about your old lady?"

"I tell you what," said Martinez. "My sister-in-law Faith is American. I know she'll come over if I ask her."

Miguel decided to notice him again. "We'll need about four thousand," he said. "You sure you can trust her? I don't want nobody to know where we are."

"Sure. If we pay her."

My godfather's face was a picture. Here was this son of a bitch who'd screwed up all down the line expecting *us* to pay one of *his* goddamn relatives to get *him* out of trouble.

"How much?"

"Well, what do you think? I figure $500 would be fair."

Miguel looked at me, and I shrugged.

"Go do it," he said. "Get her here tomorrow. Tell her to see my old lady for the money."

The next afternoon, I drove out to the airport with Martinez to meet her, and she bitched at him the whole way back into town.

"Your brother, he's a bum," she said. "He don't want to work. He thinks he's too good to work. 'I want a business of my own,' he says. A business of his own. 'What kind of business,' I says to him, 'lying around the house all day? A mattress-testing business?' He's a goddamn lazy bum. You got to talk to him, José. It's making real trouble between us."

"Sure, sure," he said. "Don't worry. If things go the way I plan, he'll get what he wants. You both will. We're working on a deal here could make me a couple of hundred thousand dollars. Then we can all retire—right, Georgie?"

"Sure," I said. I didn't know what the hell he was talking about, but I had news for him. He was already retired.

We sent her back to Miami early next morning, and got ready to leave on the two o'clock flight to Haiti. It had already been decided that I was going to carry two of the suitcases, including the new one, while Martinez took care of the other, and when the time came to leave, I was really looking forward to it. I don't care how tough you are, normally you're going to tense up a little when you're running two kilos of dope past a customs post, but this time I was so hung up on showing Martinez how it should be done that I didn't even think about the risk. I checked the bags through, and got on board without a care in the world.

The flight was very short; hardly worth unbuckling the seat belt. We climbed out of Santo Domingo, and as soon as the plane reached cruising height, it was time to come down again, over range after range of mountains cut with valleys and rivers, and then right down over the red dirt—and Jesus! I couldn't believe it. As we touched down, the wing of the plane was skimming over huts right by the side of the airstrip. There were kids playing around almost on the runway.

There were more of them in the terminal, jumping on and off the baggage conveyor. Grown-up Haitians were doing it, too—hopping on to catch a ride and then falling over their feet, laughing like hell. We pretended we didn't know each other, my godfather and Ana Baños leading the way. They showed their papers—he was still traveling as Marcello Cabot—bought their $2 pink tourist cards, and went to claim their suitcases. Martinez was next, a few paces behind them, and then me. I could see he was sweating a little bit, but so was I. The air was hot and heavy as a blanket in there.

My bags came through and I picked them off the conveyor, giving a smile and a nod to a little black guy watching me. This was it. I got in line for the customs check. One of the agents was going through my godfather's suitcase, but not very carefully, like he hoped he wouldn't find nothing. Ana Baños had hers open, too, and so had Martinez.

Then suddenly this little black guy jabbered something at me in patois. So I gave him another nod, just to be friendly, and he grabbed my two bags and started walking out the door.

"Hey!" But he had already reached the guards, and I hung back a little, waiting to see how he made out. One of them moved like he meant to stop him, but he paid no attention. He just pushed on through, still jabbering away in patois, and now I was right behind him. I couldn't believe it. We were out in the sun, and nobody had laid a finger on the bags except him.

I gave him $5, and he almost kissed me. When the others came out, I was leaning against the wall, admiring the view.

My godfather nudged Martinez. "Did you see that?" He was grinning all over his face. "He said he'd walk it through, and that's exactly what he did. Talk about a white pigeon."

In voodoo, a white pigeon—any white bird—is very big. It's a symbol of purity and freedom. The spirits look with favor on a white pigeon.

But they were not looking with favor on Martinez, and my godfather's mood didn't last. We hopped a cab with an L on its license plate, which meant the chauffeur spoke English, and drove to the El Rancho Hotel in Pétionville, which is like a suburb of Port-au-Prince. It was hot as hell, and the roads weren't no better than tracks cut into the mountain, but already I loved the place. All along the way were people with no shoes on, carrying big woven baskets of bananas and fruit on their heads. Some had donkeys to carry the baskets, and they were whipping their donkeys, and their donkeys were kicking up the dust. And the buses—the *camions,* they call them. We passed one that was just a little Toyota with like a wooden cage at the back and benches on each side for about four passengers to sit on, and it was painted all over in bright colors. You could see the people were poor, but they were all very cheerful.

As soon as we had registered, Miguel and Martinez went on down to the dock in Port-au-Prince. They were gone about an hour. When they came back, I could see from their faces that Martinez had done it again. The boat had sailed the day before.

My godfather had fixed up what should have been a foolproof route for moving stuff into Miami. Instead of fooling around with a boat and crew of his own, he had arranged to use the M/V *William Express,* one of six Antillean Line freighters of about 1,400 tons each, owned by the Babún brothers, a Cuban family living in Florida. Besides carrying general cargo between the islands, the line also operated a scheduled round-trip service out of Miami, via Santo Domingo, Port-au-Prince, and back again, using the *William Express* and its sister ship, the *José Express.*

Through Luis the Junkman, a friend of his in Miami, Miguel had hired a Haitian seaman named Yves Alexis on the *William Express* to take the stuff aboard at Port-au-Prince and hide it in one of the ventilation ducts on the end of a length of fishing line. No way anybody could spot it. They'd have to crawl down there to find it. When the ship docked in Miami, the stuff would be left dangling there until after the usual customs inspection, and then the dock foreman, a guy named Evaristio Santiesteban, who also worked for my godfather, would pick his moment to haul in the line, unhook the package, and stroll through the dock gate with it in his lunch box. Nothing could have been simpler or less risky. All *we* had to do was not miss the boat.

The only danger in this route that we could see was not from the government but from Fidel Castro. Six months before this, in December 1971, one of his gunboats had captured a sister ship, the *Johnny Express,* off the Bahamas. The Antillean Line was a bit like Air America in Asia. The CIA used it all the time, working through Teófilo Babún, who was very strong for "the cause." After seizing the ship, Havana had said that the *Johnny Express* had shelled a fishing village back in 1970 and this time was carrying a bunch of commandos who were going to be put ashore on a sabotage mission. Like everybody else in Miami, I was ready to believe it. But right now we were more worried about the sabotage mission of José Martinez, because the *William Express* was not due back in Haiti for another two weeks.

By evening, my godfather was through being mad. I think he was now convinced that Martinez had to go, so there was no point in bearing down on him, and for a voodoo freak, the idea of a couple of weeks in Haiti was not torture. For $50 a week, we now had the exclusive services of Paul-Baptiste, the cab driver who had brought us in from the airport, and that night he took us out into the woods for a typical tourist voodoo ceremony.

We all knew it wasn't the real thing, but it was still kind of spooky, with the drums beating in the firelight. The dancers kept going for hours, clashing swords and machetes together to attract the *loa,* the spirit they were worshiping, until finally one of them went into a trance. The *loa* had possessed her, and now they had to sacrifice an animal to it. So they dragged out this goat, and did a whole number with it, and then, whoosh! The *houngan* suddenly stabbed it in the neck with his sword. The blood gushed out, the goat fell, and the woman started to come back to life. The blood of the animal had pleased the spirit, and it left her.

Ana Baños was impressed. She started to moan and fall about, too, but my godfather slapped her a couple of times, and her religious experience ended right there.

Martinez was *not* impressed. He kept trying to get us to leave. He was protecting his mother's interests. And he could see he was going to have to work at it, because next day my godfather was hungry for more. We went downtown to a little restaurant, where we had goat for lunch, and while we were eating, Miguel asked Paul-Baptiste if he knew a real *mambo*—not a tourist voodoo lady like we'd seen the night before, but the real thing. Sure, he said.

So that afternoon we drove out into the country to a village he knew. It was nothing much to look at—just a few mud huts with chickens and kids running around, and one concrete house where the *mambo* lady lived. When Paul-Baptiste went in to explain in patois what we had come for, Martinez grabbed his chance. He'd been bitching all the way.

"These people," he said. "You don't know them. Just look at this place. They don't have a pot to piss in. They'll tell you anything. You're going to get a line of shit, that's all. Tell him to take us back. You don't know this woman."

"That's what I like about it," my godfather said. "They don't know us. So I want to see what she's got to say."

Then Paul-Baptiste came out and said my godfather should go upstairs. While he was gone, the rest of us sat around drinking beer in a sort of bar they had there. When he came down, he didn't say a word.

"What did I tell you?" said Martinez. "Let *me* go up there. I'll soon tell you if she's a phony."

So up he went, and as soon as he hit the stairs on the way down again, he started sounding off.

"This woman's crazy," he said. "She don't do nothing right. She's all full of shit. Let's get out of here."

"No," said Ana Baños. "It's my turn now. Okay, Mikey? That's what we came for, right?"

"Right," he said. "You go."

She came down, looking serious. "Well, let me tell you," she said. "That old lady hit *me* on the money. She ain't never seen me in my life, but she knows things about me."

"Bullshit," Martinez said. "Just bullshit. She don't know what she's talking about. Let's go."

"Now it's George," my godfather said.

I would just as soon have passed. I don't believe in fortunetellers. But I was ready to have a tooth pulled if it would have gotten under Martinez's skin.

She was an old black woman in a bright-colored dress sitting in a smelly little room with a dirt floor and no windows. There was a candle burning. She had a bell to summon the spirits, a glass of water, and a big cigar. I gave her $2. She rang the bell and started muttering in patois. Then she puffed smoke over the water.

"There's a woman that loves you," she said, in English. "But you're not married. You live together."

Well, okay. Paul-Baptiste could have told her that from the conversations he had overheard.

"There is also another woman," she said. "You've known her a long time, and you must be careful. She lives near you, and she wishes you harm."

Well, he sure as hell didn't tell her that, because nobody here even knew about it. There was this woman named Esther in Miami who was strong on voodoo and who had it in for me. She was about forty and half crazy. I don't know what her problem was, but she'd convinced herself I wanted to kill her.

The old woman blew some more smoke over the water. "You have a rebellious spirit watching over you," she said. "That is why you have a quick temper. He was a renegade in Korea, and his name is Cosmo Lacroix. You should talk to him."

And that was all she had to say. When I went downstairs, I wasn't laughing.

Martinez then bitched all the way back to the hotel. I guess he figured that if Raquel Dumois lost out to this Haitian *mambo*, then his last hold on my godfather was gone. But he went on too long, and that night at dinner Miguel changed the subject. He climbed on Martinez's back again about missing the boat, and the six kilos of coke still sitting in his bedroom.

"Screw it," he said. "Tomorrow I'm taking that goddamn shit with me on an airplane back to Miami. I'll take it in the suitcases, just the way it is."

I knew he couldn't be serious. He was just putting Martinez on the spot.

"Oh, Mikey," he said. "You ought to think it over. It's only twelve days. To go into customs with those bags—they're not stupid. That's suicide."

"Yeah? Well, I'll be goddamned if I'm going to sit around on my ass for two weeks just because you fouled up. We ain't got enough money with us anyway. I'll get those mothers in if I have to swim them across."

"Right on, baby," said Ana Baños. "I'm with you all the way. Whatever you say, I'm right there."

That night, Martinez took sick. He said it was the water, but it wasn't that that turned him yellow. It was a case of let me leave before these people ask *me* to help carry the bags. Anyway, he wanted to fly home to Momma that day, and nobody gave him an argument.

"All right," said my godfather. "Go. Me and Georgie will work it out."

Martinez left on the two o'clock plane, but it didn't make any difference. We had already decided there was no reason why we all had to stay. We were going to take it in turns to wait out the twelve days, and whoever came back to spell the other would bring the money we needed. That night me, my godfather, and Ana Baños sat out by the pool.

"Tell me something," she said. "What do you need Martinez for? Every time you ask him to do something, he screws up. He can't do nothing by himself. Why don't you just use Georgie?"

"Yeah, I been thinking about that," Miguel said. "José's giving me headaches. Plus Frankie don't like him, don't want him around. But he knows the operation. I got to be careful."

We sipped our drinks, thinking of ways to shut Martinez's

mouth. Then he said: "José did all right on the Zack Robinson deal—I got to give him that."

"Martinez did shit," I said. "I wouldn't have said nothing, but since you brought it up, all he did was watch TV." And I told him what happened.

"Shit," my godfather said. "What the fuck is it with this guy? I give that punk every kind of a break and he just lays back on his ass."

"Well, I guess he figured I could handle it," I said modestly. "But what gets me is the way he ducked out of *this* foul-up. He should have said, 'It's my job to move this to Miami. It's bad enough you had to help me out in Santo Domingo, but now I'll stay here and take care of it.' Instead of that, what does he do?"

"He shits in his pants," said Miguel. "When we get back to Miami, you take over."

"Okay." Martinez had done it all for me. "But he ain't going to like that."

"He'll get his share. I'll find him something to do. He can look after the stash."

"He's still not going to like taking orders from *me*."

My godfather took a heavy snort of coke, right out of the spoon, and was quiet for a minute.

"José won't do nothing," he said. "But have Orlando keep an eye on him. Just in case."

That was good enough for me. From now on, Martinez was accident-prone. And if I wanted to keep Orlando out of it, Ricardo Morales owed us a favor.

"All right," I said. "Next problem. Who goes? Who stays? And what do we use for money?"

"Okay. I been thinking about that, too. Frankie owes us $16,000. Tomorrow I want you to go up there and get it. Take Ana here with you, and drop her off in Miami."

"Baby, I need some money, too," she said. "For the rent."

My godfather took another snort in the other nostril. "When you get there," he said, "give her three hundred."

If that had been Raquel Maisonet, she'd have cracked him right in the mouth.

We left the next morning. As soon as we landed in Miami, I called Anna and told her to get a thousand from our safe-deposit box. By the time we reached the apartment, she was back with the money, so I gave Ana Baños her three hundred, and Orlando drove her home. When he came back, I told him what had happened. I said he was now in with us officially, and that I wanted him to keep an eye on Martinez. My godfather was right. He didn't have the guts to do nothing, but it didn't hurt to have Orlando breathe on him a little. By then, Anna had finished packing, and so back to the airport again, and off we went to New York.

After checking in at the Skyline Motel on Tenth Avenue at 50th Street, I called Frank at the number he'd given me last time. On that first trip, after making the delivery, Miguel, Martinez, and me had gone over to get our money at an apartment Frank had up in Riverdale, not far from where my godfather used to live. It was in a plush building at 3333 Henry Hudson Parkway that was just the place for rich junkies. When Frank was out, they could try Nicky Barnes, who lived in the penthouse. Anyway, I knew the number I had was for the phone in Frank's apartment there, and when he answered the call, I expected him to tell me to come on up. Instead, he just asked me where I was staying, and when I told him, he said to stick around. He'd send somebody down to see me.

Sure enough, an hour or so later, somebody knocked on the door of our room, and there was Nat Elder, my godfather's friend, the guy who had come with Frank to the meeting over in Jersey.

"Hey, there, Georgie. How's it going, man?"

"Fine, Nat, fine. Come on in. This is Anna."

"Hi, Anna. Howya doing? Look, Frank just couldn't get away. He's sorry. He's all tied up in a meeting."

"Yeah. I heard it giggling."

"What can I tell you?" He grinned. "You know Frank. No matter how hard he tries, that poor unfortunate boy just can't seem to get enough. But he's working on it. Pretty near all the time."

"Well, I know just exactly how he feels," I said. "Because we got the same kind of problem in another area. We need the sixteen thousand he owes us to get a shipment out of Haiti."

"And that's it? Man, that ain't no problem at all. You go get yourself a bite to eat, and I'll take care of that myself."

So Anna and me had dinner at Mamma Leone's, and afterwards went to bed. I'd covered a few miles that day. Around five in the morning, somebody knocking on the door woke me up, and it was Nat again.

"Room service," he said, and he handed me a large brown paper bag. "Good night and good luck. I'll be seeing you."

Inside was $16,000 in fives, tens, and twenties. Anna couldn't believe her eyes when I tipped it out on the bed.

"Hell," I said. "We just got to blow a couple of thousand of this to celebrate. Tomorrow we hit Fifth Avenue."

We went out after breakfast with about $8,000. That was all Anna could cram into her biggest pocketbook. So I figured that first of all we'd change some into larger bills, to make it easier to carry around. Never dreamed we'd have a problem. I just walked casually up to the counter of the Chase Manhattan bank on the corner of Madison and 57th Street and asked the teller if I could change some money into hundreds.

"Why certainly," she said. "How much?"

"Five thousand."

She took a gulp and changed colors. Then it came to me, what I'd done. I was so used to dealing in big sums now, it had never occurred to me that she'd think this unusual.

"Five thousand *dollars?*"

"Er-yes."

"I'll have to talk to one of the officers," she said. "I'll be right back."

When she said officers, I thought she meant cops, and I wanted to tell her, forget it. But that could have made things worse, so while she was gone, I tried to figure out what I was going to say. She came back with a guy in a banker's suit who gave me a fishy eye.

"I understand you want to change $5,000 in small bills into hundreds," he said.

"That's correct."

"It's a lot of money to carry around."

"We found that out," I said. "We're on our vacation—we been saving our money all year—and it's too bulky. So we want to change it."

We looked at him like babes in the wood, and he relaxed. "It would be much safer if you used a savings account," he said. "That way you'd earn interest, too."

"Well, maybe we'll start one for next year," I said. "But for right now, we'd like to change the five thousand."

"All right," he said. "But you'll have to sign a form with your name and address."

So what the hell? I signed it. Crisis over. I went into Anna's purse and started to dump the bills on the counter. And dump. And dump. And all the other tellers were watching while she counted it. Took her about ten minutes. Finally she handed over fifty $100 bills, and I could feel their eyes on the back of my neck as we walked out of the bank. I never did that again.

So now Anna started to unload it. She went berserk in Bonwit Teller and bananas in Saks. I couldn't keep up with her. Every time I turned around, there was somebody else saying, "That will be $400 plus tax." Soon I couldn't manage all the shopping bags, so we bought a couple of new suitcases to carry the stuff. And it wasn't all for her. She picked out a robe and a couple of sweaters for me, and I bought myself a few pairs of shoes. Between us, we tore through three or four thousand dollars in a couple of hours. Then we went back to the hotel, packed, and caught an afternoon flight to Miami. Twenty-four hours later, I was in Haiti again.

My godfather had been busy. Right after I left, he had run into a girl he knew from Puerto Rico named Mary-Lou. She was half

Haitian and had a lot of good contacts in Port-au-Prince. They had gone out on the town together—what there was of it—and that had given him an idea.

"You know what we're going to do?" he said. "We're going to open a key club down here. We'll call it the Happy 'Gator. Very expensive. Very exclusive. We'll bring down top entertainment from the States, and it'll go like a bomb. Now we're moving stuff through Haiti, it'll make a great cover."

"Beautiful," I said. "I like it. I like it a lot."

"So does Mary-Lou. And she *knows* this town. You'll meet her tonight."

I had to hand it to him. It was a great idea. Haiti suited me. Nobody lasts forever in the drug business. It makes sense to have something solid to run to when you have to get out.

After dinner, Paul-Baptiste took us down to the Casino Internationale on the waterfront, where I won a few dollars at craps and lost them again playing blackjack, and practically the first person we saw when he dropped us back at the hotel around midnight was Mary-Lou. We sat down with her in the little nightclub there, and after a couple of drinks the bandleader, whose name was Charles, came over and Mary-Lou introduced us. He was like the Frank Sinatra of Haiti, very big down there. And he was just back with his band from a tour of the States.

We talked about that for a while, and then Mary-Lou said: "Mikey and Georgie here are thinking of starting a key club in town, and I told them they ought to talk to you about it."

"Fantastic idea," he said. "You mean a *real* key club? Not just another discotheque?"

"Right," said Miguel. "Top people only. Everything the best."

"Fantastic. And you know who'll love it? Jean-Claude."

"Charles is in tight with Baby Doc," said Mary-Lou. "President Duvalier—you know? He plays with Charles's band."

"You don't say." That rang my chime. A political connection? Shit. We're home free. "What does he play? What instrument?"

"The bass," Charles said. "When we're in town, we go over to the palace every day and rehearse. We always play the theme from 'Shaft.' That's his favorite tune."

"Then Baby Doc gets the first key," said Miguel. "In gold."

"Man, you do that, and you got it made. That's the kind of guy he is. If he likes you, you can do what you want in this country. And listen, I'll take care of the entertainment. We'll bring down some big names, and they'll eat it up."

"That's what we figured," I said. "I guess we'll have to bring in most of the things we need, like equipment and furniture and stuff. With all these political contacts you got, you know anybody in the Customs Service?"

My godfather gave me a stare.

"Are you kidding?" said Charles. "It's run by a friend of mine."

"Uh-huh." I could see we understood each other. "On top of that, we got X amount of merchandise that comes through here every so often," I said. "In transit—you know what I mean? It don't stay here. And going through customs is such a hassle. All that paperwork and shit."

Charles looked at me like I was his long-lost brother. "Money's the name of the game around here," he said. "I'm sure we can work something out."

Miguel settled back in his seat. "Let's have another round," he said.

"No, wait a minute," said Charles. "You serious about this key-club deal?"

"You bet your ass we're serious. All we got to do is get the wheels turning."

"Okay." He finished off his drink. "Then let's start right now. I'll show you where this place has got to be."

So at one o'clock in the morning we were looking at $200,000 parcels of real estate on the beach front.

I got up late. That day, I had a different kind of shopping to do. Paul-Baptiste drove me downtown and I bought a stapler and a few yards of heavy sheet vinyl on the Grand Rue. This was to give the cocaine a bit of extra protection on its sea voyage. Back in my room at the hotel, I tore the false bottoms out of the suitcases and laid the six kilo packs on the bed. The stuff was already in thick plastic bags, about a foot square, so now I wrapped each one in a big piece of vinyl, turned over the edges, and stapled them down tight. Then I locked all six in another suitcase and put it at the back of the closet. After that, I sat in the sun for the rest of the day watching a bunch of wood carvers under the trees make statues out of lumps of mahogany. There was still a lot of time to kill.

That night, my godfather told me Victoria Montalvo was coming over. Talking to her on the phone, he had raved on about Haiti until his old lady wanted to see the place for herself. So the next morning we picked her up at the airport and checked her into El Rancho.

"How much did you bring?" he said, when we were finally alone in her room.

"Three thousand," she said. "Just like you told me."

"What's that for?" He hadn't said anything to me about it. "We got enough to last."

Miguel shook his head. "I got a surprise for you. This afternoon we're going to take another run out to see that *mambo* lady. And this time she's going to do a *real* number on us. You want to come, Momma?"

"Where's the stuff?" she said. "We didn't ought to leave it with nobody here."

"It's okay," I told her. I could think of better ways to spend an afternoon. Like tiring myself out watching the wood carvers. "I got it locked away."

"No, I don't trust these Haitians." Now she was here, she didn't want to see the country; she wanted to stay in her room. "You bring that stuff in here. I'll take care of it while you're gone."

Miguel tried to argue with her, but it was just the two of us when Paul-Baptiste brought his taxi around at two o'clock.

We drove out to the same village as before. Paul-Baptiste went into the concrete house to see if they were ready and came out with the old woman, who beckoned us to follow her. This time we went through a couple of rooms downstairs and out the back into a kind of walled-in patio with a tree in the middle. The ground had been marked out in complicated patterns and drawings in chalk or flour, and on one wall was a bunch of what looked like yellow crosses. They were little candles held in place with cross-pieces of wax. In one corner there was a door in the wall, opening into a kind of hut, and sitting with their backs against another wall were three or four drummers, just starting to warm up. Besides the old lady we knew, there was an even older one, who soon showed she was the boss *mambo,* and five or six other women, all wearing the usual cotton dresses. The youngest of them was maybe thirty-five.

So now we follow the old lady into a little room off the patio, and she tells us to take our clothes off. Shit. Here we go again. I look round at Miguel, but he's already getting undressed. When we're ready, she tells us to go sit on a bench by the wall near the candles, and she hands Miguel a bottle with some pale yellow liquid in it. I figure it's *clairin,* the local firewater. So he takes a slug of it—I see his eyes open—and then he hands it to me. Well, I thought I was ready for it, but when I take a whack of that shit, my brains damn near curdle and run out my ears.

Now the drums are really cutting loose. The old grandmother has started to chant and dance in the middle drawing. She clangs the two big swords she's carrying, and grinds them together like she's sharpening them. Clang, grind, clang, grind. The others join in behind her and they dance around after this old lady, chanting and twisting and hollering. This goes on for a while, and then the lady we know comes out with a whip. Pow! Smoking and puffing at a cigar. Pow! Pow!

She calls us over and stands us side by side in front of a chalk circle with drawings in it. And the one with the swords keeps dancing near us, and clanging them in front of us, and sharpening them, and the chanting's going on, and the hollering, and the other one with the cigar is cracking the whip around us. I'm losing all track of time, and the drums are like inside my head now.

Then she tells me to jump the circle, and jump back, jump over it, and jump back. And as I'm jumping over, they're chanting and urging me on. After that, it's my godfather's turn, and they keep us hopping around there for, I don't know—ten or fifteen minutes. Suddenly it all quiets down, except for the drums, and they take us to stand in front of the crosses. They're just mumbling and muttering and shuffling around. Then the chanting starts again.

The old woman gives me a box of wooden matches and points at the crosses. She gives a box to Miguel, too, and we start lighting the candles. There's maybe twenty of them on the wall. And now they go crazy. The chanting gets heavier. The more candles we light, the more they crash the swords together and crack the whip and puff the smoke. They're dancing and twitching and jerking around and the drums are blotting us out.

Then again comes a silence. She leads us back to the circle. The others are just standing around. But something's happened. I can feel the tension. When the chanting starts again, it's got a different note to it, and the younger woman gets nervous. She's shaking, and panting, and her eyes are flipping up, white. Now everybody gets really excited. I can feel the drums in my stomach, and they're chanting faster and faster, louder and louder. Then she falls.

The old lady and the one with the whip go over to her and get her on her feet. She's breathing deep and her eyes are wide open, but she's not seeing. And she's desperate. Her head keeps turning from side to side, like she's searching for something. Then she sees me. She starts coming at me, and there's a butcher knife in her hand, about ten inches long. So I square off to belt her one, and my godfather says, "Stand still." Shit. She's coming straight at me. Her eyes are glaring. She's sweating and panting—she's really in a hectic state.

Now she's right up close. And she lifts the knife like she's going to stab me, and holds it there, trembling. A foot away from me. Holy Jesus. If she decides to bring that hand down, there's nothing I can do. It goes on and on. I'm watching her arm for the slightest twitch. And my godfather is watching her pretty close, too. Nobody says nothing. Dead silence. Even the drums have stopped.

Then she starts to ease off. Everybody lets their breath out, like a sigh. And as she relaxes, so do I. The knife comes down, bit by bit, her eyes go out, and she turns away.

Now the chanting picks up again, and the drums start in with a slower beat. It's like the Gloria in a Mass. The spirit has come and accepted me. After a couple of minutes, the old woman leads us to the door of the hut in the corner. I'm not worried any more. I figure the worst is over. But then the old woman grabs my right arm. She's got a razor blade, and she cuts me three times. Not deep. Just three little vertical cuts in the place where you get vaccinated. And the other old woman does the same to my godfather. I don't like blades. I'd rather be shot than cut.

Then she takes a big white piece of cloth and taps my arm with it to get some of the blood on there. The other one opens the door of the hut. Inside, candles are burning, like in a church. It's small, about eight feet square, and decked out with colored flags and banners. There's a kind of altar at the back with pictures of saints on it. One of them is like of a little boy with a big spear, and he's getting ready to demolish the devil, in the form of a snake. And on the floor in front of it are some sticks with strips of hide on them—wet, like they just been cut from some animal.

The old *mambo* woman chooses me to go in, but after what I've seen with these crazy people, I don't want to go. I make a sign to my godfather to go instead, but he shakes his head.

"Go," he says. "The spirit is with you. He likes you."

I look around. They're all waiting for me. So I step inside, and the two old women follow. They start to chant and blow smoke again, and the drums are rumbling outside. Suddenly the white cloth with the blood comes over my head and covers me down to about the waist. I don't like that. The chanting kind of gets to me. It's like boring into my head, and swelling it up. I'm feeling nauseated. I try to fight it off but I can't move. The nausea's rising up. I'm dizzy. It's going to get me. My head's splitting tight.

"Miguel." That's me calling out. "Miguel, I'm going to flip. I'm going to fall."

Then I'm on the ground, and I don't know what I'm doing

there. I can't remember. There's this clanging and clashing. I can see candles, little twinkles of light through the weave of the cloth, and movements. So I force myself up on my feet, pulling the cloth off my head, and now I see where I am. There's a live white chicken fluttering in front of me, beating hard with its wings. The old woman is pushing it at me. She wants me to take it. She's making motions with her hands that I don't understand.

Then I hear Miguel. He's calling out in Spanish. "Twist its neck. Twist its neck. Bust it. Drop the blood on the sticks." That's easy for him to say. I can't get a proper grip on the goddamn bird. It's fighting to get away from me.

"Hold, hold," the old woman says, like in a panic. "Break! Break!"

So now I really grab that son of a bitch by the neck, and twist and jerk and pull at it like crazy until the blood starts to drip. I manage to get a few drops on the sticks, although most of it's over me, and that seems to please her. She takes the chicken away, and the other old woman leads me out of the hut. It's all over.

Inside, I'd been groggy and confused. The minute I walked out of that hut, I felt like I do always.

"When they drop you like that," my godfather said, "the spirit is in you. He likes you. And if he likes you too much, he takes you with him."

"*Now* you tell me," I said. "How long was I out?"

"Couple of minutes. Those old ladies really had to sweat to get you back."

"Oh, great," I said. "Thanks a lot."

They gave me a little red bag with a gold metal cross on the outside covered in little black designs. Sewn into it was something soft and cushiony. I didn't even want to know what it was. I was supposed to carry the bag always on my right side, either in my pocket or pinned to my shirt. Women were not to touch it, or even see it. My godfather got one, too. They also gave him a little white cloth bag with drawstrings that contained some of the hide with blood on it. He was supposed to hang this behind the front door of his house to protect it from evil spirits. I guess that was a bonus, because he was paying. I saw him give the old woman $1,400, which is a fortune in Haiti.

As we were leaving, the younger woman, the one who had come at me with the knife, hugged me. She said she had prayed that the spirit would not want to claim my life. He had taken a liking to me because of the red shirt I was wearing when I arrived, and that was why he had spared me. Then the old one tapped me on the shoulder and said I was in good hands. But I wasn't to tell anybody about the ceremony or show them the bag, because it was sacred and Cosmo Lacroix would be angry. So the first person I showed it to was Paul-Baptiste, the taxi driver. And he showed me *his*.

The next few days I hung around the hotel while my godfather played tourist with Victoria Montalvo. Even after the voodoo, I was now completely sold on Haiti as a base for our operations and as a refuge in case things went wrong in the States. We had a good contact in Charles, and now I made another one, the local street boss of downtown Port-au-Prince.

I'd noticed this guy hanging around, sizing us up, as I was doing a little shopping with Paul-Baptiste. It was so hot that day the sun punched you in the head whenever you stepped out of the shade, so I said I'd like a beer. This guy heard me, checked with Paul-Baptiste, and next thing I knew, there was a cold beer in my hand. So I thanked him, took a pull at the bottle, and looked around for some place to set it down. "No, no, no." He waved at me, and said something to another little black guy standing there, who took my bottle and held it for me. I couldn't believe it. The royal treatment. Wherever I went, there he was, standing right behind me, holding my bottle ready. Freaked me out.

So I asked his boss to join us in a little restaurant there, and Paul-Baptiste translated for us. "I'm Antoine," he said. "This is my neighborhood. Anything you need, you tell me. I take care of everything."

Okay. If we're going to build a base here, the best way to win friends and influence people is to pay them. I tried to give him $10, but he wouldn't take it. "No, no. *Ami, ami.*" The hell with that. I needed people who owed *me* favors. I made him take it.

A couple of nights later, I went downtown at about three in the morning with Charles and Mary-Lou to get something to eat. We went into the only place open and ordered sandwiches. Maybe a minute later, Antoine walked in the door. It wasn't a coincidence. He knew we were there. He took one look at the sandwiches the woman was making for us, and started yelling and raving. Then he jumped over the counter, raising his hand to her, and she really started laying the ham on the bread. Oh, Jesus, I said to myself. I got me an adopted son here. What with him and Paul-Baptiste, Charles and the voodoo people, we were getting dug in. And we needed that.

Nothing much happened in the last few days before the *William Express* was due. Victoria Montalvo took sick from the water, and my godfather sent her home. Then we gave Paul-Baptiste the day off so we could rent a car and get rid of the suitcases with the false bottoms. After that, there was nothing to do but wait, and I was getting bored now. There are plenty worse places to kill time in, but I was really glad to see that ship tie up. We hung around the end of the pier until Yves Alexis came off, and then Paul-Baptiste drove us all back to El Rancho to get the stuff.

As Yves had nothing to carry it in, I bought a tourist bag at the souvenir shop opposite the hotel, and about $10 worth of beads and junk to throw on top of the packages to hide them. Then we drove him back to the pier, watched him go aboard the ship, and that was it. Mission accomplished. We made our reservations on a flight to San Juan next morning.

Our last night in Haiti was soft and warm. Me and my godfather sat outside by the pool, listening to the voodoo drums tremble in the distance somewhere. Life felt very good just then.

"I'm glad we're going," I said. "But I'm going to miss this."

"No, you're not. I want you back here every two weeks. We got to get in tight with these people. We need this route working perfect."

"No sweat. We just got to time it right."

"That's what I'm saying. We can't afford no slip-ups. And we need some protection down here. Right now, a kid with a BB gun could rip us off."

"Next trip, I'll have a talk with Antoine," I said. "And maybe Charles can line up a couple of people."

"Okay. But do it right. Soon as we know this route is secure, that's when we make our score. I got a nice little spot all picked out and waiting for me in Caracas."

"Yeah? You through with Miami?"

My godfather shrugged. "Drugs is a hassle. In Caracas, I'm Marcello Cabot. Nobody knows me. I got the chance to pick up a real nice numbers operation. Quiet. Makes lots of money. I don't need all this running around."

"I thought you had your eye on this place," I said. "What about the 'Gator Club and everything?"

"What's the matter? You can't handle it? That's part of the operation."

"Sure. I can handle it. I just didn't figure you were ready to retire yet."

"Listen, I need a million for the numbers business, and then I'm out. After that, the operation's all yours."

"Thanks a lot." Miguel wanted a million. Martinez was babbling about two hundred thousand. They'd both blown their brains out with coke. "I'll be a hundred years old."

"What are you talking about?" he said, as if *I* was crazy.

"You know how much coke we'll have to move to make a million dollars?"

He sat back in his chair, still eyeing me. "Who said anything about coke? I got us a Corsican connection that's just waiting on me to say the word."

"Oh, Jesus. You mean you're going to bring in some horse?"

I guess I didn't sound too happy about it, because he frowned.

"I'm not talking about a couple of pounds," he said. "I'm talking about 100 kilos of European pure. Just for openers. And that's a million dollars each right there."

10

By now the government was reaching for Frank Matthews with both hands, although the left had little idea of what the right was doing. As Gerard Miller and Group 12 went after him directly, ODALE's Group 4 closed in around Mickey Beckwith. As yet neither realized they had hooked the same fish, or how big a fish it was. They still knew so little about Frank Matthews that Beckwith was considered by some to be the more important of the two.

But not by Miller, who was no ordinary police officer. After graduating from Michigan State University, he had voluntarily spent some time in prison to find out what it was like, and also to learn something about the kind of men he would have to deal with in law enforcement. By instinct and vocation, he was a thief-taker. He had not chosen this career as one among others, or as a means of advancement; it was an end in itself, taking precedence over everything, including his family, the good opinion of others, and the prospects for promotion. Direct, resourceful, and sometimes unaware of how many toes he trod on once a quarry was in his sights, Miller, at forty-two, took a mournful pride in receiving mail addressed to Herr Miller, choosing to take this as a left-handed tribute to a Teutonic thoroughness handed down from his German ancestors.

But it was also freely acknowledged among his colleagues in the Bureau of Narcotics and Dangerous Drugs that Miller had a feeling for a case that amounted to more than the sum of twenty years' experience in dealing with organized crime in Chicago, Detroit, and Miami. When Ted Vernier, who had worked with him in Detroit, went to New York in 1971 to set up the Joint Task Force, he needed group supervisors he could depend upon, and there was none more dependable than Miller. Except that Miller did not want to go.

In the Bureau, there was no more dreaded assignment than New York. Though that city was at the hub of the illegal narcotics trade, the situation there was so bedeviled by graft, politics, and overlapping jurisdictions that it offered little scope for the direct, rule-bending methods that Miller favored. Besides, he liked Miami, to which he had been posted by the Federal Bureau of Narcotics six years earlier, and where he had just made a substantial dent in the local drug trade with Operation Eagle, the first major sweep-up of Cuban traffickers in Florida. But he went North in the end, yielding reluctantly to a combination of official pressure and friendly persuasion, and found himself at the head of twelve suspicious New York City cops who not only resented the appointment of a supervisor from out of town but deeply questioned the character and competence of *any* federal agent.

The greeting Miller received in New York from his deputy supervisor, Sergeant William "Jack" Rawald, himself a fifteen-year veteran, has become a stock greeting in the NYPD for any new commanding officer. "You do as I tell you," Rawald said, "and we'll get along fine."

And so they did, though not because Miller deferred to Rawald in anything but the sergeant's superior knowledge of the New York streets. Each quickly recognized the other for an honest, hard-working cop, and that soon went for most of the Dirty Dozen, as they had at once called themselves. It was Rawald's job to make them an elite crew, and Miller's to work that crew on a case in which their previous experience was no help at all.

His men were street cops. To be effective, a street cop has to be visible. To earn promotion, he has to make as many busts as he can without making a nuisance of himself. To stay alive, he has to be ready to use his gun. Now they had to stay out of sight, watch people break the law, and keep their guns holstered. It was a lot to unlearn, particularly for officers like Stan Martin, then the most decorated man in the New York Police Department. And there was no time for retraining. After reading Detective Kowalski's report, Miller decided that his Dirty Dozen would have to find out the hard way that landing a big fish on a conspiracy charge meant it was often necessary to allow a criminal enterprise to prosper unchecked for months while the case was assembled. They would have to learn on the job that success lay in *avoiding* a confrontation with any of the main conspirators until a net had been spread to catch them all. Which brought up another problem more serious even than a green crew.

It was already clear from Kowalski's report and the toll records of the phone at 130 Clarkson that Matthews was operating in at least twenty states. In normal circumstances, this would have meant that the case had to be passed up the line to the BNDD regional office, because the New York policemen staffing the Joint Task Force had no jurisdiction outside the city, let alone out of state. But Miller dug in his toes. Circumstances were *not* normal, he told Vernier. The NYJTF needed a good case to establish itself. If they had to hand over everything that came up with an out-of-town connection, there would be nothing left for them to do but roust neighborhood dealers, which the Police Department was quite capable of doing without federal help.

On top of that, Matthews's headquarters was plainly in Brooklyn. His out-of-town dealers came to see him there. That meant the investigation would almost certainly center on New York with the object of building a case for the U.S. Attorney to prosecute in the Eastern District. In Miller's view, that placed the burden squarely on the shoulders of the Task Force, which would naturally call on BNDD Task Forces in other cities and states for assistance as and when the need arose.

Vernier was not entirely convinced. Carried to its conclusion, the argument would have rendered all the regional offices redundant. But he allowed himself to be persuaded. At this stage, it *was* a New York case. Or, rather, it was not a case at all, but merely a promising lead. He gave Miller three months to check it out, which was less than Miller had hoped for but more than he had feared. In three months, Group 12 might well lay the foundations of a major case, only to lose it to the regional office, which would naturally take all the credit. On the other hand, in three months, his Dirty Dozen might crack it.

He put the issue to them in precisely those terms. "The first thing we're going to have to do is fight the brass," he said, thereby capturing his audience at once. They were going to have to improvise a lot, because they were short of money and equipment. They would have to work around the clock, because they were short of manpower. And they were also going to have to check their every move with him until they learned how to work on their own. After all that, they might still come up empty, because how the hell could anybody get as big as Frank Matthews seemed to be without making a lot of noise? It could turn out they had all been wasting their time. But he didn't think so.

Nor did they. It was the start of one of the most unusual investigations in the history of American law enforcement. Humored rather than supported by the BNDD and the Police Department, a handful of New York street cops set out to catch one of the most important criminals of modern times. With only the sketchiest idea of what they were doing, and with not much more to work on than Gerard Miller's hunch, Group 12 homed in on Clarkson Avenue, under strict orders not to arrest anybody or to interfere with any transaction they observed. They were simply to keep Matthews under surveillance, to note what he did, where he went, and whom he met, in the hope of collecting enough evidence to justify a court-ordered wiretap and the logistical backup necessary to do the job properly (without losing the case to the regional office).

Matthews spotted them at once. They were too few to be discreet, particularly on moving surveillance. To have followed him and his visitors without tipping their hand, they would have needed six cars at least, and with two men to a car, Miller could rarely afford the luxury of having even half that many out at any one time. Matthews had only to stay home to immobilize half of Group 12.

They were also too few for Miller to consider mounting a continuous surveillance. Now and again, his men had to be allowed to eat, sleep, and see their families. The most he could hope for was to keep Matthews guessing, to avoid any predictable pattern in the stakeout, so that his quarry could never count on the coast being clear. The game was cat and mouse—to a set of ground rules that sometimes left it uncertain as to who was playing which role. Evidently sensing that no arrest was imminent, Matthews soon entered into the spirit of the thing.

The first to suffer was Patrolman John Dworsak. Parked down the street from 130 Clarkson, he saw Matthews leave the building and drive off in one of his Cadillacs. Dworsak duly fell in behind and all went well until they neared the Williamsburg Expressway. Then Matthews suddenly accelerated, blasted up a one-way street in the wrong direction, jumped a red light, and disappeared.

After that, the game became as formal as a minuet. When he wanted to be alone, Matthews would make chop suey of the traffic laws, knowing that nobody but the fuzz would follow him, and that they would only reveal themselves if they did. He would run a couple of red lights for openers, and then, if he suspected that a stakeout car had been positioned to allow for this, throw in a couple of illegal U-turns as well, and perhaps another wrong-way dash up a one-way street. In this mood, it would have taken a Hertz-sized fleet of pursuers coordinated by helicopter to keep him in sight. At other times, when he made no attempt to shake his tail, it would soon become clear that he was not worth following anyway, that he was just out on the town or deliberately trying to tease them.

The frustrations were alarming. Group 12 was stretched so thin that stakeout teams lived in their cars for days on end, taking turns to eat and wash up at the nearest Howard Johnson's. To try to compensate for their shortage of vehicles, they rigged one car for night-time duty with a rheostat control on the headlights. By varying the brightness and occasionally switching one or the other of them out altogether, they hoped to pass themselves off as several different cars in Matthews's rear-view mirror. But the pickings remained skimpy.

On January 20, 1972, Miller mounted a maximum effort in moving surveillance. He begged or borrowed seven cars and crews, and that night disposed them in the streets around 130 Clarkson to cover most of Matthews's regular opening gambits. All evening they sat there, waiting for something to happen. Then, just as Miller was about to call off the exercise, cursing his luck in having picked one of the rare nights when his suspect stayed home, Matthews came out of the apartment house and got into Nat Elder's Cadillac.

It was obviously a business trip. He took off down the block, heading west, jumped the light at Bedford Avenue, turning south, ran through another at Linden Boulevard, turning east, and lit out for Queens with only two of the seven cars still on his tail. He shook one of those at New York Avenue by crossing against the red at 90 miles an hour, and led the remaining car toward Kennedy Airport at speeds ranging up to 120. Hanging on fearfully, not because they expected to learn anything useful, but because they were damned if they were going to let Matthews think he could do as he liked, the two officers somehow kept him in sight, praying that nothing would get in their way and that their battered old stakeout car would not disintegrate around them.

Then they lost him. Or, rather, a motorcycle cop cut in ahead of them and they had to stop to avoid running him down.

But Matthews's success in eluding surveillance was, in a sense, working against him. Group 12 had shaken down fast on this diet of discouragement. They did not enjoy being made to look foolish, nor were they pleased by the apathy and criticism they encountered at Task Force headquarters. In consequence, Matthews now had a team of highly dedicated men on his tail, with something to prove, not only to him, but to their colleagues, superiors, and the world at large. There was no doubt left in any of their minds. Matthews was big. And it was now incumbent upon them, as a matter of professional pride, to prove it. For each of them, the investigation was turning into a personal crusade.

So personal that besides working hundreds of hours of unpaid overtime, and often paying their own expenses, they also chipped in for a month's rent on a vacant first-floor apartment in a building opposite 130 Clarkson. Until then, they had lacked the means to carry out an unobtrusive surveillance of traffic on the block, but now the picture began to clear. Through most of January and into February, Group 12 watched Matthews, Elder, Gattis Hinton, McCargo, John Darby, and many others, known and unknown, come and go with suitcases and paper bags. They logged their movements, noted their license plate numbers, followed them when possible, and slowly tied Matthews into a web of drug connections radiating out of their jurisdiction and probably out of the country.

They also linked him with Beckwith, ODALE's quarry, though without then understanding the relationship between the two. On January 31, Sergeant Rawald was visiting the surveillance team on duty in the apartment when Matthews and Elder emerged from 130 with three other men. As they drove off in two of the Cadillacs strewn in the driveway, Rawald dashed out to his own car and gave chase.

This time, he was not spotted. He followed them down Lenox Road until they parked just short of 56th Street, got out, and walked around the corner. Somebody was waiting for them on the block, standing by a Buick Riviera. This obviously annoyed Matthews, who started bawling him out, and at that moment another Cadillac, a white one with Connecticut plates, turned the corner and parked alongside them. Whereupon Matthews blew his stack completely. Yelling with rage, he ordered the driver off the block, and stood there fuming until the offender hurried back on foot. It was Scarvey McCargo. After delivering himself of a few more observations on the subject of security, Matthews then led his men into 101 East 56th Street, the apartment house owned by Mickey Beckwith and his mother.

It was one of the few occasions when Matthews was seen to be really concerned about secrecy, and it aroused in Group 12 a wholly justified suspicion about what went on in the building. But, for the most part, Matthews went about his business as though he neither knew nor cared that he was being watched.

In twenty years, Miller had seen nothing quite like it. Few professional criminals in his experience had ever behaved so brazenly. Most of them lived in fear of attracting unwelcome attention by spending too much, or being seen in the wrong places with the wrong people, or by having no visibly adequate means of support, but Matthews seemed to glory in extravagance and recklessness.

He strewed money around as if it were wastepaper, paying cash for dozens of $300 suits from Jacques, in Greenwich Village. He dropped huge sums in cash at Las Vegas, losing as much as $190,000 in a session (although whether these were genuine losses or disguised premiums for the casinos that laundered his money is open to doubt). He bought cars for cash: $8,000 Cadillacs and $20,000 Mercedes—so many of them that he sometimes lost track. He mislaid one Mercedes altogether, having forgotten he had it with him. Group 12 found it months later, parked near Small's Paradise, in Harlem. Though covered in dust, it was otherwise intact. Matthews might have forgotten where he had put it, but the neighborhood had not forgotten to whom it belonged.

He paid cash for his girls. He liked them light-skinned, straight-haired, and two or more at a time. Some of them lived in the half-dozen apartments he rented around town—usually in his own name—and paid for in cash. Besides 130 Clarkson, which he shared with Barbara Hinton and the three children, André, Frank Jr., and Sean, he kept another place at 1035 Clarkson for a girlfriend and their baby daughter; a hideaway in Fort Lee for two more girlfriends; the Ponderosa and another apartment on President Street for business purposes; and his four-room pad, for business *and* pleasure, at 3333 Henry Hudson Parkway.

This last he favored more than the others, treating it as his second home. On signing the lease in 1970, he gave his occupation as real estate, which was partly true, and his income as $22,000 a year, which was wholly false. Through Mattrank Enterprises Inc., of 1475 Fulton Street, Brooklyn, he was becoming a very substantial property owner with interests in several states. As a character reference, he listed Thaddeus Owens, who handled some of his legal work, and who is now a County Court judge in Brooklyn.

Besides the apartments, Matthews was also building himself a palatial colonial-style mansion on Staten Island, for cash. At the end of 1970, he had paid $23,500 for a vacant lot at 7 Buttonwood Road, Todt Hill, widely regarded as one of the most desirable suburban areas within city limits. Among his new neighbors were the then Borough President, Robert Connor; Assemblyman Lucio Russo; and Paul Castellano, brother-in-law of the late boss of bosses, Carlo Gambino.

Before this, the only black people seen on Buttonwood Road were maids, houseboys, and gardeners, so that the prospect of Matthews's arrival was greeted with muted enthusiasm. One local homeowner, of Italian extraction, even went so far as to express in public his misgivings about the effect it might have on the quality of life in the community, an affront so wounding that it upset Matthews's driving. The next time he happened to be passing the man's house his Mercedes left the road and performed a series of high-speed slaloms that plowed up the front lawns and flower beds for fully five minutes, showering the house with broadsides of dirt, turf clods, and uprooted rose bushes. After that, Todt Hill faced up to integration without a murmur.

Matthews was always sensitive to racial slights. Once, when a Mob figure threatened to kill the next nigger who crowded his drug operation, Matthews let it be known that if such a thing were to happen, he personally would lead his people up and down Mulberry Street in a convoy of cars and shoot every guinea who moved. Forced to recognize that on past form he probably meant it, the Mob did the statesmanlike thing and chalked up still another score to settle at a more convenient time.

Meanwhile, Matthews enrolled his children, for cash, in the prestigious Staten Island Academy, and Barbara Hinton drove them back and forth each day from Brooklyn, often staying out at the house to discuss progress with the decorator (fee, $10,000 cash), the contractors ($250,000 cash), or the specialist subcontractors brought in to install the marble floors, gold-plated plumbing fixtures, the enclosed swimming pool, and so on (all paid for in cash). And when the army duffel bag of money that Matthews kept in the trunk of whichever car he happened to be using occasionally ran short, he would use his Diners Club card or Master Charge instead—both held in his own name.

This effrontery, this insolent presumption that he was untouchable, above the law or immune to it and therefore not obliged to take even the most elementary precautions against detection, was baffling—difficult to credit in an otherwise hardheaded, immensely successful drug trader. It may have been a product of his heavy cocaine habit, which commonly induces a sense of personal mastery and self-confidence amounting to arrogance, but whatever the cause, the effect was to deepen still further the determination of Miller and Group 12 to bring him down.

Whenever Matthews appeared in all his glory—in a full-length black sable coat, perhaps, or a black leather safari suit—and loaded Barbara Hinton into yet another brand-new Eldorado to hit the Persian Room on a Saturday night, the watchers would brush the Big Mac crumbs from their shirtfronts, think of their neglected wives, and ease their Plymouths into the traffic after him just a shade more implacably than last time.

And they were finally getting somewhere. Besides piecing together a general picture of Matthews's operation, they had identified his closest lieutenants and some at least of his principal dealers. They had seen him handling drugs and money, and watched him spending far beyond his declared 1971 income of $159,774.59—two very good reasons for continuing the investigation beyond the original three months conceded by Vernier. But Miller was still a long way from being able to prove to the satisfaction of his colleagues, let alone a jury, that Matthews and company willfully, knowingly, and unlawfully did combine, conspire, confederate, and agree to violate Sections 812, 841 (a) (1), 952 (a), and 960 (a) (1) of Title 21, United States Code. He was not even in a position to show sufficient probable cause to get a wiretap on

Matthews's phone. What he now needed to reinforce the observations of his own men were informants inside Matthews's organization. Somehow he had to come up with a few solid witnesses who could speak of their own knowledge about Matthews's business affairs, but in Brooklyn these were as easy to find as wild strawberries.

The mortality rate among informers was high, although, once again, the black mobs made bigger allowances for human frailty than their Italian counterparts. To do time when you could avoid it by handing over to the authorities a couple of minor functionaries you probably wanted to get rid of anyway, or better still, an enemy or competitor, was considered, not honorable, but dumb. Even Big El Bynum bought himself out of minor raps in exchange for information about other dealers. As an alternative to bribery, snitching was the only effective means of dealing with straight cops and prosecutors, and as such, an accepted business practice. But it had to be used with discretion. The big operators usually covered themselves by means of bilateral treaties, one promising not to inform on another in return for the same consideration, and both would commonly unite to liquidate any lesser third party who threatened either one of them from below.

Among the finest exponents of the art of selective informing was Dickie Diamond, who managed to combine a successful criminal career with that of a government snitch from 1964 until his arrest and conviction on a murder charge in 1972 (for which he was subsequently pardoned after cooperating with the federal government on several different cases). He made no secret of it. When he teamed up with Bynum in 1966, each agreed that, if arrested, neither would give up the other, "but only small people." In 1969, he went to work on the same basis for Frank Matthews, who "didn't care what I did so long as I looked out for him as I looked out for El." It was an admirable arrangement for everybody but the "small people," among whom Gerard Miller and Group 12 now began to rake assiduously for possible witnesses with more to lose by keeping their mouths *shut* than by helping to bring Matthews down.

They had to have something to trade. The best thing was to catch a suitable candidate in the middle of a "buy," with the stuff in his hands, or the money received for it, because that gave them fifteen years of his life to bargain with. Throw in government protection for himself and his family, support payments for as long as his services were required, and a new life with a new identity afterwards, and the prospective informant would have to be, not just dumb, but willfully masochistic to choose the penitentiary.

Again, money was a problem, and also the shortage of black undercover agents good enough, or well enough motivated, to pose as out-of-town buyers and to lure one or more of Matthews's lesser people into dealing with them. There was no margin for error. Matthews knew as well as anybody what the government had to do to get him. One slip and, instead of a useful informant, Group 12 would acquire just his corpse—and possibly that of its agent as well. With his limited resources, it clearly made sense for Miller to go further out from the center and try to breach Matthews's organization on its fringe, where his vigilance had to be less. But how could he take his New York cops to Philadelphia or Atlanta? And if he did, how could he avoid conceding that the Matthews case had thereby reached the point where the regional office should take over?

By mid-February, this last question had to be rephrased: How could he prevent the regional office taking over the case when it was quite obviously one for them? The FBI had just received the Aquarius letter.

According to a source close to the Bureau's office in Atlanta, an anonymous correspondent, signing himself Aquarius, wrote in to blow the whistle on Matthews and his operation. Written by somebody who obviously knew a lot about him, the letter listed Matthews's New York addresses and phone numbers, his principal lieutenants, and even the names and states in which his cars were registered. It did not, however, have much to say about his activities in Atlanta, which was strange, coming from an obviously well-informed local correspondent who might have been expected to know more about Matthews's business there than in New York.

For this reason, the omission was thought to be deliberate, reflecting the writer's obvious anxiety to keep his identity hidden, which he succeeded in doing, although, from the internal evidence and by a process of elimination, the agents five years later were inclined to attribute the letter to a source not far from the Carter White House.

The question of authorship, however, was of little immediate consequence. What mattered was that two agencies of the Justice Department were now alerted to Matthews, and that Group 12 could no longer hope to confine the investigation to New York, leaving it to Miller's old pals in BNDD offices around the country to follow up the out-of-town leads informally. It was still a New York case in the sense that Matthews ran his operation from there, but the operation itself was now demonstrably national in scope. Inquiries in Georgia, for example, touched off by the Aquarius letter, would show that Matthews, with Nat Elder, owned a useful piece of that state. Excluding his house (and a numbers bank) in Atlanta, his real estate interests in De Kalb, Cherokee, Pike, and Haralson counties were valued at $1.75 million. He was also found to own several interesting parcels of land directly in the path of a proposed new highway, the exact route of which was known only by a small handful of top officials in the state government.

And now Matthews's name also cropped up in Pennsylvania and New Jersey, where he had a war on his hands.

On Easter Sunday, 1972, the black elite of Philadelphia and South Jersey converged on Club Harlem, a brassy nightspot in a dismal, two-story brick building three blocks from the boardwalk in Atlantic City. Some six hundred people—legitimate, not so legitimate, and downright crooked—packed into the club after midnight to watch Billy Paul top the bill in "Easter Panorama," a floor show mounted hardly more extravagantly than the audience itself, which blazed and glittered with silks and sequins, diamonds and furs.

Up front, at a ringside table, sat Tyrone Palmer, just back

from vacation in Bermuda, and holding court as always with a retinue of girls and bodyguards. A millionaire at twenty-four, Fat Tyrone was Matthews's main man in Philadelphia.

The lights went down in the mirrored room for Billy Paul, who stepped on stage and began his opening number to a riot of applause. As Fat Tyrone settled in his chair, a heavy-set man in a black silk suit obstructed his view, and three more closed in on his table, from both sides and behind. Palmer tried to get up, but the man in the black suit shot him in the face, and twice more as he fell back. Taken completely by surprise, his bodyguards lurched to their feet, cursing as they pulled their guns, and the other three men started shooting. Down went Gilbert Satterwhite, Palmer's lieutenant, fatally wounded, and three of the girls, shot dead in the rattle of cross fire.

But the shots were now barely audible in the pandemonium. Scores of patrons dived for cover, overturning tables laden with bottles and glasses, and sending chairs flying. Scores more milled about, screaming with pain and terror as the bullets flew and the mirrors shattered. The rest stampeded for the exits.

Hampered by the panic-stricken throng, the four gunmen were slow to fight their way out, the last of them having to fire a warning shot over the head of the first policeman to appear on the scene. By the time reinforcements arrived, all four had got away, and there was little left to do but restore order and piece together eyewitness accounts of what had happened. The final casualty figures for the Easter Sunday shoot-out were five dead and twenty-six wounded.

The official explanation for the carnage was that Palmer had been untidily murdered by a Philadelphia group actually calling itself the Black Mafia, which was thought to be responsible for other multiple murders up and down the East Coast from New York to Washington. Its hitmen were said to have taken up a $15,000 contract issued by associates of Richard "P.I." Smith, a lieutenant of Palmer's, who had been executed in a crowded bar on Palmer's orders a few weeks earlier for stealing cocaine worth

$250,000. In short, it was a family squabble that had unfortunately surfaced in public: boss kills greedy underboss and is in turn killed by professional gunmen hired by friends of underboss.

This explanation left several loose ends, however. Why would experienced hitmen choose to kill Palmer so publicly, risking a difficult getaway, identification by a shoal of witnesses, and federal heat, when they could have knocked him off quietly in, say, the parking lot? Was it unprofessional bravado, or a ruthlessly professional demonstration that no one was safe from them anywhere? If the latter, at whom was the demonstration aimed? Certainly not at prospective clients, who were likely to be severely discouraged by such a messy job. So who else were they trying to impress?

Frank Matthews knew. They were trying to impress *him*. In New York, Philadelphia, and several other cities, his organization—indeed, the drug trade as a whole—was under attack by self-styled Black Muslim commando groups seeking to collect a 10 or 15 percent "tax" on sales. Palmer and Smith had *both* been killed by the Black Mafia for refusing to pay, and as a public warning to other holdouts. By preying on dealers in no position to holler "cop" when victimized by kidnapings and extortion, these so-called Muslim groups were out to get rich on narcotics without ever having to handle them—and without forfeiting the goodwill of a black community appalled by the drug problem and inclined, like the police, to blame atrocities like that at Club Harlem on narcotics gang warfare.

Charles "Swayzie" Cameron, a Matthews lieutenant and himself a kidnap victim of the Muslims in New York, later told the police: "They feel they're invincible . . . In Philadelphia, they killed and killed and killed until people paid off. They kept killing and scared the other people . . . After a while, 'Hey, let's pay off. Give them 10 percent.' For a while they controlled all the drug traffic in Philadelphia. Got their percentage. Anybody big was paying."

Including Matthews. But the Black Muslim commandos were in no position to holler "cop" either. After moving John "Pop" Darby, his fifty-five-year-old lieutenant and father figure, up from

Philadelphia to the comparative safety of a seventh-floor apartment in his own building at 130 Clarkson, Matthews declared open season on the Black Mafia. Through his Italian connections, he took delivery of a consignment of automatic weapons and sent down a few commandos of his own to take care of any self-styled Muslim careless enough to break cover while on the take. The result was a standoff—in effect, a victory for Matthews.

In New York, however, the war had taken a different turn. Though extortionist groups were active, the main threat to the drug trade was offered at street level by vigilantes who were not susceptible to the same countermeasures, and who could not be bought off, either. Moved by a simple desire to clean up their neighborhoods where the police had failed, genuine Black Muslims, Black Panthers, and even Rastafarians had taken to shooting pushers on sight—and on Matthews's own doorstep. After ten unsolved killings and an almost daily round of sniping and other shooting incidents, the area around Brower Park, once a nest of bundle and bag sellers, had been completely cleared.

But pushers were expendable. And if they were driven off the streets, it hardly mattered; their customers would find them soon enough. With the flow of heroin drying up, Matthews had more pressing problems on his mind. As for Group 12, they were not much concerned, either. Their main worry, after the Aquarius letter, was that the BNDD regional office would claim Matthews for its own before they could collar him themselves.

With just enough resources to keep the case alive, but not enough to crack it, Miller hung on, working his men into the ground, chasing down every lead that might bring them face to face with a coercible witness. Though he must have been tempted many times to arrest Matthews in possession of narcotics and put him away on a substantive charge, he was too good a policeman to settle for that and lose the chance of rolling up the whole organization. If he simply lopped off its head, everybody would just move up one place and carry on as usual, alerted to the danger and all the more difficult to catch for that reason. What Miller now needed before he could get much further was an enterprising government prosecutor to work with, a federal grand jury, political backing, and unlimited funds. In short, although there was no way he could have known it, he needed William Callahan.

One of that rare handful of American attorneys who had read law, not in law school, but as clerks in law offices, Callahan had passed his New York bar examinations in 1964, at the first attempt, and gone to work in the trial department of the prosperous New York partnership of Nixon, Mudge, Rose, Guthrie, Alexander & Mitchell, where he stayed until the senior partner left to run for President in 1968. Callahan then went into private practice, specializing in criminal-defense trials, until recruited into government service late in 1971 by Andrew Maloney, regional director of the new Office of Drug Abuse Law Enforcement. Maloney needed a good trial lawyer on his staff to take charge of an ODALE grand jury now sitting in Brooklyn and inquiring into the case of William "Mickey" Beckwith, among others.

By birth, experience, and inclination, Callahan was ideally suited to the role of investigative attorney. His father had been head of the Manhattan Homicide Squad, and at one point Callahan had thought seriously about joining the New York Police Department himself (his brother, in fact, did so). The idea of a career in criminal law had eventually appealed to him more, however, and now, after defending cases for seven years, he was eager to try his hand at prosecuting them, bringing to the job a flexibility of mind, a dislike of red tape, and an impatience for results more commonly associated with private practice than with government service.

Like the Joint Task Force, ODALE was also looking to make a name for itself—indeed, it was under extreme pressure from the White House to do so—and among the cases it had either taken over or originated in New York, that of Mickey Beckwith had seemed the most promising. Starting with a tip-off, it had been nursed along almost singlehandedly by Detective Michael Bramble for two years, waiting, like Miller's investigation of Frank Matthews, for somebody to come along with grand jury backup and adequate funds.

When Callahan arrived on the scene with almost the entire resources of the U.S. government behind him, this requirement was more than satisfied, but it was precisely at this point that the Beckwith and Matthews investigations converged, and ODALE was forced to recognize that it had backed the wrong horse. It was now obvious that Beckwith worked for Matthews, who was already the subject of a BNDD Task Force inquiry. Stalemate. Callahan and ODALE's Group 4 could go no further without the cooperation of Miller and Task Force Group 12, while Miller's Group 12 was bogged down without the backup and funds of Callahan's Group 4. The stage was set for a classic merger, particularly after Beckwith himself appeared before the ODALE grand jury in May and took the Fifth Amendment on every question put to him.

But neither side was at all anxious to embrace the other, though both were arms of the Justice Department. If Beckwith had proved a cooperative witness, ODALE might well have snatched Matthews from under the BNDD's nose, and Miller was well aware of it. But that was only one of the reasons for mutual suspicion that lingered on even after that possibility had receded. There had always been a good deal of rivalry among the various agencies responsible for enforcing the drug laws, some of it constructive, but most of it not. Many important investigations had been fragmented by their in-fighting, with one group jealously withholding witnesses or information badly needed by another. With the launching of ODALE, however, it had looked for a while as if those already in the field might almost unite in common mistrust of what was widely regarded as a naked Nixon grab for a law-and-order issue on which to campaign for reelection. To veterans like Miller, hard-pressed to keep an important investigation going, and with his men partly financing it out of their own pockets, the setting up of yet another agency—especially a headline-conscious crew of Hollywood-style gangbusters—must have seemed like a wanton diversion of resources from where they would really count.

Aware of this resentment, ODALE's agents, and its New York counsel, William Callahan, set out to show the world how wrong their critics were. There was also a temptation, not always resisted, for ODALE to justify itself by belittling the performance of the older agencies, by suggesting that ODALE had been founded to make good their deficiencies.

In this atmosphere of mutual distrust, neither side was prepared to greet the other with more than a chilly politeness—not, at any rate, until Miller and Callahan got to know each other better; until Miller realized that by working with Callahan he could broaden the case as much as he liked, without fear of losing it, and until Callahan realized that by working with Miller he could lift a far more illustrious scalp than Beckwith's.

Until then, they shadowboxed cautiously.

Still trying to identify and list Frank Matthews's business connections, Miller sent Officers Roger Garay and John Dworsak on a photographic surveillance mission. The results are still a treasured memory among that generation of New York policemen.

Matthews was driving a brown Mercedes that day, and the two officers followed him uptown to Harlem in a florist's station wagon with a roof rack carrying a coffin-sized cardboard box of the sort used for wholesale flower deliveries. Garay was at the wheel, and Dworsak was in the box.

The idea was that, whenever Matthews stopped for a street corner chat with somebody, Garay would slow down to allow Dworsak to take pictures of them through a hole in the box as he drove by.

Success depended on careful positioning. Matthews had to be allowed to get far enough ahead for him to stop and begin his conversation before they passed, but not *so* far ahead that they risked losing him.

As Dworsak had the better vantage point, and it was up to him anyway to choose the moment to take his pictures, Garay had agreed to follow his instructions, speeding up or falling back, moving out from the curb or closer in as directed. The only difficulty was that the traffic noise sometimes made it hard for him to hear what Dworsak said.

They crossed 125th Street with only a taxicab between them

and the Mercedes. Then Dworsak called out something, but a horn blew simultaneously nearby and Garay missed it. He asked Dworsak to repeat what he had said, but there was no answer. He asked again, taking his eyes off the road for an instant as he leaned out the window to catch his partner's reply. In the same split second, the cab in front of them stopped abruptly, and so did Garay. He ran into the back of it.

Dworsak shot out of the box like a torpedo out of its tube. He thumped down on the hood, slithered across it diagonally, arms extended, and disappeared over the left fender.

Mesmerized with shock, Garay paused for a moment, collecting his wits, then threw open the door to go to his partner's aid. He reached him at the same time as the taxi driver, and the two were then joined by Frank Matthews, who had heard the collision and come back to investigate.

All three looked down at Dworsak, lying in the street cursing and trying to untangle himself from the straps of his camera, light meter, and photographic bag, which were threatening to choke him.

Matthews stooped to help him up. "You all right, buddy?"

Garay suddenly realized that neither Matthews nor the taxi driver, now inspecting the back of his cab for damage, had seen Dworsak shoot out of his box. They had both assumed he was a pedestrian whom Garay had knocked down.

"Goddamn cowboy drivers," said Matthews, brushing at the dirt on Dworsak's jacket and glaring at Garay. "Man, they ought to lift your license."

He straightened up to look over the heads of the gathering crowd.

"Shit," he said. "Never a goddamn cop around when you need one."

11

Four days after we got back from Haiti, my godfather said, "We need some money. Go up and ask Frank for $100,000."

"You think he'll give it to me?" I said.

"Why not? He knows you. Tell him to come on down here if he wants. And don't say nothing about the heroin deal."

So I hopped a plane to New York that night, checked into the Skyline Motel, and called Frank the next morning. He told me to meet him at his apartment on Henry Hudson Parkway.

Nat Elder let me in, and we joined Frank in the living room. They looked like two guys with a problem.

"Hey, Georgie, how's it going?" Frank said. "And if it's like bad news, man, don't tell me."

"No. Things are going pretty good," I said. "We got a load of shit coming in from Haiti, and I need $100,000."

"You got it," he said, not batting an eye. "How much stuff you got coming?"

"I don't know. Ten or twelve keys?"

"Okay. But I need more. A whole lot more. Like I mean ten times more. I need every goddamn spoonful you can get me. You tell Mikey."

"Sure," I said. "That's why we need the money. You want I should take it, or you want to take a run down there with me?"

He looked at Nat. "Sure. Why not? I'll get us a couple of reservations for tomorrow."

So he did that, but then I had to cancel until the day after because he got tied up, and it was June 4 before we finally made it on Eastern's night coach from La Guardia.

We met at the airport about twenty minutes before flight time. Two guys brought him out in a car, and one of them handed him a big, black leather shoulder bag, which he threw my way as soon as he saw me standing there. It was heavy. That son of a bitch must have weighed 30 pounds.

I already had my ticket, so I waited while he got his at the counter, and then we went to stand in line for the security check. Nothing to worry about there because paper don't show up on those X-ray machines, but the strap on that lousy bag was cutting into my shoulder.

"Oh shit, man," I said, handing it back to him. "You carry your own goddamn wallet. That's too heavy for me."

He laughed, and balanced it on one hand like it was empty. Frank was a strong guy. He passed through with no trouble, but as I went to follow him, one of the marshals stopped me.

"Would you mind stepping over here a minute?" he said.

It didn't sound like I had much choice, and with his partner standing behind me, I got a really thorough body search.

Frank didn't even look back. I watched that black bag out of sight, thinking that maybe my godfather hadn't wasted his money on that voodoo routine after all. Cosmo Lacroix had just saved us a hundred grand.

"Can I have a reason for all this?" I said, as the marshal got down to my ankles.

He stood up, holding out his hand for my flight bag. "Just a routine check," he said.

"Yeah, but why pick on me?"

The other one shrugged. "You look like an Arab."

"Yeah? Well, what can I tell you?"

Frank had taken a window seat. I sat down beside him. The black leather bag was under his legs.

"I got stopped."

"Show me your ticket," he said, and I gave it to him. "See that? It's one-way. When you travel, always get round-trip. Don't matter you don't use it—one-way tickets make them jumpy. The guy on the desk tipped the marshals to check you out."

"Makes air travel kind of expensive, don't it?"

"Expensive? Oh, man." He laughed. "That one-way of yours damn near cost you a hundred thousand."

We talked about luck after that, and then about Haiti. When I told him about the voodoo, he got so excited I had to promise he could have a ceremony done on him as well as soon as he could meet us down there. I could just see him in a white suit and beads on 125th Street. Which was exactly what my godfather was wearing, under a Maurice Chevalier hat, when he met us at Miami Airport. Frank put a hand to his head and staggered back.

"There he is," he said. "There's the Preacher. Howya doing, Mikey?"

"Hey, Frank. Glad you could make it. I figured you'd be too busy."

"Yeah, well, you know how it is when you've got a hundred thousand things on your mind." He patted the case he had hung on my shoulder as we got off the plane. "But I just came for the ride. I'm not staying."

"Not staying? You mean, you don't even got time for a snort?"

"Man, I thought you'd never ask," he said.

My godfather had brought his old lady's car, a gold Nova, and he drove us over to my place. Frank sat in the back with the money, but I carried it into the apartment, and I could see Anna was jumping with curiosity. Out came the coke, and right away Miguel and Frank were into their snorting and bullshitting routine, so I took her with me to buy hamburgers from the Steak and Egg place behind the house.

"What's in the bag?" she said. "What you got there?"

"Lots of money, sweetheart. Lots of money."

She was dying to see it, and she got her chance after we finished eating.

"You want to count the money, Georgie?" Frank said. "Make sure it's all there?"

"Hell, if you say it is, Frank, that's good enough for me."

"I didn't check it that close, man. Better you count it while I'm here."

So I opened the bag, and inside were ten big packages wrapped in Christmas paper. That was Frank's trademark. He always liked to wrap his money in Christmas paper. And in each package there were twenty bundles of $500, most of it in twenties, but with some fifties and hundreds, and even a few fives and tens. Anna's hands were shaking as we counted the bundles. There were two hundred of them. She wanted to take a picture of the whole pile, but we wouldn't let her. Instead, we stashed them in a suitcase, and hid it under the bed.

Then Frank asked me to call Delta to see if they had a flight to Atlanta that night, which they did, at 3:50 a.m. It was only around midnight at this point, but he said he had some things to do at the airport while he waited, so I offered to drive him over. As Miguel was leaving, too—he had a date some place—that left Anna to look after the money. I gave her my old .38 with the silencer, locked the door from the bedroom onto the balcony, and drew the curtains.

"You going to be okay?"

"I'm just fine," she said. She was sitting cross-legged on the bed with the gun in her lap. "Anybody wants to take that money, I guarantee they'll have to kill me."

"Oh, Jesus," said Frank. "When Georgie gets back, don't you shoot *him*, you hear? Him and me's got work to do."

On the way out to the airport, he didn't stop talking. The coke had put him in a very good mood.

"Mikey says you're working on something real big," he said.

"Yeah, well. You know how it is. Takes a little time."

"You got it, baby. I ain't worried. You just keep that stuff coming. All you can get."

"Sure, Frank. When we got this new route down pat, I'll bury your ass in the stuff."

"Man, that's great. That I want to see. Last year I must have dealt damn near a thousand kilos, so I got a good-sized ass to bury."

I almost ran off the road. He had to be kidding. But he didn't look like he was kidding.

"Let me tell you something," he said. "I got $80 million out working for me, so you stick close, Georgie. Anything you need to keep that stuff moving, well, you just ask, you hear me?"

"I hear you, Frank. I hear you."

After dropping him off at the airport, I drove back home to play with the money. When Anna finally let me in, we tipped the bundles out on the bed and started counting them again. We were about halfway through when my godfather came back for another look, too. He helped himself to a couple of thousand, and we all stared at the heap for a minute.

"Okay," he said. "This is what I want you to do. Medina and Diaz are over in Miami Beach, at the Carillon. In the morning, I want you to take them a down payment on the next shipment."

"How much?"

"Ten thousand. They got to travel with the money, so pick out some of the bigger bills; otherwise, it's a hassle."

"Okay."

"And take $15,000 for yourself."

"Okay." I figured that was fair. "How about the rest of it?"

"Stash it," he said. "Some place handy. We got another deal going down."

I was taking over the operation, but that didn't mean he was going to sit down and explain anything. It wasn't his style. I was still going to have to make do with his telling me things I needed to know as we went along. Nothing I could do about it. Except that, after he'd gone, I took $18,000 instead of $15,000.

Then me and Anna picked out $10,000 in big bills for the Venezuelans, and by now Orlando was with us. There were so many of those little bundles. I tossed Anna a couple, and although Orlando hadn't really done nothing yet, he'd spent a lot of time running around with me, so why not? Here's a bundle for you, too. When we were down to $70,000, I figured it was time to stop horsing around. As soon as the bank opened, I packed as much of the money as I could into the safe-deposit box and left the rest in the suitcase under the bed.

Then I drove over to Miami Beach to deliver the $10,000.

Medina checked out with it right away, heading for the airport, but Diaz was going to spend a few days in Miami with his wife. Miguel had invited them to stay in the little one-room guest apartment he had fixed up in back of his old lady's house. I ran into my godfather there around noon.

"I been looking for you," he said. "You know where Ernesto Marinero lives?"

"Sure. In that blue and white building on 3rd Street."

"Okay. Meet me there at two. And bring the money."

"All of it?" I didn't have nothing against Ernesto, but when you go visiting strangers with $70,000, you got to think twice.

"All of it. He's got seven keys, maybe more."

"Okay. You want I should bring a piece?"

My godfather hesitated. "Hell, I know this guy for years. If you got one with you, I don't know about it."

Already I didn't like the smell of this deal. I got there a little early, with the money in the trunk, and parked in front of the building to wait for Miguel. But Marinero showed up first, in a white Chevy, and I decided to go in with him, because that way there wouldn't be no reception committee. Couple of minutes later, my godfather arrived, and now the three of us waited, not saying much.

Came another knock at the door. I didn't know who the hell was out there, or if he was going to come in with the coke or an M-16, so I stood up against the wall where I could see him but he couldn't see me unless he turned around. Then Marinero let him in, and it was just a neighborhood guy I knew who was trying to get started in the bookmaking business. He came in, put a bag down on the table, and went out again without a word.

Now Marinero brought out a scale, and my godfather weighed the stuff. Near enough seven keys. Then he broke out a sample and tested it in the palm of his hand and on his tongue. I could tell just by looking at it, this wasn't the quality we were used to. The stuff had already been cut.

"How much?" said Miguel.

"Nine thousand a shot."

He thought about it. To me, the price was a bit steep, but at least the load was right there, no ifs or maybes.

"Okay," my godfather said. "Go get the money, Georgie."

So I counted out $63,000 onto the table and that was that. Miguel went off with the coke, and I took what was left of the money over to his old lady's house and stashed it in her bedroom closet.

That night, I met my godfather at a two-story white house on SW 11th Street, where José Martinez was cutting the stuff. When I walked in, he was working on a huge pile of cocaine on the table. Marinero's seven keys. I tried a bit in the palm of my hand, and still wasn't too crazy about it.

"You thinking of hitting this again?" I asked Miguel.

"It'll take a light one. We'll make three out of two."

I didn't say nothing, but if it had been me, I would have moved the load just the way it was. You could see the difference when you compared it with our own six keys, which had just been brought off the *William Express*.

"We'll be finished around eleven tomorrow, Georgie," said Martinez. "You can pick it up then."

Miguel stepped in before I could answer. "I want you to take the stuff up to Frank," he said.

"What, all of it? How about Zack?"

"No, just the Marinero shit. Eleven keys."

"Well, if Zack gets the rest, you want me to take that up, too?"

"You just do like I tell you," he said, which meant that Zack was going to get screwed.

I didn't like that. I could run into him up there. And he knew Frank. But I wasn't about to give Martinez the satisfaction of hearing me and Miguel bandy words. I went home and made reservations on the noon train to New York for Anna and me. To hell with the bus.

By this time, Anna knew how deep I was into this business. That $100,000 from Frank had really turned her on. Now she wanted to be in on the action, too—not just knowing about it, but doing something, making money. And this was her chance. She used to joke with us about what she would do when she got big in drugs. She was going to buy herself an island. She was going to have a big house there, and a pool with sharks in it. Anybody she didn't like, she was going to throw them in. When I laughed at her, she used to say, "Well, that's the way I feel. If I have the power, I want the best." She was really living it up in her dreams.

Also, there was another reason I wanted to take her. She was nervous about staying alone in the apartment. Since the voodoo ceremony in Haiti, some funny things had been happening around the house. We had a bamboo blind in the bedroom, and every so often it would give off a long rattle, like somebody was giving it a hard shake. There was no draft or nothing, and it had never done that before. And Feo would suddenly jump off the bed for no reason and start barking at nothing. It was kind of spooky.

Orlando said it was Cosmo Lacroix. I still didn't go for that stuff, but I had to play the role. The first time I dressed all in white, I couldn't hardly believe it. Look at this shit I got to be going through. But I had to do it. The belief was too strong. I was not supposed to talk about what had happened in Haiti, but I told Orlando, and he said, "Goddamn. That's the real shit, man. You really got worked over. You got to keep those people happy. You take care of Cosmo Lacroix."

So I had to set up a little voodoo shrine in the house. Nothing fancy, because Anna wasn't supposed to know about it. On a red handkerchief, I stood a carved wooden figure I'd brought back from Haiti. It was a statue, about a foot high, of a black slave in chains, down on one knee and begging for his life. Then next to that I had a card with Cosmo Lacroix printed on it, the red bag the old woman had given me, and a brandy snifter full of water with a crucifix in it. But the real secret was in half a coconut shell. You had to peel it, cut the meat out, clean it, and dry it yourself, and then talk to it and smoke to it.

Orlando came over to check mine out. You're supposed to

light up a cigar and blow the smoke real slow into the shell. If it just sits there, doing nothing, or comes right out again, that means the spirit is rejecting it. He's pissed off with you. But if it swirls around, that's good. That shows the spirit looks on you with favor. So I blew smoke into my shell, and right away it started to swirl around like crazy.

"Hey, the man is with you," said Orlando, all bent out of shape with excitement. "Look, he's accepting. He's really sucking on that smoke. That's Cosmo. He's really happy with you."

Well, Anna wasn't too happy with *him*. She didn't feel like staying behind with Cosmo Lacroix, and I figured 11 kilos was a lot to carry anyway. So I booked us two rooms on the train in different names, and around 10:30 next morning I went over to Martinez's new house on SW 18th Street to pick up the stuff. They weren't ready for me. Medina was there, back already from Caracas, and so was Pedro Diaz, but there was still a big pile of cocaine on the table, unbagged.

"Hey!" I said. "I got an hour. We got to move our ass here."

So Martinez and Medina weighed the stuff up in half-kilo bags, while me and Pedro sealed them, and twenty minutes later we had twenty-two bags in a long cardboard box. Raquel Dumois was home, but there was no voodoo shit this time. She must have heard about Haiti. I just loaded the box in the trunk and drove back to Anna, who was all packed and ready.

Seeing she was so anxious to get in on the action, I put fourteen of the bags in her suitcase and eight in mine. "This is a business trip, right?" I said. But I should have known better. That night on the train, I got to feeling horny and tapped on her door. "Hey, it's me," I said. "Let me in."

"Nothing doing," she said. "This is a business trip, right?"

She wouldn't even let me help when we got in at Penn Station, although she could hardly lift the goddamn suitcase. "No," she said. "Leave me alone. I don't want nobody to do nothing for me. I'm earning my money."

So I left her to watch both cases while I called Frank at the Fort Lee number he'd given me last time. To avoid too much talk on the phone, we'd agreed that a call from me to say that I was in New York would mean that we should meet outside Leighton's men's store on Broadway an hour later. After I gave him his cue, I went back to Anna, who finally agreed to share a cab with me up to the Skyline.

As soon as we had registered, I took a stroll over toward Broadway. Dead on the hour, as I was looking in Leighton's window, I saw the reflection of the black T-bird pulling in at the curb behind me. I crossed the sidewalk and Frank got out to meet me.

"Hey, Mr. G. How are you doing? Hop in while I check out those threads."

In the front passenger seat was a thin, well-dressed black guy wearing a derby. I climbed in the back, and he gave me a nod. Then we sat and waited a few minutes while Frank looked at the clothes and chatted with some guy he ran into, a real obvious pusher. That shook me up a little. It wasn't too smart, keeping that kind of company. I had Frank pegged for a big wholesaler. Never occurred to me before that he might be selling all the way down to the street.

"Say hello to Slim, Georgie," he said, as he got back in the car. "Slim's my main man. When I ain't around, you talk to him, okay? Or Nat."

I found out later that Slim was Gattis Hinton, but for right now I was listening to this little warning bell ring. I knew they didn't come no bigger than Frank Matthews, but the bigger you are in drugs, the more careful you got to be to stay clean. You got to keep away from the stuff. You got to stay off the streets, and you got to line other people up to take the fall if there's trouble. But Frank was right in there doing it. Him and my godfather were two of a kind. Instead of keeping the noise down, they both went around like they was running for mayor.

"So what's the story, Georgie?" he said. "How much have you got for me?"

"Eleven."

He frowned a little bit. "Yeah?" The Preacher told me it was going to be twenty-five. So how come only eleven?"

That's when I knew that Miguel must have promised him our six keys as well, cut one-on-one to make twelve. I'd had a bad feeling about this deal from the start, and it wasn't getting any better as we went along.

"Gee, I don't know, Frank. He just told me to bring up the load. All I know is, it ain't from our usual connection, so could be there's more on the way."

"Yeah." He still looked thoughtful, but I could see he wasn't blaming me. "I guess it's okay. Where's the stuff at?"

"I got it back at the hotel. The Skyline."

"Fine. Then let's do it right now. Are you ready for us?"

"Sure," I said. "Give me ten minutes."

He drove me back to the hotel, and as I went to get out, he laid his hand on my arm.

"I know that Preacher man," he said. "So I'm counting on *you*, Mr. G. You going to make us all rich?"

That was a pretty good line, coming from a guy with $80 million. "Sure as hell going to try."

"That's my man." He patted my arm. "Next time, you make it 50 keys, okay?"

"Well, it's cooking, Frank, it's cooking. But we got to go slow till we're sure of the route."

I went upstairs, transferred the stuff to a couple of shopping bags from the No Name boutique, covered the top of each one with towels, and ten minutes later Slim came up to take delivery. Thanks a lot. See you soon. Mission accomplished. Anna and me went to bed. It wasn't a business trip no more.

Around two in the morning, the phone rang. It was Frank.

"Georgie, come on down here. I want to talk to you, man."

The tone of his voice was not the same. He sounded mad. Oh, fuck. Something was wrong, and I guessed what it was right away. This was the Marinero shit, and they'd hit it too hard.

I got dressed in a hurry. He was outside on the sidewalk with Slim, and steaming.

"What's the matter, Frankie?"

"Don't give me that, Georgie. What are you doing to me? Look at this goddamn shit here."

He handed me a piece of foil with a bit of coke inside. I took some, and it was pretty bad.

"See that? All powdery and shit? Goddamn it, Georgie. Narcotics is a hard game, and I ain't got time for this."

Now I had to be careful. Somebody could wind up dead, trying to unload garbage on a guy like Frank Matthews, and it wasn't going to be me.

"You telling me this is what I brought you?" I said, like I couldn't believe my eyes. "*This* shit?"

"You know it, Georgie. So don't fuck around. This comes from your people."

"Jesus." I tried it again, and shook my head. "Well, I got to find out about this. All I done was bring it up. But somebody's been fucking around with this shit, no doubt about that." Now I started to get mad as well. "And when I find out who, I'll kill the son of a bitch. I'm sorry, Frankie, but you got my word it won't happen again."

"You bet your ass it won't, Georgie. This ain't what I'm used to."

"I know that. From now on, anything you get from me I'll guarantee is okay. You got my personal word."

"Shit." Frank was a fair-minded man. I watched him cool off. "It ain't your word I need, Georgie. I got to have stuff I can move. You got to take care of me. I pay you up front, and you give me this bullshit. You know that ain't right."

"Listen," I said. "I don't blame you for bitching. I'm just telling you it won't happen again. If you want, I'll pay back the money and move the load some place else."

I knew I had him there. The stuff was bad, but he could still make money on it.

"No," he said. "It's okay. But I want to see the Preacher. I want to talk to him. So you just get him up here."

"Okay, Frank. I'll take care of it."

I went back upstairs, looking for blood. I was mad at myself for not checking on the stuff when they bagged it up, but I was a hell of a lot madder at Martinez. That scumbag. It was Miguel's fault, too, for letting it happen. Frank's a noble guy. I liked him. And these bastards were fucking around with my reputation.

First I got Ana Baños out of bed. "No, Mikey's not here." Then I got Victoria Montalvo out of bed, and he's not there either.

"Well then, find him," I said. "And tell him from me to get his ass up here quick. Because the man ain't too happy with what's going on."

We hung around the hotel all day, waiting for some word, but nothing. Nothing the next morning, either. Then he suddenly shows up in the middle of the afternoon, acting like it's *my* fault that things have gone wrong.

"What the hell's the matter now?" he says.

With all this time to think about what could have happened if Frank had turned nasty, I wasn't about to take that attitude from nobody. There was going to be some changes.

"You know goddamn well what's the matter," I said. "You fucked this thing up. You send me here with a bunch of shit and then ask *me* what's the matter? The man is bitching. And he's right. That Marinero stuff is garbage. He's got a legitimate beef."

My godfather wasn't used to that tone, but he could see I had reason.

"Then what the fuck did José do to it?" he said. "I told him, just half a key cut to every key."

"Yeah? Well, it wasn't so hot to start with, that shit. And he stepped on it hard. The punk. Frank's really disgusted. And I'm not bound to lose a customer like him over this scumbag. From now on, I do everything. Martinez is out."

That was pushing. My godfather just stood there.

"If it was up to me," I said, "I'd give him to Frank. He'd make chopped liver out of that son of a bitch. I ain't giving Martinez a second chance to play with my life."

Miguel thought this over, still looking at me. "Okay. You got it. Martinez is out."

"Okay. Now what about Frank?"

"Don't worry about it. Just get him over here. I'll take care of Frank."

I didn't think he would find it that easy, but I called, and Frank came over at about seven that night. When he phoned up from downstairs, I gave him the number of my godfather's room, next door to mine, and went out in the hall to meet him.

"Mikey took his time getting here," he said, as he stepped out of the elevator.

"Had a little trouble tracking him down," I said. "He hopped a plane as soon as he heard."

"Sure."

Frank was still pissed off, but he wasn't the kind of guy to go crazy just because somebody screwed up somewhere. I took him along to the room, and as soon as he put his foot inside the door, Miguel went into his bullshit routine.

"Hey, Frankie. How's it going? You're looking good, man."

"Yeah, yeah, Mikey," he said, "but you're fucking me around. You gave me a bunch of shit there, man. You're not taking care of me."

"No, Frank. Don't say that." My godfather tried to look reproachful, which wasn't easy for a guy whose happy face would frighten a barracuda. "It was a mistake. The guy either stepped on the stuff too hard or he ripped us off. I got to find out."

"Don't tell me your problems, Mikey. I got my own headaches. All I know is, you sold me 11 keys of shit, and I don't go for that."

"Listen, *I'm* the one that's hurting. You think I'm dumb enough to try a thing like that on my best customer? You think I want to put myself out of business? Come on, Frank. I got a reputation to consider. This asshole has screwed us both."

"Then, Mikey, you ain't minding the store. It's your people did this to me. What's the matter? You don't like me any more?"

"Man, I can't watch every son of a bitch every second. The scumbag who did this is dead, okay? What can I tell you?"

"You tell me what I'm going to do with 11 keys of shit, Mikey."

"Aw, forget the 11 keys, for Chrissake." My godfather's patience was getting ragged. "I got bigger things on my mind."

Frank went still. I knew he wouldn't try nothing. I never saw him carry a piece anyway. But I had to wonder if we would make it out of New York. Oh, Jesus.

"Bigger things, Mikey?" he said.

"Yeah." And my godfather smiled. "Like this 100 keys of smack I got lined up."

Frank hit his forehead. He was punishing himself for even thinking bad things about us. I never saw a man turn around so quick. One second, Miguel's a bug he's got to squash. Next second, he's Santa Claus.

"Oh, *man*," Frank said. "You're putting me on. Did you just tell me like 100 *keys?* Let's hear about it, baby."

"Sure, Frank." Now my godfather knew he had him, he wasn't going to let him off that easy. He turned to me first. "How much does Frankie owe us, Georgie?"

"About $16,000," I said.

Frank couldn't believe it. He looked from Miguel to me and back again. "You're kidding," he said, not mad, but like he admired our nerve. Next to 100 keys, just about everything had to be a joke. "*I* owe *you* sixteen thousand? After the last load of shit you just gave me? God*damn*."

"Didn't I say I'd take it back?" I said. "Frank, you got 16 big ones on the tab."

"God*damn*." He shook his head. "All right, all right. So let's hear it."

"Okay," my godfather said. "Now I don't want no bullshit. I got this 100 kilos coming in, and I'm going to make you my partner. All right?"

"All right, all right—tell me."

That Miguel. Partner, nothing—Frank was about to get screwed. He was going to have to front the money and would end up buying the shit anyway—at $20,000 a kilo. *If* it existed. My godfather hadn't mentioned this 100 keys since Haiti, and I hadn't asked him because I hoped it was just a pipe dream. I wasn't comfortable with heroin. If this deal went down, it meant 220 pounds of poison out on the streets. I'm not saying that cocaine is good for you, not when a guy like Frank uses it to mix with smack and make speedballs, but it don't wreck people the same way. And you got to be rich to afford it. Anyway, I wasn't too sure about my godfather's Corsican connection. I knew Miguel. The way he was selling it to Frank, it sounded to me like he was trying to sell himself on it as well, so for his sake I hoped it was solid. Disappointing Frank with 11 keys of shitty coke was one thing. Disappointing him with 100 keys of imaginary horse was something else.

I figured I ought to take out a little insurance.

"Look, I hate to butt into this love match," I said, "but let's get something straight here. You're partners on this heroin deal—fine. That's strictly Mikey's connection. I don't know nothing about it. But we also got a cocaine business running here, and that's *mine*. That's separate, okay? We carry on like before. I bring Frank coke and he buys it, right?"

"Right," said my godfather. "I just gave Georgie the whole operation. I got to work on this other deal now."

"So you're not *my* partner, Frank," I said. "You're my buyer, right?"

"Right." He would have agreed to anything. The 100 keys had just unraveled his imagination. He acted like Mikey had just saved his life, and maybe he had. For a whole year now, it had been nothing but bust, bust, bust. People were getting popped everywhere. With his connections, Frank had to be picking up a few keys here and a few keys there, but the whole East Coast was in a panic. Cut down to around 4 or 5 percent, 100 keys of European pure could turn the whole goddamn situation around. *If* my godfather could get them. The way they were both talking now, Frank was going to take delivery tomorrow, and to me that spelled nothing but trouble.

"Listen," he said, "I want you guys to see my new house."

We knew Frank was building a place out on Staten Island; he'd told us that last time. He couldn't leave the city, but he wanted to give his kids a break. So he had bought a piece of property out in the Todt Hill section, and they were just moving into a brand-new Southern-style mansion. Cost over half a million, he said, so naturally we were curious to see what you got for that kind of money. I went back to my room, told Ricky Acosta, who was there watching baseball on the color TV, to take off, warned Anna to keep the door locked while I was gone, and joined Frank and my godfather downstairs in Frank's gold Mercedes convertible.

He was on a real charge that night. As we drove downtown, the car radio was tuned to some black station, and Elijah Muhammad came on.

"That's my *man*," Frank said. "You eat your ham sandwiches, you little white mother-fuckers. It's peanut butter and jelly for me."

"Get *him*," said my godfather. "You ever hear such bullshit? The guy swallows a lima bean and figures he's a Muslim."

"Not your style, Frankie," I said. "You got to go down to Haiti with us. See your people in action."

"Yeah, Mikey, we got to do that. Georgie told me what you did down there—about the voodoo, and all. I got to catch that routine for myself."

"Any time, Frank," said my godfather. "Georgie's getting in pretty good with those people. He's going to open a key club in Port-au-Prince with some guy who's tight with the president. Right, Georgie? You going to give Frank here a key for the Happy 'Gator?"

"Am I, hell," I said. "No niggers allowed."

Frank laughed. "Man, you're out of business already. I hear that's all they got down there."

"No, they got a lot of light-skinned too. And *they* got the money. You ought to look at it, Frank. Buy some of that beach-front property near the city. You'd be a king down there."

"Well, listen—check it out for me, Georgie. I mean that. Makes a lot of sense to build some solid contacts overseas. Then you always got a place to go."

Meantime, he had this place out at 7 Buttonwood Road—a beautiful white two-story house with columns outside supporting the roof. Inside there was a big lobby; marble, with a semicircular staircase up to the second floor, and a crystal chandelier. On one side, there was a fantastic room with an Oriental carpet, a piano, and bookcases against the wall, and on the other side, a huge living area, all the way through to the back. He had a plush dining room, too, with steps down to a big yellow kitchen full of the latest equipment and with like a built-in centerpiece for preparing the food and everything. Out back was a patio, and a place for the swimming pool already staked out. Beyond that was a good bit of ground. He was going to have it landscaped into a golf course—just a couple of holes for chipping and putting.

Then we went upstairs to look at the bedrooms. Frank's was as big as a baseball field, with a queen-sized bed and a walk-in closet like a two-car garage. But what really caught my eye was his bathroom. The tub was a round, sunken pool, in marble, with gold faucets. And the whole room was mirrored, the walls, the doors, the ceiling. Wherever you looked, you could see yourself, a dozen different ways.

"Jesus," I said. "An ugly nigger like you with all these goddamn mirrors?"

"Now how can you say I'm ugly?" he said, admiring himself this way and that. Then he caught my eye, and pretended to get mad. "And you calling me nigger? Hmmm." He flexed his muscles, and they were big muscles. Frank had style.

He was a confident man. You didn't have to treat him like he was special. He knew he was. And you could trust that. He was too proud to screw anybody. If he gave you his word, you could make book on it. A lot of these guys have to keep reminding you all the time who they are, but not Frank. Just never occurred to him you might forget, so he never pushed people around for no reason.

Never needed hangers-on, like most of them do. Never had bodyguards around him all the time. Never went armed—not that

I saw. And yet nobody ever messed with him. It's known Frank has dumped five or six people. If you take a shot at him and miss, that's your ass. If you cross him, you got to kill him on the spot. If you steal from him or threaten him in any way, then you better find a deep hole to hide in. Because he *will* put $50,000 on your head. And if that ain't enough, then $100,000. If there's black people around, there ain't nowhere he can't find you.

And that was why I had this worry in the back of my mind. After all the talk, if my godfather goofed—if it all came down in the end to a load of Miguel bullshit—we could both wind up in a case of dog food. But for now we were family. Nothing was too good for us. After seeing the house, my godfather was in the mood to snort a little cocaine.

"Hey, Frank," he said, as we got out of the car at the Skyline. "I need an ounce. And none of that shit I just sent you. I mean the real stuff."

Miguel just loved to live dangerously. A couple of hours before, Frank wouldn't have laughed.

"You got it, baby," he said. "Come on, Georgie. We'll take a run out to Brooklyn. We got to take care of the Preacher."

So off we went again. Frank was quiet for a time. Then he said: "Okay, Georgie—we're tight, right?"

"Sure," I said. "We're tight."

"Well, we got to work this thing out now. For the 100 keys."

"Sure, Frank. But, like I say, right now I don't know more than you do. He ain't talked to me about it."

"Okay. But you'll be bringing it up through Haiti? I mean, like that's the route you got, right?"

"Yeah, I guess so."

He looked at me a couple of times, in between carving up the traffic. "You got something on your mind, Georgie?"

"Me? No. I'm just the cautious type, that's all. I got to find out what's going on."

"All right. But I'm ready. Anything you need, you got. You just tell me."

"Sure, Frank. That's good to know."

He took me to an apartment he had on Clarkson Avenue. On the dining-room table was a half-kilo bag of coke already busted open. He gave me a big piece of tinfoil.

"That's dynamite stuff, Georgie. Take what you want."

So I took a good ounce, and as I turned around, I caught him looking at me kind of funny.

"Something wrong?" I said.

"No. I got a coat that's small on me. I just bought the goddamn thing at Leighton's. And if it's small on me, it might fit you. Just hold it right there."

He came back with a beautiful white jacket that must have cost $200 at least, and held it open for me. "Here, try it on."

It fitted like it was made for me.

"That's got to mean something, Georgie," he said. "I want you to keep it. Me and you are going to make a name for ourselves."

"Don't say that, Frankie. I don't want to be famous. I want to be rich."

"We'll take care of that, too." He walked me to the door. "Just bring me more of those big rocks, man. My people are waiting on me. They say I got the godfather connection."

"Sure, Frank. And thanks for the coat."

"You take care, now. You got cab fare?"

"Yeah, Frank. I got it."

Jesus. I just hoped Mikey knew what he was doing. I hopped a cab on Flatbush and darted back to have a little talk with the godfather connection. First I gave him the ounce.

"Listen," I said. "Before you blow your brains out with that stuff, I want to ask you something. This 100 keys—is that solid? And no bullshit now. You save that for Frank."

"It's solid." He took a big snort, right out of the spoon, and opened his eyes wide. It was several seconds before he could speak again. "I told you. I know this Frenchman in Caracas. He's got big connections in Marseilles."

"Yeah, I know. You said that. But Frank's talking like he's going to get the stuff next week."

"He's hurting. He needs it." My godfather blasted his other

nostril with a second spoonful, and blinked like he'd walked into a wall. He sighed, several times. "But Frank knows better than that."

"Does he? You talked like it was all set. Already he's asking me how we're going to handle the delivery."

"So tell him." He pushed the tinfoil package my way. "You want some?"

"No," I said. "Tell him what? I don't know a goddamn thing about this deal."

"You know enough." He looked at me a bit sharp. "And so does he. That's pretty good stuff. I wonder where he got it."

"Shit."

"What's the matter?"

"Well, shit—either I'm in this deal or I'm out of it. And if I'm in it, I ought to know what's going on. I don't even know what I'm supposed to do."

"I told you." My godfather frowned. "You're going to bring the stuff over from Haiti. How you get it to Frank is your business. That's all you got to worry about."

"What, 100 keys? On the *William Express?* You're kidding me."

"Not all at once. Jesus Christ. It'll come in four or five loads. And we'll use the other boat as well—the *José Express*. Evaristio's got a guy on that one, too."

That was better. "The stuff comes in at Caracas?"

"Right."

"How are you going to move it to Haiti?"

"I don't know. Why don't you let *me* worry about that. I may buy an airplane."

Oh, Jesus. "Frank wants to know. He asked me already."

"Fuck Frank." The coke was shifting his gears in front of my eyes. "We're gonna put him on top of the whole goddamn heap. Frank waits on *us*. All *he's* got to do is come up with a million dollars."

"Is *that* all?" I said. "Oh, well . . ."

"He can do that. Certainly he can do that. Easy. Seven thousand a shot to the Frenchman—makes $700,000. Plus a thousand a key moving it to Haiti. Plus another thousand getting it to Frank. $900,000, right?"

He lined up another spoon and fired it in, rubbing the side of his nose to make sure it was still there. Then his eyes unfocused, and he sat like a statue for a while.

"For that kind of money, he's got a right to take an interest," I said.

My godfather laughed unexpectedly. "Yeah, I guess he has. Maybe I'll take him down there with me. Introduce him to a few people. You know what this is going to mean to that guy? The way things are right now? He's got to make himself a clear 10 million, just on this one deal."

"Yeah, well—could be," I said. "With 100 keys of pure hit—what? Twenty times? Twenty-five?"

"Pure?" Miguel looked at me like he was in pain. "*Pure?* You crazy? He ain't getting no pure. We're going to hit that shit one-on-one like always."

Oh, my lord. Now we were talking about *two* hundred kilos.

"Hey, wait a minute," he said. "Suppose we cut the stuff in Haiti. Why not? We could do all the delay work there before we even hit Miami. Luis the Junkman can handle it. We'll find a place and get him over there with a couple of guys."

That made sense—except it doubled the number of boat trips. But Miguel had shifted into overdrive and was running ahead of me out of sight.

"Hold it," I said. "Frank still gets a hundred?"

"Right. Costs him two million, okay? That's just for openers. Henry Morgan says he'll pay up to thirty thousand a crack for good merchandise, so let's say we throw him fifty. What's that? Another million and a half? Okay. Same thing in Puerto Rico. The whole goddamn island is dry. We can get thirty thousand a key there easy. So what have we got? Five million? Minus a million up front? That's two million dollars each."

I didn't know what to say.

"*Plus*," he said, "we sell Frank the connection for another two million."

I shook my head in a daze.

"Unless you want to do it again," he said, misunderstanding.

"No, no," I said. "That'll do. I'm not greedy."

Not being as souped up as Miguel, I was slower to take this all in. At the head of the line, we would help ourselves to the first slice, but the real mind-blowing numbers came after. With a panic on, our 100-key load would make maybe three tons of junk by the time it got down to the street. Worth, what? $75 million? $100 million?"

It was just beginning to get through to me that, because of famine prices and shortages and everything, we were probably talking about a deal that would gross up into one of the biggest single crimes in history.

"So when's it going to happen?" I said, a bit shaky.

"When I get down to Venezuela and start turning the wheels."

"And when will that be?" I asked him.

He dragged his fourth spoonful into his second nostril and pinched his nose tight, staring at me bug-eyed.

"Soon," he said. "Soon."

12

The big squeeze was starting to hurt. So far, New York had been the least affected of the major cities, although the East Coast shipping strike that summer had sharply reduced the level of imports. The wholesalers still operating had tried to maintain New York's supplies at the expense of other markets, but prices were already 25 percent up since the first of the year. This meant not only that addicts had to steal more but also more addicts. Every stretched-out junkie from out of town who could thumb a ride or raise the bus fare was now homing in from the cold.

Outward signs of distress, however, were less dramatic than usual (except for a fever of street crime). This time, methadone had taken the edge off the panic; the number of sweating, gray-faced addicts found doubled-up in their own puke in West Side doorways was much smaller than in previous dry spells. But below the surface the situation was dangerously unstable. As the flow of narcotics tapered off, many dealers took their vacations early, heading South to avoid importunate clients, to seek new connections or wait for happier times. Others, like Big El Bynum and Louis Cirillo, went away more or less permanently at the government's expense. The rest—those with something to sell or the resources to corner such supplies as there were—grew richer and more powerful every day. In Boston, a kilo of pure heroin sold by the ounce could now fetch $800,000 *wholesale*. Little by little, mostly by default, the whole of the drug trade was falling into the hands of the few big operators remaining in business, and most of these bought from Frank Matthews.

With almost a year's work behind them, Miller, Rawald, Garay, and the rest of Group 12 went on watching him with a near-physical yearning to punish his insolence. They were still not much closer to bringing him down, but their persistence had at last been recognized. On June 5, 1972, a federal grand jury was empaneled in Brooklyn, in the Eastern District of New York, to inquire into Matthews's activities, which meant that the overall direction of the case now passed to Robert A. Morse, United States Attorney for the Eastern District, and in particular to Assistant U.S. Attorney Francis J. Sheerin.

In practice, nothing much changed. In theory, the power to subpoena witnesses and question them before a grand jury with none of the inhibitions laid upon a prosecutor in open court, or even upon a police officer interrogating a suspect, should have made a decisive difference, but the mere knowledge of *whom* to call, based on Group 12's observations, was not in itself sufficient to make anybody speak. People who knew Matthews were generally more frightened of him than the law. All but a very few of the witnesses called in the early days of the grand jury took refuge in their Fifth Amendment right to remain silent, and those who did not were invariably those with little or nothing to offer. The only immediate effect of Miller's having to share the responsibility for running the investigation, therefore, was that the U.S. Attorney's office now shared in the general frustration.

The best potential witness they had so far was Norman Lee Coleman, a small-time drug dealer and courier from Baltimore whose credibility before a trial jury was not likely to be enhanced by a police record ten times longer than Matthews's. But it was a start. Coleman had known Matthews on and off since 1968, when he had bought some cocaine from him in Atlantic City. Since then, most of his merchandise had come from Bighead Brother Carter, Matthews's lieutenant in Baltimore, and Coleman could place Matthews in many a compromising situation there.

But until March 1972 he had no incentive to do so. An early victim of the heroin shortage, Coleman had gone back to running narcotics for James "Turk" Scott, one of Matthews's best customers in the city. A prominent local Democrat, Scott operated under cover of a bail-bond and insurance brokership, and was outwardly so respectable that Maryland's Governor Marvin Mandel later appointed him to fill a vacancy in the state's House of Delegates. In January 1972, however, Scott was more immediately concerned with the seven kilos of heroin that Coleman had just ferried down for him from New York. As a reward for his efforts, he gave Coleman a full kilo for himself on consignment, a gesture so munificent as to have set him up for life, had Coleman not sold some of it to a federal undercover agent. Arrested for doing so in March, and with state charges for possession of heroin already hanging over him, Coleman agreed to cooperate with the government in return for lenient treatment.

(Scott's political ambitions were subsequently interrupted by his arrest in April 1973 on the strength of Coleman's testimony. Three months later, they were terminated by gunmen in an underground garage, probably on Matthews's orders, just before Scott was due to stand trial.)

With Coleman in the bag, the next step was to snare Carter, with the idea of either securing *his* testimony against Matthews or else indicting him as a co-conspirator. Having nothing to lose but thirty years in jail, Coleman agreed to go back on the street and carry on business as usual—with a difference. When he went to see Carter, he would be wired for sound with a Kelcom one-way transmitter. About the size of a cigarette pack, the device had a range of a little over a mile, so that Coleman's conversations with Bighead Brother could be simultaneously monitored and recorded at a safe distance.

Besides opening up a line of attack on Matthews's flank, Coleman also helped to get a frontal assault moving in New York. On June 27, he appeared in Bronx County before Judge William Kapelman of the New York Supreme Court to give evidence *in camera* supporting Group 12's application for a wiretap on Matthews's telephone in apartment 5J, 3333 Henry Hudson Parkway. Now that he was living out on Staten Island, Matthews had routed most of his business calls through that Bronx number, which was covered twenty-four hours a day by an answering service. Added to the results of a year's surveillance, Coleman's testimony was deemed sufficient probable cause to justify the issuance of an interception order, and from that moment on, the case shifted perceptibly into higher gear.

Though they rarely discussed business in anything but disguised or general terms, Matthews and his callers were quite astonishingly indiscreet on the telephone. While obviously aware that it might be tapped, they invariably forgot or lost patience in moments of heat, stress, or mutual incomprehension. From day one, Group 12 was showered with names, numbers, and more or less cryptic allusions to people, places, and events, so that the whole nature of the investigation suddenly changed. Instead of spending most of their time on close but random surveillance, scratching about for leads, the Dirty Dozen could now spend *all* their time actually checking out the leads they were being given, or on surveillance with a set purpose in view, to verify a connection or to observe a particular transaction.

Interesting things were happening in Philadelphia, too, where Matthews controlled the narcotics trade through his senior lieutenant, Pop Darby; his main distributor, David "Rev" Bates; and Darby's wife, Flossie, who stayed behind as Pop's eyes and ears after Matthews moved him up to New York. Although Matthews's overriding concern was securing enough cocaine and heroin to keep his organization together, he had to contend as well with an equally critical shortage of cutting materials. A 5 percent bag of heroin is also 95 percent quinine, mannite, milk sugar, Epsom salts, or some other soluble, non-toxic base, so that by the time a 100-kilo shipment of pure reaches the street at 5 percent strength, it will have been cut with over two *tons* of filler. At 3 percent, it would need about three and a half tons.

Quantities of that sort are not normally available over drugstore counters. Indeed, any abnormal purchase of materials suitable for cutting drugs is like sending a telegram to the local narcotics squad. Quinine, the preferred adulterant, was particularly hard to come by. After 1971, a license was needed to buy or sell it, and many drug dealers diversified into pest control, one of the few businesses left that could use quinine legally on a large scale. Other drug dealers relied on more traditional methods. They corrupted security guards and production workers in pharmaceutical houses by paying up to $70 an ounce for a product worth perhaps $4 an ounce on the legitimate market.

Needing it by the truckload, Frank Matthews did both, and still could not get enough. By the late spring of 1972, his stockpile of cutting materials had run so low that he was unable to cut and distribute some 50 kilos of heroin he had on hand, though every dealer in his empire was begging for a "package." Without a new source of supply, the mills would have had to shut down, a prospect so dire that Pop Darby undertook to talk the problem over with his old friend Walter Rosenbaum, whom he had known for twenty-five years as a Philadelphia bail bondsman, but who also ran a general merchandise business from his office at 1721 North 17th Street. Perhaps *he* could buy in bulk for them.

After being turned down by several American drug companies, Rosenbaum came up with the answer. Mannite was an Italian product, so why not import it directly? He called the Italian consulate in New York for a list of manufacturers and wrote off to them, asking for prices and delivery dates.

Darby was delighted, and so was Matthews when he heard. He told Darby to bring Rosenbaum up to New York, and the three of them met with Mickey Beckwith, his production manager, at 130 Clarkson. After some discussion, they agreed to a trial shipment from Santana Progal of Genoa of 252 kilos of mannite—more than a quarter ton of laxative—for immediate delivery by Alitalia air freight upon receipt of a certified check for $1,814.40.

If it worked out, they told Rosenbaum, he could order them 50,000 three-quarter-ounce bars—about two and a quarter tons—every three months. And did he think he could get them 10,000 ounces of quinine a month from the same source? If so, they would pay him $100,000 a shipment.

Rosenbaum said he would try. On June 13, Darby called at his office with the money, and the order was placed with Santana

Progal. But Rosenbaum had been thinking. Five hundred and fifty pounds of mannite could be explained away without too much trouble, but from then on, he would be in over his head. Even if Santana Progal had no knowledge of American restrictions on the distribution and sale of quinine, U.S. Customs officers certainly did. What was he supposed to tell them if they wanted to know what the stuff was for?

On June 17, Rosenbaum called in at the Philadelphia office of the BNDD, identified himself, and made the agents a sporting proposition. If they would allow him to bring in $50,000 worth of cutting materials and take his profit, he would then tell them when and where to seize the stuff. As a bonus, he would also turn in Darby, Beckwith, and Matthews.

To his entirely justified amazement, the offer was rejected out of hand. Even more remarkably, no effort was made to keep an eye on Rosenbaum after this interview. Not content with rejecting a chance to incriminate three major violators of the drug laws, the local agents also omitted to ensure that Rosenbaum did not go ahead with the deal in any case, which, of course, he did. When the mannite cleared customs at the end of June, he and Darby arranged for its collection from the airport and its delivery to a stash on Sherman Avenue in Newark, New Jersey.

(In BNDD's defense, it might be argued that the Bureau would have laid itself open to severe criticism if it had knowingly allowed an informant to profit from a criminal conspiracy, but elsewhere its agents were finding ways around this kind of problem every day. Nobody ever questioned, for example, the practice of paying informants. The Philadelphia office could therefore have seized both the goods *and* the $50,000, and paid Rosenbaum for his information a sum equivalent to the profit he had expected to make on the deal. Everybody would then have been happy, except for Darby, Beckwith, and Matthews.

If the objection remains that this would simply have put a gloss on what was still unethical conduct, then standards of decorum in John Mitchell's Department of Justice were higher than previously supposed. And even if they were, there is no explaining the assumption that Rosenbaum would abandon the project just because the Bureau had refused to countenance it.)

Rosenbaum went on to become a valuable associate of Matthews's, although the closest he ever came to importing quinine for him was to inquire if Santana Progal could supply it. With Darby, and Frank Matthews's personal check for $15,000, he set up a company called the Herald Corporation, with the object of buying stock in a new bank about to be formed in Philadelphia. When it came to laundering street money, there was nothing quite like owning a piece of a bank—unless it was owning a casino. With the prospect of legalized gambling in Atlantic City, Rosenbaum and the Herald Corporation also began to take a close interest in the real estate market there.

But if the BNDD had lost, temporarily at least, a good witness in Rosenbaum, it found another in Babe Cameron, Matthews's main man in his home town of Durham. Thanks to District Attorney Anthony M. Brannon, who induced Cameron's lieutenant Dan Barbee to turn informer, Cameron caved in after being charged with dealing narcotics, and also with the murder of one of his customers, who had died of an overdose. No stranger to prison—he had spent ten of his first thirty years behind bars—Cameron found the idea of another fifteen years to life in the penitentiary was more than he could bear.

In New York, Donald James now saw the light as well. Already cooperating with the Brooklyn District Attorney as a witness against his partner "Dutch Schultz" Daniels and the other principals of New York's leading street-level drug ring, James was also in pawn to the federal government for selling "weight" to a BNDD undercover agent on two occasions a year earlier. Set up, therefore, for a one-two, state-federal combination punch that could knock him out of circulation for thirty years or more, he was inclined to risk Matthews's future displeasure to avert the present danger—particularly as the government was prepared to offer him its protection as well as freedom from prosecution.

With Coleman, Cameron, and James; with many smaller fry contributing a lead here and a hint there; with the intimidating powers of a sitting grand jury at their back; and with a tap on Matthews's business phone, Group 12 were now better equipped to stalk their man than ever before, although they still resented having to share their quarry with anyone else. Having uncovered Matthews's tracks in twenty-one states, however, they had finally come face to face with the situation they had always feared: they had converted the doubtful to a belief in Matthews as the supreme criminal of his day, before they were ready to bring him to trial.

The witnesses so far available to Sheerin were too far from the center of Matthews's operation to carry enough weight. Furthermore, they were all of bad character and had each been bought with the promise of leniency. Someone closer to Matthews was needed—a supplier, or a lieutenant in day-to-day contact with him. Someone like Beckwith, perhaps.

Miller went through channels to see if he could get access to ODALE's files, and met William Callahan coming in the other direction in search of material on Matthews.

The moment for a merger was exactly ripe. Forced by the logic of events to assess each other as potential allies rather than as actual rivals, they resigned themselves with as much grace as they could muster to a conference called by their respective superiors, and found that double harness fitted them perfectly. Callahan, with ODALE's funds and political heft, would run the grand jury, in liaison with Sheerin; Miller, with his BNDD Task Force group, would continue in charge of the field investigation, working out of town through the ODALE connection whenever his own informal contacts proved inadequate.

For a shotgun marriage, it was made in heaven. An immediate bond between them was a mutual determination to keep everybody else out of the case, no matter how broad or complex it became.

Meanwhile, they had a lot of wiretap tapes to listen to. On one of them was a call taken by Matthews's answering service at five o'clock in the afternoon of July 2.

"Mr. Matthews," announced the operator. "Hello?"
"Could I please leave a message there, ma'am?" asked the caller.
"Surely. Who's calling?"
"Georgie."
"Georgie?"
"Yes, ma'am."
"And your number?"
"445-1127. Area code 305. In Miami."
"305-445-1127?"
"Yes, ma'am."
"What's the rest of the—?"
"Call me as soon as possible."
"Okay."
"Thank you."
"You're welcome."
The caller hung up.
"Who the hell is Georgie?" Miller asked.
Nobody knew.
But his business with Matthews was obviously urgent, because at 1:43 the following morning he called again, and again left his Miami number with the operator.
On July 6, Miller was presented with another puzzle. Matthews's service answered a call from a New York operator, who said: "There was a call made and billed to this number going to Caracas, Venezuela. Is that acceptable?"
"Who's making it?" asked the woman on the service switchboard.
"Umm—he said he was a preacher's son. It was going to Mr. Marcello Cabot."
"This is an answering service, honey. I don't know . . ."
"It was *his* answering service."
"Oh. Okay. Yes, it's okay."
"Thank you."
This obviously wasn't good enough for the overseas operator, who came back on the line seconds later to clarify matters.
"Mr. Matthews," said his service, picking up.

"This is overseas operator."

"Yes, operator?"

"Mr. Frank Matthews is making a call from another telephone and would like to have it charged to this number."

"That's—that's okay."

"Thank you."

She hung up.

"Who the hell is Marcello Cabot?" Miller asked.

Nobody knew.

13

My godfather was in no hurry to get to Caracas. Me and Anna left him at the Skyline, and it was a couple of days before he showed up in Miami. Ricky Acosta was with him.

"He wants in on the action," Miguel said to me.

"Aw, shit. We don't need him."

"Yeah, but I owe the guy. And he needs the bread."

"Then why don't I talk to Orlando?" I said. "See if he can cop 100 pounds of grass some place. They run it up to New York, maybe they'll both make a little money for themselves."

"Okay. Ask him. I'll check with José Martinez."

"Suit yourself," I said. "But Orlando could use the exercise. All he does is hang around with Ricardo Morales."

Before Orlando could get his ass in gear, Martinez made a connection for 80 pounds at $225 a pound.

"How about it, Ricky?" my godfather said.

"Hey, listen. I can get $500 a pound for it up there without even trying. That's if I had $18,000."

"I'll front the money." And when Ricky started to thank him, Miguel cut him short. "But you better know what you're doing, because I'm making you responsible for this shit, understand? I want the eighteen thousand back, plus $100 a pound, plus whatever I give you for expenses."

"You got it, man. That's like money in the bank."

"Okay. Then you take care of it, Georgie."

So Georgie took care of it. While I went to get the money, Ricky fixed the time and place with Martinez, and that night we drove over to a house on 11th Street, between 17th and 18th Avenues. Martinez let us in. He seemed nervous.

"The guys will be here in a minute," he said. "I got a gun over there on the sofa. Under the pillow." And he led the way upstairs.

Ricky didn't follow right away. "What's he telling *us* for?" he said to me. "If he needs a gun, he can go get it and use it, right? He wants *us* to use it? What is it with this punk-ass son of a bitch?"

Nobody talked much for five minutes. Then somebody knocked at the door and Martinez went down to let in these two kids.

"You got the stuff?"

"We got it," they said. "Eighty pounds."

"Okay. Start getting it up. I'll come out with you and open the gate. You can bring the car into the back yard."

The load was in one-pound bricks, and as they brought them up, we weighed them. It looked like pretty good stuff, but that whole weed scene turned me off. Amateurs, all of them, and full of romantic bullshit about having adventures and feeling like heroes. They dumped the last of the load on the table and waited while we checked it. Then I tipped out on the bed the $18,000 in my flight bag, and their eyes popped.

"I told you these were the real people," said one of them.

Oh, Jesus, I said to myself, what the hell *is* this? I should have let these sons of bitches handle the deal themselves.

"Better count it," said the other one. "Make sure it's all there."

"It's there," I said, and I pulled out my pipe with the silencer. "So just get the fuck out of here. Unless you want to start counting the holes in your head."

They left.

"Now all I need are some wheels," said Ricky.

"Tomorrow I'll take you to this dealer I know," I said. "And José will have this shit all packed up and ready to go, won't you, José?"

He looked like he might say something, but changed his mind. "Sure, Georgie," he said.

Next morning I fixed Ricky up with a clean little Dodge Dart for $1,800 cash and drove with him around to Martinez's place to pick up the grass, which was now taped into four big black garbage bags. We loaded them into the trunk, and I counted him off $1,000 for expenses on the road.

"Okay, I guess you're ready," I said. "Grow wings and fly, baby."

And that's exactly what he did. He got in the car and left for New York. Just like that.

Next problem.

"I couldn't let you go, Orlando," I told him. "I need you here. Martinez is out. Mikey's going to Caracas. I got to build an organization, and you're it."

"Well, shit, Georgie—I could really have used the bread, man. I'm just about busted on my ass."

"You're not hearing me, man. Will you listen, for Christ's sake? You're going to be my stash now. You're going to take the shit up to New York for me. You're in, man. This is where you really start to make it. Only I need a contact for some lactose."

"No sweat," Orlando said. "I got a connection in a drugstore. The one on the corner of 9th Court and 8th Street—right next to Isabelita's."

"Okay," I said. "Great. You're on stand-by."

Next problem.

My Corvette, which I'd had for like a month. One night—Anna and Orlando were with me—I was coming off the Expressway after dicing a little with another Stingray, and the front suspension broke as I went to make a right turn. Big moment. Couple of minutes before that, we'd been doing 100. Cosmo Lacroix must have been holding it together with his bare hands. Anyway, we pushed the son of a bitch into a garage, and I told the guy to call Don Allen Chevrolet in the morning and have them send a wrecker.

Next day, I went over there myself. The goddamn car was still in warranty, and I wanted to see the guy I bought it from. So while I waited for him I looked around their Corvette showroom, and boom! In love again. There was this pretty white one with a red interior, and it spoke to me. So did the sticker. It said $6,800.

Something told me, Don't buy it. But something else said,

What the hell? When the guy came over, all apologetic about the car they just towed in, I told him I wasn't happy with it no more.

"I want that one," I said.

He thought it over, figuring out sums in his head the way they do. "Tell you what," he said. "You give me the car you got, plus thirty-five hundred, and it's yours."

"It's mine," I said. "Don't go away."

I was goddamned if I was going to pay for it myself, not after all the bullshit aggravation in New York with Frank, and now with Ricky Acosta. So I went to see my godfather.

"Hey, look," I said. "I need $4,000."

"Take it," he said. "Don't bother me."

Next problem.

Well, the next problem was getting him off his ass and over to Venezuela. It was now the end of June already. Every day I'd check to see what was happening, and mostly he was over at the African Pet Shop, getting himself cleansed of evil spirits before the trip.

"Georgie, come and pick me up at Barbarito's," he'd say. And there he'd be, in the middle of killing a goat or something in the big room with the dirt floor that Barbarito used for his voodoo ceremonies. Since Haiti, Raquel Dumois was no place. Barbarito had taken over as our spiritual godfather, our *padrino en palo*, and this was the real thing, with dead spirits and blood sacrifice.

One morning, I got over there and Barbarito met me in the hallway, by his life-sized statue of Santa Barbara.

"Miguel is just finishing up," he said. "He's about ready to go now."

"Good," I said. "Because we got things to do. He's supposed to be in South America."

"Unless the spirits are with him, he will accomplish nothing. Such things cannot be hurried. But I can tell you this. Miguel has promised the spirits that when he leaves for Venezuela the cocaine operation is yours."

I guess that made it official.

"And you know why?" Barbarito said. "This ceremony today has proved your loyalty to Miguel. He could not leave before the spirits showed him whom he could trust. And they say you would give your life for him."

"Yeah?" I wasn't completely sure about that. "Well, I guess he'd do the same for me."

"I guess he would," said Barbarito, but he didn't seem completely sure about it, either.

Anyway, Miguel was ready, and he went out that night to celebrate his departure.

"Look," I said. "We both know you're going to get drunk on your ass, so don't drive. Do us both a favor. Take a cab, okay?"

"Sure," he said. "Don't worry about it."

Next morning, about 6:30, the phone woke me up, and it was Ana Baños.

"Your godfather's in jail," she said.

Shit!! I was out of bed like somebody fired a thousand volts through it.

But then I thought, what could be so bad? We were clean—unless they found cocaine in his goddamn pocket. There was no big deal going down they could have caught him at.

"What did he do?"

"He wrecked the car," she said, and I started to breathe again.

"Bad?"

She laughed. Apparently he had left a bar, very drunk, climbed into his Pontiac Grand Prix, and driven it flat out into the back of the car parked six feet in front of him—a car belonging to the guy he had just been drinking with. Hearing the crash, the guy came out on the sidewalk just in time to see my godfather reverse out of the wreck like a crazy man and take off, everything screaming. Being a friend of his, he didn't call the cops or nothing, figuring he'd catch up with him later, when he sobered up, but then a prowl car latched on to Miguel anyway as he went storming down the avenue. And all he had to hear was that siren. He just floored that son of a bitch and hauled ass.

They chased him for half an hour. The bastard was having the time of his life, blasting through red lights, charging the traffic coming at him on one-way streets, sideswiping other cars or forcing them off the road. Finally, when he had half the prowl cars in the city on his tail, he took one chance too many and drove into a wall, giving himself a big lump on the head. So they fished him out of what was left of the Grand Prix and drove the body over to Dade County Jail to sober up in the drunk tank.

"How much is the bond?" I asked her.

"Two thousand," she said. "I posted it already. I'm at the jail-house now."

"Okay. Wait there. I'll come and pick up the pieces."

My godfather was a sadder and wiser man. They had booked him for driving under the influence, failure to have a vehicle under control, and leaving the scene of an accident—six counts.

"What the hell did you *do*?"

"I don't remember," he said. "And don't bug me. I got a headache."

"Yeah, so have I," I said. "When are you going to Venezuela?"

"Never mind Venezuela. I just want to go home."

So we put him to bed, and later that morning I went over to Packer Pontiac to see about his car, which had been towed in there. How he got out of that thing with just a lump on the head I'll never know. The Grand Prix looked like it had been worked over from end to end with a 20-pound sledge. I was shaking my head over it when one of the mechanics I knew there came up to me with a funny look on his face.

"You got anything to do with that car, Georgie?" he said.

"It belongs to my godfather. Why?"

He looked around to make sure nobody was listening. "Well, I'm not supposed to say nothing about it," he said, "but we just had a couple of federal agents around here asking questions. You in any trouble, Georgie?"

"No," I said. "But it looks like my godfather is."

Federal agents? It didn't make sense. Why would they be interested in a drunk-driving case?

"How long will it take to fix this thing?" I said, still trying to figure it out.

"You better talk to the office," he said. "There's some kind of problem with the insurance. They want $2,000 cash up front before we put a wrench on it."

"What kind of problem?"

"I don't know," he said. "The guy who wrecked it told the cops his name was Cabot or something, but the car's insured in some other name. Why don't you talk to the office about it?"

"Yeah, I'll do that."

But first I went and talked to a lawyer I knew. I laid $500 on his desk and told him to call me the minute he found out what was going on. Then I went home to wait, not worried exactly, but unsettled by all this bullshit. When you're tied in with two guys who make as much noise as my godfather and Frank Matthews, then you got to wonder about the future.

Couple of hours later, the lawyer called back, and it seemed Barbarito had been right—the spirits *were* with my godfather. There was a New York warrant out for him since 1970 for failing to answer a gun charge. When they'd booked him for drunk driving that morning, the Miami police had naturally taken his fingerprints, but with a tank full of drunks, they hadn't gotten around to processing them until *after* his bond was posted. As soon as they did, of course, the guy they had booked as Marcello Cabot—because that was what his papers said—turned out to be Miguel Garcia, a fugitive from New York, which made it a federal matter.

It was bad enough, but not as bad as I'd thought. I hopped in my new Corvette and set a new course record to Normandy Isle.

"Oh, there you are," he said, obviously feeling better. "I just heard from the Venezuelans. You better go up and see Frank. We need $30,000."

"Never mind about that," I said. "Right now, we got to worry about you. You really opened a can of worms with this shit." And I told him what had happened.

Luckily, there was a phony address along with the phony name on his phony papers. Otherwise, he would have heard about it already from the federal agents. I got him packed and over to the airport inside an hour, put him on the first plane out heading south, and waved Marcello Cabot goodbye.

Next problem.

"I hope he gets arrested," Anna said. "I hope you all get busted on your ass."

"Oh, thanks a lot," I said.

"Coke I don't mind. That's for rich people. But heroin? That's sick. You know what it does to those kids?"

"Yeah, I know. I'm not too crazy about the idea myself."

"Then stay out of it. We don't need that. It's dirty money."

"I tried to talk him out of it, baby—honest. I told him, 'Shit, the same way we can move 100 keys of horse, we can move 100 keys of coke.' "

"So what did he say?"

"He said there's not the same profit, and he's right. We'd have to bring in 400 keys of coke to make the same."

"Dirty money. I don't want it. I hope they bust the son of a bitch."

"Don't say that, baby. You know if he gets stuck I'm not going to turn my back. Even if I *did* stay out, somewhere along the way he's going to need my help, and then I'll be in it, anyway. So I might as well be in it from the beginning and get the thing over with. Don't you see? I'm going to have to stick my hand in it, one way or the other."

"Then you're going to do it without me."

"Aw, come on, baby—we're talking about a million dollars. Then we retire."

"It's dirty money. I don't want it."

"Well, you think about it. Because I got to go see Frank now and get us another $30,000 of his dirty money. Because that's what you're wearing, baby. That's what pays the rent and buys the groceries—Frank's dirty money."

"I never thought I was hurting nobody," she said.

A few days later, I called Frank a couple of times to let him know I was coming. By this time, I figured Ricky Acosta would have unloaded the weed, so I called him as well and told him to meet me at Newark Airport.

"I got $12,600 for you," he said. "The rest is on the way. You want it now?"

"No. First, I want you to run me by Frank Matthews's place up in the Bronx. We'll do our little bit of business later."

But Frank wasn't home, and neither was Nat.

"Come on, Georgie," Ricky said. "Let me give you the money. I don't feel easy with all that dough around the house."

So we went over to his place, and after he counted out the money, he ran me over to the Renaissance Motel in New Jersey, where I was staying this time. It was still early—around three in the afternoon—so I tried Frank again, and got him. Come on up to the apartment, he said, and back I went again, by cab.

Nat was there. "Hey, how's it going, Georgie?" he said. "I hear you're going to make us all rich."

I took hold of his lapel, like I was feeling the quality. "Man, I wish I was as poor as you," I said. "How are you, Frank?"

"Hanging in there, Mr. G.," he said. "Just waiting to hear from Santa Claus."

"Yeah, well. He got a little high and crashed his reindeer."

"Yeah, I heard about that." He was talking light, but that didn't mean he was kidding around. "So I guess that puts more on you, right? If he ain't coming back?"

"No," I said. "Mikey gets the stuff to Haiti. I get it to you. Same as before. If he takes care of his end, I'll take care of mine."

"No ifs, baby. All I want to hear is *when*."

"You better talk to your partner about that." I didn't like the trend. I wasn't going to take pressure from nobody. "I ain't heard a word since I got him out of town. And for right now I need thirty thousand."

He must have caught the change in my voice, because then he relaxed and got up smiling.

"I know. He told me. But *he* said forty."

"No, thirty's enough."

Son of a bitch. He was playing games. He was trying to make *me* responsible for what my godfather did.

I unbuttoned my shirt and stowed the money away in the belt I was wearing underneath. It was all in new hundreds, but checking myself in the mirror, I looked like I'd suddenly put on 30 pounds.

"You stopping over, Georgie?" said Nat. "We could check out a couple of places tonight."

"Hey, nothing I'd like better, but I got to get back." That was all I needed, to be seen running around town with a dope dealer. "I got a rock pile waiting in Haiti."

"That's my man," said Frank. "Just you move it on up here. You got a car?"

"No, I came by cab."

"Then wait a minute. I'll run you downtown."

Frank in a hurry was like my godfather drunk. He was going to drop me off as soon as we found a cab—and we found one all right. He drove into the back of the goddamn thing as it stopped for a light on Riverside Drive. Not that hard, but enough to shake up the driver, who came back ready to make trouble. Before he could open his mouth, Frank was wagging a $50 bill under his nose. The guy looked at him for a second, hating his guts so much it was turning him gray. Then he took the money and walked away without a word.

"All you need is love," I said. The guy had started yelling at his passenger through the cab window.

"Yeah," said Frank. "But a million or two don't hurt." And I couldn't disagree with him there.

Now I had the money, I figured I might as well head back to Miami. But first I wanted to buy some shoes, so when we finally tagged a cruising cab, I told the driver to take me to a Nunn Bush store I'd seen in Times Square. I was the only customer they had right then, and I worked the clerk pretty hard before I found four pairs I liked. Without thinking, I opened my shirt to get at the money to pay for them, and the poor son of a bitch damn near fell on his ass when he saw that great thick belt full of hundreds.

It was just careless, like the time in the bank. That's the big danger when you're into something illegal. You get used to it. You go about your business, thinking nothing of it, and it's only when people react like he did that you suddenly remember what's normal to you is far out to them. Anyway, I looked him straight in the eye, so he shouldn't get no ideas, and started loading the money into one of the shoe boxes. That really hurt. He looked around like he was saying, I don't even want to *see* this. Then I put the string back around the box, loaded it into the shopping bag he'd given me, and walked.

Times Square didn't seem too healthy now. Even shoe salesmen have friends. So I hopped the first cab that came along and rode back to the Renaissance. It took only a few minutes to move Ricky's $12,600 from under the mattress into the other shoe boxes, and I was on my way to Newark Airport.

I was looking forward to a few days at home with Anna. I'd been running around a lot, which never improved her temper, and I had to make her understand I was on a three-and-two count with my godfather. After he gave me the whole cocaine business, there was no way I could refuse to help him. But it was strictly a one-shot deal, and I wanted her to know that. Once it was over, I was going to retire from the dope business and spend a few years seeing the world before settling down to something else, something legitimate.

I had it all worked out in my mind, what I was going to say to her, but the phone started ringing the second I got inside the door. It was Pedro Diaz. They were going to be in Haiti with the next load in two days' time.

Anna wasn't pleased. She wasn't any happier about the heroin deal either, but she'd cooled off enough to realize I just couldn't walk away from it. We spent the rest of the night working on our relationship.

Next morning, I went out to buy some lengths of vinyl and a

good stapler. On the way back, I called in to see Barbarito. Miguel had made me promise to do that before every trip, and I knew Barbarito would tell him if I didn't. It was times like these when I really felt I was earning my money.

"Go to the grocery store," he said, "and buy some split peas, some white beans, some red beans, and some cornmeal. Put them in a little sack, and stand at the door of your house, facing outward. Then brush yourself down with the sack—long strokes, and away from you, like this"—and he showed me how. "When you've done that, take the sack to the railroad track and throw it down on the rails. The train's a traveling thing. It'll carry away the evil spirits."

And me with a plane to catch.

After that, I had to run over to Normandy Isle to leave some money with Victoria Montalvo. I'd started out that morning figuring I'd keep $5,000 out of the $12,600 I'd collected from Ricky and give the old lady the rest, but after the Barbarito bullshit, *she* got the five thousand, and *I* took what was left.

It was getting late now, and I had to make San Juan that night if I was going to catch the Air France flight on to Haiti next morning. So we rounded up Orlando to drive me out to the airport, and on the way I gave him $500 to buy some lactose and get his apartment set up for the stash. The main thing he had to find was a big mirror, about five feet by four feet, to use as a table top for cutting the stuff.

In San Juan, I checked into the Caribe Hilton and called Willie Moto. His real name was Willie Dipini, and I'd met him a couple of times in Miami with my godfather. Willie was pretty big as dealers go on the island, and remembering what Miguel had said about throwing a few keys his way, I figured it wouldn't do no harm to see what *he* could do for *us*. One way or another, it looked like I was going to need an army to handle this deal, although naturally I didn't say nothing about it when he came over. As far as he was concerned, it was strictly social.

So what did we talk about? Voodoo. Willie was having lots of troubles in Puerto Rico, mostly because the place was dry. But the last time he was in Miami, Miguel had told him it was probably on account of his spiritual condition, and I'd gone with them to Barbarito's to get it checked out. Seemed poor Willie was in a bad way. Those evil spirits were really crowding him. The minute Barbarito sat him down and cut loose with the weeds and throwing stuff on him and shaking and everything, he could tell right away—they were going to have to go the whole route. So after a real long ceremony there, they left him alone in Barbarito's big room with a big hairy sheep and a butcher knife. He had to sacrifice this sheep by stabbing it in the neck and feeding the blood to *la nasa,* Barbarito's little pile of sticks and skin in front of the altar, like they had in Haiti.

Well, this goddamn sheep didn't want to go, and fought Willie to a standstill before he finally got it. Then they sat him down and cut the shape of an arrow on his forearm, and after that there was a lot of chanting and blowing smoke around. And the smoke took different forms and swirled about, which showed the spirit was with them. And so it went on. They kept the poor bastard there for damn near a week, just working him over to get him clean.

"Made all the difference—right, Willie?"

"Yeah, well . . . Yeah, I guess so."

"Well, you got to keep it up, you know," I said. "Next time I talk to Mikey, I'll ask him what you got to do next."

"Oh, shit," he said.

And now finally it was the Venezuelans' turn to give me a hard time. I copped the Air France connection to Haiti next morning, skimming into Pétionville again over those crazy huts along the runway, and took a cab to El Rancho. Since the last trip, diplomatic relations had been restored between Venezuela and Haiti, and so the whole team was there—Perez and Medina, with their girlfriends, and Diaz, who had come alone. The hotel was full, so I checked in with him.

"Something wrong, Pedro?" I said, after we talked for a couple of minutes. He was acting like his pet dog had died. "We got problems?"

He shrugged. "You got the money?"

"Well, of course I've got the money. Why wouldn't I have the money?"

"Okay. Then let me go talk to Medina."

He left me wondering. And I understood even less what was going on when Medina came back with him and they stood by the door fidgeting and waiting for each other to say something.

"Come on, fellers," I said. "What's the bad news?"

"It's the money, Georgie," Medina said. "Can I have it?"

I looked them both over pretty hard. "What's this?" I said. "Something new?"

"It's the Doctor," Pedro said. "He wants to see the money first."

"Oh, yeah? Well, *I* want to see the stuff first. Fuck *him*. What the hell's the matter with Albino?"

Medina could see a storm blowing up, and looked to Pedro to help him out.

"Ah, Georgie, it don't mean nothing. He's just a little touchy, that's all."

"So am I a little touchy," I said, getting madder by the second. "Why all the goddamn drama? How much have you got?"

"Four."

"Four? Only *four?* What the fuck's going on here?"

Medina tried to palm me off with a chicken-shit grin. "It's like Pedro said. He's just a little touchy."

"What about?" And now I was really yelling. "You got what you asked for. I gave you $10,000 in Miami, right? If you wanted more you should have said so."

"I know, Georgie. But what can I tell you? He says if he don't see the money up front . . ." And he shrugged.

So I sat down on the bed, taking my time.

"Let me tell you something," I said, like we were now discussing the weather. "Albino's got a choice. He can either deal fair and square with us like always—no hassle, no surprises, everybody happy. Or he can fuck us around and see how he likes dealing out of a pine box."

Medina looked at Pedro, who showed him his empty hands.

"You go bring me the stuff," I said, "and I'll give you the money. Like always."

Five minutes later, they were back with the four kilos. Without a word, Medina unloaded them onto the bed from a suitcase.

"Fine," I said. "Four keys. That's sixteen thousand, right? Or has the price gone up, too?"

"No, no. The price is the same."

"Okay. We give you ten already, so we owe you six." And I counted out sixty $100 bills, right into his hands. "Now we're square, right?"

"Right," said Medina. "I'll take it to him."

"Wait a minute."

He stopped at the door like I had a gun on him.

"You forgot something." I tipped the rest of the money onto the bed alongside the cocaine. "$24,000. That's six more kilos paid for up front—and don't bother to count it. Just ask that asshole if he's happy now."

Pedro helped Medina pack the money in the suitcase but stayed behind when he left with it. As the door closed behind him, he shook his head and laughed.

"Fucking Indians," he said.

"Yeah, yeah—but I don't have time for this horseshit. You're the one we're counting on—I told you that. We got to keep these guys moving. Four kilos—shit! I got a man who'll take all I bring him. He's crying for it. We got to get this up to 10 or 15 keys a trip."

"Well, we can get them for you—ain't no doubt about that. I'll lean on José a little bit, and we'll talk to Albino some more."

"Well, you look out for us, Pedro, and we'll take care of you—you know that."

"Sure," he said. "Just leave it to me."

We stapled the four kilos into the vinyl I'd brought, and stashed them in the closet. Then we went to check on the boat, and waiting outside the hotel was Paul-Baptiste, who greeted me like a brother. So I threw him a fifty to be getting on with, and we drove down to the pier.

I had four days to wait before the *William Express* was due in, which was fine by me. I needed the time to follow up on my contacts and spot locations. Next morning, Medina took off with his girlfriend, and later on the Doctor went, too—I never did see him on that trip. But Pedro was in no hurry to get back to his wife, and so we rounded up Antoine and set out with Paul-Baptiste to win friends and influence people.

Top of the list was Charles, the bandleader. With 100 kilos of horse coming together in Marseilles, I badly needed that introduction to his friend the customs boss, but there we struck out. Charles was away with his band in the islands some place, and I couldn't find Mary-Lou either. But I lined up a couple of ideal spots on the edge of town where we could do the delay work on the shipment, and by the time the boat came in, I had a whole bunch of people ready to adopt me.

It didn't take much. Haiti is a poor country. On my shopping list of stuff for the next trip were kerosene lamps and support hose for the voodoo people; a stereo tape set for Paul-Baptiste; shoes and shirts for Antoine; and a shoulder holster for the .38 caliber Special worn by the secret police agent who worked in the harbor master's office. They weren't high-level people—I needed Charles to open those doors. But if I wanted some workers in a hurry or a little muscle for local protection or if I had to disappear for a while, then I now knew what to do. I'd made myself at home.

So I picked up another tourist bag from La Belle Creole department store for the four kilos, piled the usual beads and stuff on top of it, and Yves Alexis walked the load on to the *William Express* without a hitch. It was so easy. He could have carried a grand piano on board and nobody would have noticed.

"Well, I guess that about wraps it up," said Pedro. "You going to cut that stuff the way I told your godfather—with the lactose and acetone?"

"Hey, now tell me again about that," I said. "We were going to do it a couple of loads back, but we run out of time."

"Yeah, it takes a little longer, but it's worth it."

And as Paul-Baptiste drove us out to the airport, Pedro explained exactly what I had to do.

There are lots of different things you can use to cut coke. I know people who do it with aspirin, bicarbonate of soda, Epsom salts, boric acid, and even plain old table salt. If you want to be fancy, and you got a drugstore connection, then benzocaine and procaine are good. So is mannite, which Frank also used to cut heroin. But, for my money, the best thing when you're dealing "weight" is lactose. It's not hard to find, which is important when you need a lot of it, and it won't hurt nobody. The only trouble is it leaves a sweet taste, which some coke freaks don't like, and it turns the coke all brown and shitty inside a couple of weeks. Once you cut it with lactose, you got to move the stuff fast.

But Pedro's new cut got rid of those problems. First, you put the lactose in a big plastic pan and pour in enough acetone to cover it. Then you add two cc of citric acid for every kilo of lactose, and give it a good stir with a plastic paddle to get that lactose really wet. After that, you let it work for an hour or so, stirring occasionally, and at the end of that time you pour off any acetone left on top of the mixture. Now you spoon the stuff out onto a flat surface and let it dry. This takes six or seven hours, but you can speed things up if you want with a couple of heat lamps.

When it's ready, the stuff looks as hard as a rock, but it crumbles into dust when you pinch it or push it through a strainer. And it's not sweet any more. The acid has given it a bit of a bite, a ting that goes well with the freeze of the coke.

Better yet, it won't go bad either, so if you miss your connection after cutting the load, you don't have to go crazy trying to move it some place else. It was a bit more trouble, but it sure as hell improved the shelf life of the product.

So now I was real anxious to try it. After what happened with the last load, I was going to make certain Frank had nothing to bitch about this time. Instead of cutting the four keys one-on-one to make eight, I was going to make just six and, with the new cut, really knock him on his ass. As soon as I got back to Miami, I sent Orlando around to his drugstore friend with a list of what we needed. He came back all proud of himself.

"No problem," he said. "I put the order in, and Aguero says he'll have the stuff in a couple of days."

"Fantastic. What's it going to cost us?"

"Oh, maybe forty, fifty dollars."

"No, I mean what does he want for himself?"

"Nothing," Orlando said. "He's my friend."

"Oh, come on. All the more reason. If he's a friend, why not let the guy make himself a few hundred dollars?"

"Hey, it's not me. He don't want it. He told me."

"I don't get it," I said. "Don't make sense. If he thinks the cops will give him a break if we're busted and he tells them he didn't make no profit, he's crazy."

"No, he's like that. He's just doing me a favor, that's all. What do *you* care?"

"I *care*. Guys like that make me nervous."

But a couple of days later he came through on schedule, and I took a run over by Evaristio's house on North River Drive, right opposite the Antillean Line dock, to check on the load. The *William Express* was due in about thirty hours, he said, and I should call him half a day or so after that to give him a chance to get the stuff off. I also found out my godfather hadn't paid him for last time, which was typical. Evaristio was supposed to get $1,000 for every kilo he brought ashore, but that wasn't all profit. Out of that he had to pay Yves Alexis on the ship, and also a percentage to Luis the Junkman, who had fixed up this deal with my godfather. So I told him I didn't have the cash right then, but he'd get it as soon as I moved the stuff coming in.

After a bumpy start, my first solo run was now going good.

When the time came to call Evaristio, sure enough the ship was in, and that night me and Anna picked up the four kilos at his house. Then we drove them over to Orlando's place, our new stash, and got ready for cutting it next day.

This was Orlando's big moment. So far, he hadn't made much. I'd slipped him a few hundred dollars here and there, and out of the last couple of loads, I'd given him an ounce of pure at a bargain-basement price to hustle on the corner. That way he could hit it a couple of times to make it four, and turn them over at maybe $500 a crack. Out of the $2,000 he cleared, all he had to pay me was three or four hundred for the original ounce. I didn't feel it, and it gave him a few dollars in his pocket so he could play the big man in front of Ricardo Morales.

But now he was in with a chance at the real money, and the first thing he had to do was help me with the new cut. We got over there late next day and spent the whole evening following the recipe until finally the lactose and acetone mixture was all spooned out on the mirror ready for drying.

The fumes would have knocked out an elephant. I told Orlando he ought to rent a motel room for the night, but he wouldn't hear of it. Anybody wanted to separate him from the stash, he said, they would have to carry him out feet first—and that was damn near what I had to do next morning. When I got over there around nine, he had flipped out from the acetone. He didn't know where the hell he was. I had to send him over to his friend Aguero in the drugstore to get unraveled, and it was nighttime again before we started on the cutting.

We didn't hurry the job this time. Everything had to be exactly right, and it was. Before we bagged it, I sniffed the stuff, just to test it, and the top of my head blew off. Feo checked it out, too. He was snuffling around like always, when he suddenly let out a howl and went crazy. All Pekinese got bulgy eyes, but his were popping right out of his head. He ran around chasing things that weren't there, jumped up in the air, turned somersaults—that dog was so high he took a week to come down. Feo always had expensive tastes. Home-cooked chicken. Strawberry ice cream. And now the best goddamn coke in the country.

We finished around midnight. Orlando was feeling okay again, so me and Anna arranged to pick him up at seven and run him over to the bus station. He wasn't exactly sure where he would take the six keys, but he gave me the phone number of a friend of his in New York, a guy named Mike, who had worked as a bartender on the U.S.S. *Constitution.* As soon as he got settled, Orlando would leave word with Mike, who would pass the message to us when we called.

So next morning we saw Orlando off on a Trailways bus and had the rest of the day to enjoy ourselves. As it was the first chance I'd had to give the new Corvette a workout, I took Route 41 and headed into the Everglades. Anna was dozing. After a while, she woke up and looked off to the side to see where we were.

"Just look at those trees go by," she said.

"Honey," I said. "It's not the trees."

I had just touched 130.

Later on, we found a quiet spot and parked because I had something else to try out—my first legal gun. Like my godfather, I figured the best cover I could have was as a jewelry salesman. They generally carry a lot of cash. They move around a lot. They always have an attaché case with them—for their samples. And they need a gun for protection. So, as a licensed businessman, I had just bought myself a brand-new Smith & Wesson .38 and registered it.

We shot a lot of trees that day, and when the ammunition ran out, we raced the car some more. Life was pretty good.

Next morning, we flew up to New York and checked in at the Howard Johnson's on Eighth Avenue. When I called Mike, he told me Orlando was staying at the Hotel Wilson, just off Columbus Circle, so I phoned him there and had him come on down.

The trip had gone off all right, but he had had a couple of bad scares on the way. The first one was when the police stopped the bus at a roadblock. The moment he saw those lights flashing, his balls wrinkled up—that's not a fun scene when you're carrying—

but they didn't come on board. Turned out they were just diverting traffic past a bad accident. Then, at the next rest stop, some guys broke into the bus while it was parked and started busting open all the suitcases. By a miracle, they didn't get into his, although they smashed one of the locks.

I called Frank, and we arranged to meet at the hotel that night around ten o'clock. He arrived soon after we got back from dinner at Mamma Leone's, and as soon as he called up from downstairs, I told Anna and Orlando to take a walk.

He came in very high, like an entrance on stage. In that sort of mood, he could fill a room all by himself, he was that overpowering. So after the usual bullshit, I figured I'd get off the bad news first.

"Now listen, Frank," I said, "I only got six keys—but don't get your feathers ruffled. It's dynamite stuff, and there's a whole lot more on the way. I'm planning on pushing through twenty-five or thirty kilos a time from now on."

"Yeah?" he said. "You mean you got a big load of rocks coming in?"

"That's what I mean, Frank. And it's going to cost you. I'm going to need seventy thousand in about three weeks."

"Man, if you got the rocks, I got the cash. Don't worry about it." He really wasn't paying too much attention. It was like he was expecting me to tell him something else. Something more important. And he couldn't sit still. "Let's go take a ride," he said.

He could hardly wait till we got in the car. "Did the stuff come in yet?"

I couldn't pretend not to know what he meant. "The horse? No. I would have heard."

"Well, you know I was down there?" he said. "I was in Caracas. I took him some money."

"No, I didn't know." Right away, I had a bad feeling. "I ain't talked to Mikey since he left. I been busy. You better tell me what's going on."

"Shit, we had a hell of a time down there. Whoo-eee." He

laughed, and ran a red light. "We really tore up that town. I met the Frenchman—the Pimp. You know him?"

"Not yet."

"You know what he did? He sent three girls up to my room. *Three.* And I was so coked up, I kept them all. Never thought I'd live to see the morning."

He hung a right at 57th Street that damn near gave me a coronary and left taxi horns blowing for a couple of blocks back.

"Oh, my God," I said. "I can just imagine. You two bastards on the loose over there? Oh, Jesus."

"You should have seen me, Georgie. Three of them. I took the Preacher a hundred thousand, and if he hadn't put me on the plane, I'd have stayed down there till I blew it."

"You mean, like another couple of days?"

"You got it, man. Shit. That's my kind of town. I'm going to buy a hotel down there. The Pan-Americana. Mikey's setting up a meeting with the owner."

"Oh, Jesus. What's *that* going to cost you?"

"Who knows?" He blasted across Seventh Avenue, scattering pedestrians like pigeons. "Five million? We bought a plane, too."

"Oh, my God." They must have woken up every cop for a thousand miles. "What the fuck for? What kind of a plane?"

"Who knows from planes? It's a plane. Some old two-motor job. The Preacher says he's going to fly the stuff to Haiti in it."

"Yeah? Well, it sounds like you two could have done that without a plane," I said. "I got to think about this."

"Well, don't take too long, man. That stuff's going to get there any minute."

If I'd believed that, it would have been the worst moment of my life. Nothing was ready. Nothing had even been decided yet. But I knew my godfather by now. When he was coked up, whatever he *wanted* to happen was as good as done as far as he was concerned. These two bastards had bombed each other out of their skulls down there, and were treating their dreams for real. But the plane was serious. God only knew what they had stuck me with. If I left this to them, it wasn't a million dollars I'd be looking forward to, but a million years.

"I'll talk to Mikey," I said. "Now what about these six keys? You want them now?"

"Sure. Why not? But you'll have to stick around for the money. I got $200,000 tied up for you to take down there for the first load, plus the hundred I took already, so I'm a little short. Just give me a couple of days."

"No, I can't spare the time," I said. "I'll take what you got, and you owe me the rest. I got to work on this other deal."

"Well, I can let you have about $13,000." He swung right down Fifth Avenue, tires squealing, just under the nose of a bus. "I'll have to see what I got in the trunk."

"That's okay. Why don't you drop me off at the hotel and come back for me in an hour? I'll have the stuff ready."

We made it back to Howard Johnson's without killing anybody, and I sent Orlando over to his hotel to stand by the load. Then, while we waited for Frank, I filled Anna in on what had been happening. Talking to her always helped me get my head straight.

If Frank was right, if the first shipment was on the way, my godfather would just have to keep it in Venezuela until I was good and ready to receive it in Haiti. Nobody was going to stampede me with this airplane bullshit. It would be *my* ass that was up for grabs, so the job would be done *my* way. And the more I thought about it, the more conservative I got. So far, I was clean. No record. Nothing known. If these noisy sons of bitches brought down the heat, the worst that could happen to me was maybe a very thin conspiracy charge. All that anybody could prove was that I knew them, and since when was it a crime to know a criminal?

So I had to keep it that way. When the stuff *did* arrive in Haiti, I would have to make damn sure they didn't bring no heat with it. And if Frank thought I was going to haul the shit up to New York for him, he had another think coming. He was going to have to get off his ass and take delivery in Florida.

When he called from downstairs, we drove over to the Wilson

Hotel, and I left him parked a little way up the street. The desk clerk gave me the eye as I went through the lobby on my way to Orlando's room, so I made Orlando carry the stuff down and hand it to me in front of him. If the guy saw me go up empty-handed and then come down carrying a bag, I figured he was liable to start hollering cop, what with all the hotel robberies going on.

So I walked the load up the street and dumped it on the back seat of Frank's car.

"Don't run no more red lights," I said.

"You kidding me? I'm going to drive that stuff home like I was eighty years old and half blind. You going back tonight?"

"No, it's late. We'll go tomorrow."

"Fine. Don't make it too early. Maybe I'll get the money for you. I'll give you a call around six."

"Okay. I got a couple of people I want to see anyway."

One of them was Orlando's brother, who lived in the Bronx. He was an ex-junkie who had done five in Sing Sing for robbery. Orlando wanted to help him out, which was fine by me, so long as he was off the needle, because now I had to put an organization together in a hurry. I knew the guy anyway, from Miami. When he was sick, his wife used to come around to my place and call through the window.

"Georgie, have mercy," she would say. "My children haven't eaten today."

So I would get up and say to her, "Celia, what the hell are you doing out on the street?" It used to be twelve at night or later, and she would have these two little innocent kids with her, four or five years old. This went on for a month. I'd go get them something to eat, buy a gallon of milk and take them home—they were living in a motel down by the railroad track on 2nd Avenue in Miami.

I used to try to talk to the guy about it, but he was wrecked on that shit. He would sit on the bench, all jittery, and he was a dangerous man when he got like that. He'd find somebody to drive for him, and they'd stick up one garage after another. He'd jump out, put a gun to the guy's head, take $50 from him, and then go three blocks and do it again. But now he was running clean. He knew the moves. There was the blood tie with Orlando, and you could see he would bust his ass for anybody who gave him a break. So we put him on stand-by, although I wasn't sure where I could use him yet.

By six, we were back at the hotel, but I didn't hear from Frank for another couple of hours. When he called, he was downstairs, and we went for another ride.

"Georgie, I'm sorry," he said. "I got all tied up today on another deal. I can only give you the thirteen for right now."

"Hey, man—I told you. No sweat. I know you're good for it."

"Okay." It was the nearest I ever saw him to being embarrassed. "Another couple of days and I'll have money coming out of my ass, but you hit me just wrong. Another couple of days and I'll have the two hundred thousand for you as well. You want I should send somebody down with it?"

"No, let's just wait on that," I said. Jesus, it would have been so easy to rip him off. "I don't want to leave that kind of money lying around. Let's wait until we know for sure the stuff is on the way."

"Oh, it's coming," he said. "The Frenchman told me. All we got to do now is decide how we're going to work this deal."

He had quietened down a lot from the night before. He was even looking where he was going, so I figured it might be a good time to straighten him out on a couple of points.

"I been turning this over in my mind," I said. "That's a lot of stuff. Word gets out, and we'll have every scumbag in the country buzzing around like flies on a shitpile."

"So what do you want to do, Georgie? You need some guys down there? You need guns, or what?"

"Could be. I'll let you know. But what I'm thinking about now is breaking the shipment up more. We get unlucky—if I put it all on the ship and we get hit, we lost the whole load. If I split it up, bring some in another way, and they hit us, then we still got most of it."

"Right. Makes sense."

"Sure it does. That goes for the law, too. You guys been making a lot of noise down there, so if anybody's watching, let's make it hard for them. We can run some of the load on the route we got going now, and the rest higher up on the coast maybe, where it's quieter. We're going to need boats, and I'll have to plan this down to the second."

"Hey, man," he said. "I'm glad you're on my team. What kind of boats? We got a big cruiser in Sheepshead Bay."

"No, I'm thinking about two or three 24-foot Formulas with extra gas tanks. They're fast and handy, and nobody'll look at them twice—they got hundreds down there. But I'm going to need at least $100,000 to set all this up."

"Georgie, I told you," he said. "Let me know what you want and you got it. And when you make the drop, let's stay out of the big cities. Let's use a nice quiet town where there ain't too much heat around, and nobody knows us, okay?"

"I'm glad you said that, Frankie. I already decided I can't send my people all the way up to New York with that shit. You got to come South for it. I'll find some small town up in northern Florida with a motel or something just off the highway and we can work the switch there."

"We'll play it any way you want, Georgie," he said. "You just tell me when and where."

And he meant it. I was going to bring him 100 keys, so I could have anything and do anything I wanted. A free hand—that was what I'd asked for, and that was what he had given me. Then why did I feel like I'd been sentenced to death? Because I'd been conned. I'd just taken charge of the whole operation, that was why. Anything went wrong now, my friend Frankie would have me chopped up for dog food.

"One more thing," I said. "Don't call my godfather in Caracas. Anything you want to know, you ask me. I'll keep you posted anyway."

"I hear you, Georgie." He was smiling, but we both knew how much *that* was worth. "You're the boss."

We kicked it around a while longer, tidying up a few more details. I'd convinced myself now I needed to mount machine guns on a couple of powerboats to protect the load against rip-offs. Anybody who connected Frank with my godfather in South America would have to be pretty dumb not to guess what was going down between them. All they'd have to do is watch and wait for the right moment to make their move.

The weak spot in the route, the one time when the stuff was out of my hands and unguarded, was after we put it on board the *William Express.* If somebody knew where to look for it—and there were several people who could sell that information, including Yves Alexis and Evaristio—the best place to hit the shipment would be at sea, and at night. Out in the Gulf, they've sunk many a boat for 100 pounds of marijuana, so it wouldn't be hard to organize a boarding party for millions of dollars' worth of horse. But with a couple of powerboats, I could either sucker the hijackers by putting a decoy package on board and running the stuff in myself, or I could give the *William Express* an armed escort into Miami.

And I didn't want to rely only on Frank for protecting the stuff once we got it ashore. It was safer not to. He had met the Frenchman in Caracas, so he knew the connection. He would have paid out a million or more already to the Corsicans and for expenses, so once he got his hands on the load, he might just be tempted. Instead of handing over another two million, he would find it a lot cheaper to pay us off with a couple of slugs in the head. He was our friend and all that, but you got to think of these things.

As we were going to hold 100 keys back after cutting the load, I could buy some insurance with that. I could go to Zack Robinson and say, "You want 20 keys? At a good price? Then give me five or six of your best men." And the same with Henry Morgan. I had to get me a few checks and balances in there.

By now we were over the bridge into Brooklyn, and Frank stopped on a quiet street. We got out, and he opened up the trunk, where he kept his loose change—about $20,000 in an army duffel bag.

"You sure you don't want to wait?"

"No," I said. "I got a million things to do. You can give me the rest next trip."

"Okay." He counted out $13,000.

"Now tell me again what you're going to need," he said. "You want seventy thousand in three weeks?"

"Right. Plus another hundred for the boats and expenses."

"Plus the two hundred I got for the first load," he said. "Plus the twenty I owe you from this deal."

"Twenty-three," I said, and he laughed.

"Okay. Twenty-three. What's that? Around four hundred thousand?"

"Near enough."

He patted my cheek. "Keep in touch, Georgie," he said. "Don't let me get nervous."

"You owe *me* money," I said. "Why should *you* get nervous?"

Neither of us stopped smiling.

"Come on, Georgie," he said. "I'll drop you off at the hotel."

I picked up Anna and Orlando, and we caught the 1 a.m. flight to Miami. It was August 2.

14

Miguel Garcia owed his Corsican connection to Rolando Gonzalez-Nuñez—the same Gonzalez who, before his involuntary immigration to Venezuela, had given Matthews a start in the drug business.

Though his departure from New York had been hurried, Gonzalez had not gone empty-handed. Arriving in Caracas with two suitcases full of $100 bills, he had found a ready welcome among that city's Cuban exiles, and was soon shuttling back and forth in his white Lincoln Continental between a luxurious apartment on the Avenida Andres Bello and a hardly less comfortable office suite on the Plaza Venezuela.

Among a variety of business interests, he had done well as a broker between the Corsicans, like Antonio Simon Orsatti-Serra, also known as the Pimp, and the Cubans, like his old friend Miguel Garcia, also known as Marcello Cabot. For a consideration, Gonzalez could also effect useful introductions to past and present members of the Venezuelan government, police, and security forces.

On learning that Garcia needed a connection, Gonzalez had passed him along to Antonio Orsatti, who owned the Coco Rico Bar, a popular night spot and pickup palace on the Calle San Antonio, Sabana Grande. A naturalized Venezuelan, Orsatti was a forty-nine-year-old native of Porto-Vecchio who had arrived, via Marseilles, during the great Corsican invasion of South America in the sixties. Like Gonzalez, he had done well in his cover business and even better behind it—as a procurer, and as agent for several leading heroin exporters.

But Orsatti was not particularly impressed by Marcello Cabot, seeing him (quite rightly) as more of a freelance adventurer than as a sober businessman of the preferred Italian sort. It was partly to improve his credit rating, therefore, that Garcia agreed to Frank

Matthews's descent on the city soon after his own arrival there, booking him into the Hotel Club Americana from July 7 to 10. But the main reason for Matthews's visit was that Garcia needed $100,000 to pay for the DC-3 he was buying through Miguel Sanz.

Sanz was another of Gonzalez's useful contacts. A former officer of DISIP, the Venezuelan secret police, he was the local equivalent of Ricardo Morales—a heavy enforcer with government connections who survived, even prospered, by carefully balancing the shadiness of his private deals against his usefulness to the authorities. Garcia had quickly recognized that Sanz held the key to all the logistical backup required in Venezuela. Besides providing a plane and crew for the onward journey to Haiti, he could also arrange for the courier bringing the stuff in from Marseilles to avoid the usual customs inspection at Maiquetía Airport. Sanz would simply relieve the courier of his baggage-claim stubs as he got off the plane and walk the load through himself. He knew the right people out there. As part of the same service, he would also take charge of security for the shipment for as long as it remained in Venezuela.

If Frank Matthews was needed to reassure Orsatti, therefore, then Sanz was needed to reassure Frank Matthews.

So was Joseph Jules Gabriel Sereni, a plumply handsome twenty-nine-year-old Corsican from Sartène, whom Orsatti had introduced to Garcia as a possible courier.

Sereni had first appeared in Caracas at the end of 1970. A much traveled young man with vague aspirations to a career as a nightclub and television entertainer, he had managed to live quite well in Venezuela with no visible means of support. Though holding a foreigner's Cedula of Identification, he showed no signs of settling down there. He had been back to France at least once, ostensibly to see his girlfriend and family, and he was perfectly willing to go again, as Garcia discovered during dinner at the Hotel Tamanaco one evening, when he offered Sereni $10,000 to take care of a little errand for him in Marseilles. On July 6, Sereni renewed his passport at the French Embassy.

When Matthews arrived on the following day, therefore, he had nothing to do but unload his money, which he did with an abandon that Orsatti, Sanz, and Sereni found most gratifying. Garcia had taken care of everything. Matthews had merely to admire the efficiency of the Corsicans and the elegance of the delivery arrangements before taking to his bed in Suite 1385 with a week's supply of women (from Orsatti) and high-grade cocaine (from Gonzalez). When Garcia dug him out eventually to put him on a plane back to New York, Matthews left with the distinct impression that the shipment would be on the move in a matter of days—knowing, indeed, that Sereni was leaving for Paris on the eleventh.

Sereni's mission, however, was simply to activate the Corsican machinery and report back in person to Garcia, who knew as well as anyone, except Matthews, that no merchandise would leave France until it was paid for. Nor had Garcia told Matthews that the initial order would be for 20 kilos only, priced at $5,000 a kilo, f.o.b. Marseilles. If all went smoothly, he intended to follow this up with a further order for 100 kilos for delivery in September.

No sooner had Matthews arrived back in New York than he started telling everyone about his trip, including Group 12's wiretap crew. Gerard Miller was particularly interested to hear about it, because although he knew Matthews had been away, nobody had known where.

On the very day he returned, they listened in on a call between Matthews and his friend Sheila Frazier, the actress, who had just finished making *Superfly*, a film which many street people took to be about Matthews, and in which Frazier played the female lead.

"You one of those gangster man's wife?" he asked, after she had explained what the movie was about.

"Well, you see, I'm like—I'm very much against all that," she said. "I'm pretty much sheltered from this business, and whatnot."

"Oh."

"But never mind that. What you been doing? Where you been at?"

"I just come back from South America today," he said.

"Oh, you did? Did you go to Rio?"

"No, I went to Caracas."

"Caracas?"

"Uh-huh."

"Oh, so you stayed there?"

"Uh-huh. I stayed a couple of days down there. Yeah, I just walked in the house. Ain't been asleep all goddamn night."

"Well, you mean you just got back? Like today?"

"Right. Yeah. I just walked through the door."

It was obvious that Matthews's trip was connected in some way with the call he had made to Marcello Cabot in Caracas a few days before. And thanks to Cabot's eve-of-departure escapade at the wheel of a white Pontiac in Miami, Miller now knew him to be Miguel Garcia, a known narcotics wholesaler. Putting one and one together, he smelled a deal in the wind that BNDD agents in Miami and Caracas ought to know about.

As Matthews had flown in that day, it was also fairly simple to trace his movements back. Routine inquiries showed that he had returned on Pan Am Flight 218 to Kennedy Airport, and that a blond German stewardess remembered him. He had pinched her bottom.

"What do you do?" she asked him, trying to put their relationship on a more intellectual plane.

"I'm in the movies," he said. "Hard-core. You want a part in my next picture?"

"No, really," she said. "I'd like to know."

"Well, if you must know," he said, "I'm a big-time dope dealer." And they both laughed.

Other stewardesses had taken him more seriously. He employed several who worked for domestic airlines to carry packages of drugs around the country, paying them up to $4,000 a drop. To make a delivery in Atlanta, for example, he would arrange for the load to be stashed in a luggage locker at the appropriate New York airport, and for the key to be given to a stewardess flying that route. On reporting for duty, she would pick up the stuff, packed usually in one of her airline's flight bags, and leave it in another luggage locker at the Atlanta airport upon arrival. All that then remained was for her to pass the key to her Atlanta contact at the first convenient opportunity.

Oddly enough, although Matthews booked his flight back from Caracas as Frankie McNeal (his mother's maiden name) and filled out his U.S. Customs Declaration in the same way, he traveled on a legitimate passport in the name of Frank Larry Matthews, and no one apparently noticed the discrepancy. BNDD agents in Caracas, acting on Miller's inquiry, discovered that he had stayed at the Club Americana as McNeal also, and that Cabot had been registered there at the same time. Though they were unable to find out what the two had been up to, as a matter of courtesy they informed the Policia Técnica Judicial, the Venezuelan federal police, of Cabot's true identity and record.

Miller still had nothing useful on Mr. G., however. The Miami number he had left with Matthews's answering service was listed to a George Ramos, which accounted for the G, but he had no criminal record—not under that name, at least—and BNDD, Miami, could find no reference to him in its intelligence files. Short of a photograph or a positive eyewitness identification, there was no way of knowing whether they had seen him or not, whether he was one of the unknown males whom Matthews had met while under surveillance.

Nor was there any sure way of knowing whether the South American trip and Mr. G. were even relevant to the investigation or just two more of many lines of inquiry that had started out promising and led nowhere. For the time being, Miller and Callahan preferred to press their attack on surer ground. They subpoenaed Mickey Beckwith to appear before the grand jury, and were subsequently intrigued to overhear a telephone conversation between him and Matthews in which they discussed the advisability of Beckwith leaving town for a couple of months.

In fact, he did leave town with Matthews and John Darby in July to go to the Quarry *v.* Ali fight in Las Vegas, where Matthews as usual entertained a party of major dealers at the Sands. And, instead of returning with them afterwards, Beckwith went on to Los Angeles, where he moved into the Century Plaza Hotel, with the evident intention of staying for some time.

Though it would have been a simple matter for Callahan, Sheerin, and Miller to have brought him back, there were several sound reasons for letting him stay. One was Beckwith's obvious interest in expanding the organization's connections on the West Coast, where Mexican brown heroin was not hard to find, and another was the note of distrust, sometimes almost of hostility, that had crept into relations between Beckwith and Matthews. They had started out more or less as partners, but now Beckwith plainly resented Matthews's total dominance of the business, and had turned awkward, secretive, and possibly disloyal, treating some of the deals he made as though they were personal, when they were clearly meant to be with the organization. From the telephone discussions that Group 12 overheard, Matthews was not yet ready to take issue with his old friend over this, but his impatience was very evident. Beckwith's absence might well reinforce the growing sense of alienation and grievance between them, and perhaps soften him up as a potential witness.

A third good reason for leaving him in California was that it made life a little easier for Group 12, who were trying to find out what was going on in Beckwith's place at 101 East 56th Street, in Brooklyn. That Beckwith should still be operating at all was remarkable enough, after appearing before one grand jury and being summoned to another; somehow they had to see inside without disturbing the rats' nest. With luck, a well-timed raid might produce enough physical evidence to convict Beckwith and, with the prospect of fifteen years at least in a federal penitentiary, turn him finally against Matthews.

A badly timed raid, on the other hand, could easily produce nothing. It might also reunite Matthews with Beckwith, out of a sense of common danger, put their whole organization on its guard, and cost Group 12 a year's work.

In these delicate circumstances, the J & R Paint Co. was founded by Sergeant Jack Rawald and Roger Garay.

Discreet observations by ODALE's Detective Bramble and latterly by Group 12 had established that the mill—if there was one—occupied the first floor of the detached three-story building. There was no possibility of getting close enough to see through the windows facing the street, even if their blinds were *not* permanently drawn; a fenced-off basement area with a tree saw to that. But there were three more windows, heavily barred, along the side of the house at first-floor level, and these looked out on an alleyway separating the building from its three-story neighbor. Although the alley was fenced off from the street by iron railings, and a basement area again made it impossible to reach the windows without a ladder, there was at least a chance of climbing up to look in without at once being spotted by everyone on the block. And the best time to do it would be early in the morning, when not only were there fewer people about, but the sun was at the right angle to light up the interior.

The question was, who might legitimately be up a ladder against the wall of an apartment house peering in through the window shortly after sunrise?

On the appointed day, a battered old station wagon bearing the sign of the J & R Paint Co. on its side and an assortment of ladders on its roof turned onto the block from Linden Boulevard at about 6 a.m. and parked a few yards short of Number 101. The two men who got out in paint-splattered overalls unloaded their gear quickly and quietly, as any considerate workmen might be expected to do so early in the morning, lifted it over the railings into the alley, and were both off the street in a matter of seconds.

The story of what happened next varies in detail, according to which member of the Police Department tells it, but most seem to agree that the two men then propped a ladder against the wall of 101 and that Garay started up it from the basement area toward one of the three first-floor windows, carrying a paint can in one hand and a brush in the other. On reaching it, he realized that once again they had gone to a lot of trouble for nothing. Through the bars, all he could see was a sheet of plywood nailed to the window frame from the inside. The other two windows had been similarly boarded up.

As he looked down and around to signal the bad news to Rawald, he noticed a man leaning on the railings, watching him.

They stared at each other for a moment. Then Garay nodded, and briskly plunged his brush into the paint can. It came out bright yellow, and he hesitated.

"Goddammit, Jack," he called out. "I know this ain't right. Can't be. You sure we got the right house? Take another look at that work sheet."

The sergeant, who had seen the man, too, fumbled in his overalls and pulled out a piece of paper, which he pretended to scrutinize closely.

"Well, I don't know," he said. "I guess it could be a seven."

"You mean, it could be one-oh-seven?"

"No. I mean it could be seven-oh-one."

"Oh, shit," said Garay. He shoved the brush back in the can and made his way down the ladder, shaking his head.

Two minutes after this pantomime, they drove off the block with their equipment, and the J & R Paint Co. went into liquidation.

It was now, in the month of July, that the East Coast's heroin shortage finally dipped to panic level. On the fifth, two days before Matthews flew to Caracas to spur delivery of the 100 kilos Garcia had promised him, Myles J. Ambrose, director of ODALE and President Nixon's commander in the drug war, announced the interdiction of the enemy's supply lines. In consequence, he said, "there has been a continuing decline in the quality of heroin, and there also has been a rise in the price of it."

This was confirmed by Nat Elder in a telephone conversation with John Darby on July 15. After talking about "Old Hairy Face" Beckwith, who was still in Los Angeles, and their Baltimore dealer, Liddy Jones, who had recently escaped from jail, they turned their attention to the situation in New York.

"How's everything?" asked Darby.

"Man, man, there ain't nothing," sighed Elder.

On the eighteenth, not to be outdone by ODALE, the Bureau of Narcotics and Dangerous Drugs published comprehensive statistics of drug seizures in the twelve months to June 30, and ten days later the crisis became official when *The New York Times* reported that nearly 400 kilos of heroin had been intercepted in the East during the previous year.

For Matthews, his colleagues, and his competitors in the drug business, however, this did not necessarily mean that all of it had been lost, although it certainly meant that they would have to pay for it twice. Since 1969, substantial quantities of heroin confiscated by the New York Police Department and signed in by the Property Clerk at the Department's warehouse on Broome Street had been quietly signed out again by detectives who hated to see it go to waste. Before the leak was discovered in December 1972, they sold about 180 kilos back to the trade, often to the same importers and wholesalers who had handled the stuff in the first place.

Though Beckwith bought substantial amounts of it for Matthews, he never dealt directly with the detectives concerned, however. They would sell only to the Mob, whom they felt they could trust not to presume too far on a business relationship. Indeed, the whole operation had an Italian flavor. The 180 kilos were signed out on nine vouchers, five of them bearing the name of Detective Joseph Nunziatta, a fifteen-year veteran. Variations in the signatures led later to the suggestion that they might have been forged, but by then it was too late to put them to the test, because Nunziatta had been found dead in his car, an apparent suicide, in the Greenpoint section of Brooklyn.

On the day of his death, he had had an appointment to see U.S. Attorney Whitney North Seymour, Jr., who was offering him immunity from prosecution in return for his cooperation in an investigation of corruption among narcotics agents and police officers. A few hours before the interview, Nunziatta apparently drove out to Greenpoint, wound up the windows, and shot himself in the left side of the chest with his .38 caliber service revolver.

Although his widow claimed later that someone else had done the shooting, a three-page, handwritten note was found in the trunk of his car, which said that he had been driven to suicide by the actions of others, unnamed. Among those questioned after his death were Sergeant Frank King—later described by Special Prosecutor Maurice Nadjari as the "prime suspect" in the theft of the 180 kilos, although no one has ever been charged with it—and Nunziatta's friend, Detective Edward R. Egan, of "French Connection" fame. Nunziatta had actually played a bit part in the movie made from Robin Moore's book, before being assigned to the newly created New York Joint Task Force in June 1971.

A hundred and eighty kilos, however, was like a planeload of rice in an Indian famine. As far as Matthews was concerned, with the federal government on his tail and the Garcia–Ramos connection as the one bright hope in the supply situation, it was time to start thinking seriously about the future.

He was enormously wealthy—not even he could tell exactly how much he was worth—but every cent was at risk, tied up in the organization as working capital. If he had been forced to leave without notice, literally on the spur of the moment, all he could have taken with him was the cash he had on hand, and that might have been as little as the $20,000 he kept in the trunk of his car. Indeed, it was not hard to imagine circumstances in which he might have been compelled to leave with nothing at all, except for the clothes he stood up in, and there was no guarantee that his people would be able, or even willing, to finance him once he had gone. The organization, and with it his money, would pass automatically to those left behind, who would make it their own.

On the advice of Don Andrews, his Mob-appointed financial consultant, Matthews began to squeeze the operation for cash, no longer with a view to reinvestment in the business, but for the acquisition of real property and the build-up of capital funds overseas. Outwardly, nobody noticed much difference. He still went to Las Vegas every few weeks to launder his money through the casinos, and there was always enough on hand to cover a buy, but before very long he was exporting the profits of his organization at the rate of a million dollars a month.

If the business had been running at its normal, pre-panic level, this apparent drop in the cash flow might soon have been obvious, but in the summer of 1972 the effect was masked not only by a lower cash requirement—there was less stuff around to buy—but also by the higher profits being earned on a sellers' market by such merchandise as he *did* lay hands on. The only one of his immediate associates to notice a brief shortage of cash was George Ramos, and he thought nothing of it. He was preoccupied with plans for bringing in the 100 kilos, and with the urgent necessity for a conference with his godfather, who had just flown into San Juan, Puerto Rico, from Caracas.

Following Gerard Miller's inquiries about Garcia, alias Cabot, and George Ramos, the BNDD office in Miami had been taking a routine look into their affairs to see if a case could be developed against either of them independent of the Matthews investigation, which was out of their region and therefore of little direct interest.

Nobody in Miami could tell them much about Ramos, except that he had just bought a $7,000 Corvette, paying for it with the big money he was making as a courier for a guy known as Scarface. But when Scarface was identified as Garcia, it was enough to put all of BNDD's agents in the Caribbean on full alert, because a lot was known about *him*. If Garcia was active, sending drugs to New York, then his links with Frank Matthews and his association in Venezuela with Rolando Gonzalez suggested the possibility of a very big case, indeed.

On July 28, a Puerto Rican agent lounging around San Juan Airport noticed a rather sinister-looking figure with a scarred face get off the plane from Caracas. He reported this to Don Harper, special agent in charge of the local BNDD office, who in turn checked with Miami.

Within the hour, reinforcements were on the way from the

mainland with orders to keep Marcello Cabot under surveillance around the clock. Picking up his trail at the Hotel Americana, Isla Verde, they watched him check out next morning with Barbara Maisonet and followed his cab to the Caribe Hilton, where the two of them moved into Room 606. On learning from the desk clerk that Cabot was planning to stay for at least a week, Harper ordered a command post to be set up in the hotel.

On August 1, two middle-aged men checked into the hotel and reported to Cabot. Their names were Marcello Lacour and Juan Serra, and they had just flown in from Caracas, where inquiries revealed that they both held pilot's licenses.

And on August 3, Harper learned that Cabot had arranged to meet George Ramos that night at the airport, and advised Miami accordingly.

15

The day after I got back to Miami with Anna and Orlando, Pedro Diaz called from Caracas to say that he would be in Haiti in three or four days with another load. A couple of hours later, around noon, my godfather called from Puerto Rico.

"I just talked to Pedro," he said. "You coming over?"

"Right," I said. "I'm on the nine o'clock Eastern flight."

"Fine," he said. "I'll pick you up at the airport. And don't forget to go see Barbarito."

Barbarito sold me a duck, a live duck. This was *abre camino*, to open the road, before traveling.

"Take the duck and buy a melon," he said. "Then go with them both to the ocean. When you get there, break open the melon in front of the duck. You're giving him food, an opportunity to eat if he's hungry. Then let him go and watch his flight. The faster and farther he flies away, the safer your journey will be. He'll clear the way for you."

So I did like he told me, and that son of a bitch really hauled ass over the water. I watched him till he was out of sight and then went home to wait for Orlando, who was going to drive out to the airport with Anna to see me off.

I got in to San Juan around eleven o'clock, and my godfather was there to meet me with Rudi Cutty Sark. We called him that because that's what he handled—he was a sales representative—but his real name was Rudolph Ostheimer.

He should have been in jukeboxes. We hit a few bars along Ashford Avenue, and there was no scotch to be had but Cutty Sark. No J & B. No Ballantine's.

"What the hell *is* this?" my godfather said. "You don't let these people sell nothing else?"

He just cracked a smile. "Well," he said, "they only carry quality stuff. What can I tell you?"

Finally we got to his apartment in Isla Verde, and he had a couple of girls up there, which made my godfather happy. Then Willie Moto came by.

"Hey, Willie. How's it going, man? You doing better now?"

"Shit," he said. "I don't know, man. About the same, I guess. There just ain't nothing here. Business is flat on its ass."

"Well, that's how it is when the spirits ain't with you," my godfather said. "What you had done in Miami is good, but you got to keep up with it."

"Yeah, Georgie told me. But I ain't going to wrestle no more goddamn sheep. That's *out*."

"How about a duck?" I said.

He looked at me.

"Yeah, a duck is good," my godfather said. "Go buy a duck. We'll take him to the ocean, and then you just cut him loose."

"Yeah?" That was better. "Okay. I'll buy a duck."

"Yeah. That should do it. Now how about seeing if you can cop us a little coke?"

"You got it, man," he said. He was really grateful. "You want to take a ride with me, Georgie?"

So we went and ran around a few bars until Willie finally connected for a few grams of coke. When we got back to the apartment, I put a bit of it on the back of my hand, and it was poison.

"How can you take that goddamn shit?" I said, as they all dug in.

"Like this," said my godfather, and he snorted up a pile of it on the end of his door key.

I left them to it and went and poured myself a Cutty Sark. After a while, he joined me on the balcony.

"So how's it going?" I said.

"Just fine. The Frenchman's standing by to go pick up the load. It's all working out fine."

"Yeah. Well, I was up there in New York—I took Frankie six keys—and he tells me you bought a goddamn airplane."

"Yeah, that's right. How about that?"

"And he wants to buy a hotel or something? You been up to your shit again, you two? Don't we got enough headaches?"

"Listen, I got it all down pat," he said. "There's no problem. I got a couple of pilots here with me, and tomorrow we'll go over the whole thing."

"Yeah, well, that's good. But what did you bring the pilots *here* for? We could have talked to them in Caracas."

He was only half listening to me. He kept looking along the balcony like he expected to see somebody.

"They're coming to Haiti with us," he said. "We got to pick a location for the drop."

"What drop?" I said, but he didn't hear me. All of a sudden, he had jumped backward, and was brushing at himself like he'd walked into cobwebs.

"Hey, Rudi," he shouted, and he sounded real scared. "Quick. You got some cologne?"

"Cologne?" Rudi said. "Hey, what's wrong, man? Something bite you?"

"Cologne. Gimme some cologne."

"Well, I don't know, man. I got after-shave. You want after-shave?"

"Yeah, give it to me." My godfather kept brushing, trying to sweep something invisible off the balcony. "And hurry up. For Christ's sake, hurry up." He was going crazy.

Rudi took off for the bathroom, looking like he wasn't too sure which one of them was nuts, but I knew this routine because my godfather had pulled it on me several times. He'd seen something. A spirit had come by. I never saw nothing, but he generally claimed *he* did, and the answer was always perfume. Spirits don't like it. It drives them away.

By the time we got rid of the spirit, I could see we weren't going to talk no more that night, and I went back to the hotel. It was already around 2 a.m., and I was pretty tired from all the traveling I'd been doing lately.

Early next morning, Willie woke me up to go buy a duck. I told him he better not do nothing with it until he consulted the master, so we put it in the trunk of his car and drove back to the hotel to see what was happening.

All hell had broke loose. Ana Baños had flown in from Miami and caught my godfather in bed with another woman. Not Barbara, because she couldn't have said nothing about that, but one of the girls from Rudi's apartment. So Ana was having hysterics, and my godfather, who had a king-sized hangover, was getting ready to shoot her. I sent Willie downstairs to wait while I sorted it out.

Seemed my godfather hadn't sent her any money since he'd left for Venezuela. No reason why he should have, but she claimed he had promised to pay her rent. After he refused all her calls, she had come to San Juan to collect in person, and found him screwing around with some whore.

That was pretty good, coming from her, but a promise is a promise. When they both calmed down, my godfather told her to stick around until the following day and he'd give her $400. Not generous, but then again, not a bad rate for one night. She was much better-looking than the girl he'd just had, and he was always a practical man.

I stuck around, making soothing noises while he took a shower and got dressed, and then he said, "Come on, I want you to meet the pilots."

They were in the room next door: Marcello Lacour and Juan Serra. My godfather had already told me he'd found them through some big political contact of his in Caracas, so I was expecting to see a couple of sharp young professionals, but they turned out to be kind of seedy—two middle-aged guys who looked like professional losers to me.

"This here is my godson," Miguel said. "He takes over the shipment in Haiti. I want you to explain to him what we got in mind."

So they pulled out a big chart of the waters around Haiti and went into a long spiel about how the DC-3 my godfather had bought was the best thing around for this kind of job. They were going to fly the load first to Guadeloupe, then come in, wave-hopping under the radar, and drop the stuff in my lap in a flotation bag. And when they showed me where on the chart they were going to do this, I saw my lap would have to be one hundred miles off the coast out at sea. It was just Mission Impossible bullshit.

But I let them speak their piece, while my godfather listened, all proud of himself, and when they'd finished, I said, "Okay, we'll talk about this later," and took him back to his room.

"You got to be kidding," I said. "This isn't for real."

"What are you talking about?"

"This James Bond routine with the airplane. You can't be serious."

"Sure I'm serious." And now he looked it. "The deal's all set. That's how we're going to do it."

"Not with me, you're not. Drop it in my lap? I wouldn't trust those guys to shit straight in a toilet."

"They're qualified pilots," he said. "They say they can do it, they can do it."

"Then good luck to them. But what about *me?* How do *I* get out there—swim? And then swim back one hundred miles with 25 keys between my teeth? Shit. Why don't they just fly their fucking flotation bag up to New York and drop it in Central Park reservoir?"

I was really pissed off, and he could see it, so he kept his cool.

"We'll get a boat," he said. "We'll buy one here. I always had that in mind."

"We'll probably buy *two* boats," I said. "But not here. And not for that. It isn't so simple. You got to register the son of a bitch. You got to do a hundred things they can tag you with."

"Then we'll rent one in Haiti."

"No, we won't. It's the same deal. And even if we *did,* who the fuck knows how to steer the goddamn thing to some exact spot one hundred miles out in the goddamn ocean? I'm telling you, Mikey—it won't work."

"We'll pay somebody to take us out there. You know how many boat captains you could buy in Haiti for $10,000?"

"Okay. So what happens if the weather turns bad? Or the engine breaks down? Or we get there late? Or *they* do? Or they drop the stuff by the wrong goddamn boat? Tell me that."

He shook his head, but I could see I was getting at him.

"And what about these goddamn pilots and boat captains and boat-yard people and all the other guys we're letting in on this deal?" I said. "What do we do with them afterwards? Kill them? No, Mikey. Let me tell you—when I want to commit suicide, I'm going to do it the easy way."

"You really think it's that bad?" he said.

"I really think it's shit. I got to wondering when Frankie told me you guys had bought an airplane, but I never dreamed of nothing like this. I figured you were going to wait on me to get a contact with this customs guy in Port-au-Prince and then fly the plane in there while he turns his back, which is a different deal altogether. But there's no way I'm going to play any part in *this* shit. No way in hell. Unless we can get that customs contact and fly the stuff in there, the plane deal has got to go."

So he walked around the room, muttering to himself and pulling faces.

"We got $65,000 tied up in that plane," he said.

"Okay. Then sell it. And if you drop a little on the deal, so what? It ain't *your* money."

"Well, for right now, I got to get something to eat." He wasn't about to say so, but it looked like I'd won. "We're going to have to discuss this some more."

"Goddamn right—if you want *me* to have any part of it. If we can't get the customs guy in time for the first load, then I say we bring it in with mules."

"What? Twenty-five kilos? Shit, it'll take six mules with two suitcases each."

"So? Six South American tourists. Who's going to look? The coke comes in that way, don't it? It's a nice quiet way of doing business."

So when he got through grumbling, we went downstairs and had a late breakfast with Willie. After that, I made reservations for me, my godfather, and the other two jokers on the Air France flight to Haiti next morning, and we went out on the town, winding up for the evening at Rudi Cutty Sark's pad.

Around midnight, I called it a day.

"Hey, Rudi," I said. "Keep an eye on Miguel. Tonight I can't have him screwed up. We're traveling tomorrow. Early."

"Got you," he said. "Don't worry. I'll see he gets back in good shape."

As I stepped out in the hall, Willie suddenly let out a shriek like I'd caught his balls in the door. I went back inside to see what was wrong, and he grabbed hold of my jacket. His face had gone green, and he was so scared he couldn't speak.

"What the hell's the matter with you?" said my godfather.

Willie looked around without seeing nothing. "The duck," he said. "I forgot the fucking duck."

"Oh, Jesus," I said. "Willie bought a duck this morning. It's in the trunk of his car."

"Okay." My godfather smoothed down his white suit and was ready to do his *palero* bit. "You got a melon, Rudi?"

"A melon?" he said. Last night it's cologne; now it's a melon. "I don't know. Maybe."

"Well, take a look. We need food for the duck."

"Yeah?" He screwed up his face like he was in pain. "I don't know what ducks eat. Do they like Rice Krispies?"

"If you don't got a melon," my godfather said, "bring some bread. We're going to the beach."

So we all went down with the bread, and when Willie opened up the trunk, the duck was dead.

"Oh, Jesus," said my godfather, shaking his head. "That's *bad*."

Willie went down on his knees. "Look what you guys have *done* to me," he said. He was practically in tears. "Oh, my God. It's still warm. It just happened."

"You should have taken better care of it," Miguel said. "I don't know what's going to happen now."

"It's not *my* fault." The guy was brokenhearted. "There must have been something wrong with it. Oh, God, the saints will punish me. You tell me to take a duck and let it go, and now it's died on me. Oh, Jesus. I can't believe it. The spirits will kill me for this."

And maybe they did. Willie was quite a young guy, but it wasn't too long after this that he had a heart attack and died.

Anyway, the next morning I got out of bed around five-thirty and went in to wake up my godfather and Ana Baños. The night before, I'd told the pilots what time we were leaving and arranged to meet them at the gate just before the flight, but there was no sign of them out there.

"They're supposed to find me in the middle of the ocean?" I said. "They can't even find the goddamn airport."

My godfather went off, muttering under his breath, to put Ana Baños on a plane to Miami while I called the hotel. There was no answer from their room.

"Maybe they checked out," he said, when he came back.

"No. I asked the desk."

"Then try again."

Our flight was already being called. This time I made the operator stay with it until one of them answered.

"I just woke them up," I said. "They're still flat on their ass."

"So leave the sons of bitches, then," Miguel said, and he walked off. Exit two pilots.

"Okay, stay there," I told them. "Don't follow us. Stay in the hotel, and I'll see you in a couple of days."

I was careful not to say another word about it on the way over, but as we circled Duvalier Airport I pointed out to my godfather a bunch of U.S. Navy ships in the harbor.

"You still want them to fly that thing under the radar?" I said. "Or you want to trade it in for a submarine?"

He didn't say nothing, but from that moment on we both knew we were doing it with mules. And why not? The simplest way is usually the best, and we had the system going like clockwork.

"We got six keys for you," said Pedro, when we met up with him at El Rancho. "And I talked to the Doctor about upping the shipments to ten or fifteen."

"Yeah? What did he say?"

"Well, there's a little problem with the Indians, but he figures he can do something. If the money's there."

"*If?* The creep. Didn't I pay for this load up front? Didn't I? What does he want, for Christ's sake? A Dun & Bradstreet rating? Shit. The guy's got no class."

"No, but he does have the stuff. And he's here, so *you* tell him."

"Don't worry," said my godfather. "Where's he at, this son of a bitch?"

"No, take it easy—he'll do it. He's just the cautious type, that's all."

"Yeah. Me, too," I said. "But we'll get to that later. First, we got a little business to attend to."

Miguel didn't have nothing to contribute here. It was my operation now, and I figured he would soon get distracted with something else if we changed the subject. So after we wrapped the load in vinyl as usual and stapled it up securely, I went downtown with Paul-Baptiste to see about the boat.

This time, we were right on the money. The *William Express* and Yves Alexis had gotten in that morning. We picked up a few carvings at Aux Artisans before driving back to the hotel to collect the package, and Alexis carried it off in an old suitcase Pedro had brought with him.

"So who needs an airplane?" I said to my godfather. "Next time they come, these guys are going to bring 15 keys. No sweat. We'll put them on the boat, just the same as those six. So none of your bullshit. Fifteen keys, 25 keys—what's the difference? We know it works, so why fuck around?"

He didn't say I was right. He wouldn't give me the satisfaction. "You don't got your 15 keys yet," he said.

"Want to bet? I'm going to talk to Albino right now."

I didn't know what I would say, but this was one of those times when I couldn't be beat. I guess Cosmo Lacroix was right in there swinging, because Albino Perez didn't hardly put up a fight.

"Look, I got a millionaire in the United States," I said. "A big man. He don't have time for no six or seven keys. We got the money. Bring me fifteen next time and I'll give you the sixty, seventy thousand, cash on the nail. Whatever's necessary, okay? So what's it to be? If you can't handle it, then I got to look elsewhere."

"No, no," Albino said. "I'll talk it over with my people. Maybe we can help you."

"No maybes, Albino. I want fifteen next time. But I'll settle for ten."

He looked at Medina, and they both shrugged.

"Okay," he said. "Have the money. I'll see what I can do."

That night we went looking for Charles, but he was still out in the islands some place, and that clinched it. No customs contact, no plane.

"Nothing more I can do here," I told my godfather. "When we know for sure the shipment's on the way, I'll come back over with Luis the Junkman and set it all up. But for right now I got to go see a man about a couple of powerboats."

"You want to get rid of the pilots?" he said. "You going back to Puerto Rico?"

"My pleasure," I said. "But I only got four, five hundred dollars on me. You better give me some money."

"If you ain't got enough, get hold of Rudi and tell him to lend you a few hundred. Or Willie. He thinks he's got 10 keys coming."

"Well, don't he?"

"What, Willie? Where's *he* going to get three hundred thousand from?"

"We could front him the stuff."

"After he killed the fucking duck?"

Poor Willie. I called him from Port-au-Prince, and he was so anxious to get lucky, he even came out to the airport to meet me with the five hundred I figured I would need to pay the hotel bill for those jokers, the pilots.

"You didn't miss nothing," I told them. "You're on stand-by. Check in with my godfather when you get to Caracas."

He could tell them the bad news. So then Willie drove me back to the airport, and I hopped the first plane out to Miami.

With a few days to spare now before the *William Express* came in, I planned to take Anna up to Fort Lauderdale to try out the Formulas, and if they looked good, to get the boat yard started on fitting the long-range tanks. I also had a few things to work out with Orlando and Luis the Junkman. But I was still in bed the next morning when my godfather called from San Juan.

"Hey, listen," he said. "Get your shit together. We're going to take a little trip down South."

I looked at Anna and came close to giving him an argument, but I'd never been to Caracas, and I figured that was what he had in mind. And after the routine with the airplane, it suddenly didn't seem like such a bad idea to check the whole deal through. So I called Orlando over to the house and gave him a couple of hundred to get the cut ready for the six keys we had coming. I told him if I wasn't back to call Evaristio around the tenth, and if the load had come in, to stash it and wait for me. Naturally, he wanted to know about the heroin deal, so I told him it was coming together, but I had to go check it out in Caracas. He was very impressed.

The next afternoon, I joined my godfather in Puerto Rico. With all the traveling I was doing, *I* was the one who should have bought a plane. And maybe I would just *do* that, once this thing was over. It would come in handy, living in Haiti.

"I've been thinking," he said. "I want you to take a look down there. I want you to meet these people. Because I'm nothing to them no more. You're the godson—the man with the big connection, and that's who they want to see."

"Yeah?" It was just his little joke, of course.

"Yeah. And you can talk to Medina and Diaz as well—get your shit straight with them."

"Okay."

"It was Frankie did it," he said. "He talked a lot about you down there. Georgie this, Georgie that. So now they figure you're the one that pulls the strings, the guy they got to deal with. The guy that fixes everything."

"Yeah?"

"Yeah. So go fix a couple of tickets to Caracas."

Just a little touch on the leash. Typical Miguel. But he meant what he'd been saying, because he came back to it on the plane next day.

"Now you watch yourself," he said. "They're going to treat you like a king. This deal means a lot to them. It's been nothing but bust, bust, bust, and they're hurting a little. So right now they need us."

"Us or Frank?"

"To them, it's the same. Frank's the biggest buyer they're going to see. There ain't too many around like him no more, and they think we got him in our pocket."

"Sounds like we're in for a hell of a good time."

"Right. Anything you want, they got," he said. "King-size. But don't let that fool you. They'll be watching. Give them something to use, and they'll use it. It's a hard game, and no love lost."

"Then we'll beat them at it."

Above the customs area in the terminal building at Maiquetía Airport is a glassed-in enclosure where people who have come out to meet arriving passengers can look down and spot them on their way through. I saw Pedro Diaz up there as I came in from immigration, but then there was a holdup. My godfather had lost his smallpox vaccination certificate—or so he said; I'm not sure he ever had one. Anyway, a girl took him away some place so he could show her the mark on his arm, and left me there stewing. These little fuck-ups always got to me. There was no need for them. If you're in business, do it right, or don't do it at all.

A couple of minutes later, he was back, grinning all over his face like he had put one over on me. I figured he had shown her a $20 bill as well as the mark.

"Well?" he said, seeing I was annoyed. "I'm vaccinated, ain't I?"

"Yeah, you're vaccinated. She'll remember *you* all right."

He didn't care, and again I got that sinking feeling. This was positively my last time out with these guys.

Then Pedro latched on to us, and now the news was all good.

"Hey, we're going to have a ball, Georgie," he said, as we reached downtown. "You and me, we're going to stand this place on its ear. Starting right now." And he parked outside the first of about a dozen bars we hit that day.

"Yeah?" I said. "You mean, we got something to celebrate?" For me this was still a business trip, although that would soon change.

He winked, and as soon as we sat down inside, he leaned across the table.

"You're getting your 15 keys, Georgie," he said. "I got it squared away for you."

"How much?"

"Seventy thousand."

I pretended to think about it; my godfather was watching. "Okay," I said. "It's a little high, but that's on delivery, right?"

Now Pedro pretended to hesitate. "Yeah, I guess so. In Haiti. Three weeks."

"You're a good man, Pedro." As far as I was concerned, this was now a vacation. "That's how I like to do business."

A few bars later, we reached the Coco Rico.

"This is it," said my godfather. "The Corsican owns it—Antonio Orsatti."

"The Pimp?"

"Yeah, but don't call him that. He's kind of sensitive."

Miguel made an entrance like Little Caesar, and the flunkies came running. Then *I* got the treatment, with the bowing and smiling and washing of hands. It was just like Frank said. Dark, expensive, and full of good-looking broads—a high-class meat market.

Orsatti turned out to be a stocky, black-haired guy in his forties, who spoke Spanish with what I guess was a French accent. He was a quiet man—especially next to my godfather—but he had the same kind of eyes, and when he said something, people listened. Even Miguel.

"We heard a lot about you, Georgie," he said. "For a young man, you got plenty responsibility on your shoulders."

"Well, I heard quite a bit about you, too," I said. "And from what Frank tells me, you're making it real easy for us, so I guess I'll get by."

"Yeah, I got a feeling you will at that," he said, and he led us to a table. Pedro started to follow, but when my godfather gave him a look, he decided to stay at the bar.

"Well, the wheels are turning," Orsatti said, after we'd given our orders. "Sereni's all set, and things look good. We should have the first shipment of 25 kilos here inside two weeks."

"Fine," I said. "Frank will be happy to hear that. I got $200,000 cash waiting to cover it as soon as you say the word."

"Good, good. But we're not sure yet about the arrangements for payment. We may want the money in France, we may want it here. I'll let you know about that."

I looked at Miguel. "The deal was payment on delivery. That's what Frank told me."

"Right," he said, and turned on Orsatti. "What's the idea? Why the switch?"

"No switch." Orsatti smiled, and turned out his hands. "Sereni is working for you, no? So you take delivery when he does—in Paris or Marseilles. But it's not certain. Maybe we'll save you the trip and take the money here, I don't know. This I must clarify."

"Yeah, do that," I said. I didn't mind the idea of a trip to France, but the risks were too high. "We're paying him, but Sereni's *your* man—he's one of your people. If *you* can't trust him to get the stuff here, why the hell should we?"

Orsatti laughed. "Now I know why we hear so much about the godson," he said. "But don't worry. It's a detail. A technicality. After the 25 comes another 75, maybe 100 kilos three weeks later, so why should we argue about where the money is paid?"

"Right," I said. "I don't give a damn, so long as it's in Caracas."

Orsatti's smile shrunk a little bit, so my godfather jumped in.

"Yeah, well, I'll take care of that," he said. "We got a lot to discuss, but let's get acquainted first. Look at Pedro. He's doing all right."

And he was. He had three or four of the best-looking girls around him I ever seen in a joint like that.

"Compliments of the management," said Orsatti.

"Well, I don't know," I said. "The kid looks in trouble. I better go help him out."

I'd made my point, and there was no sense getting in a hassle with the guy. Like he said, my godfather would take care of it. So I joined Pedro at the bar, and it took till three in the morning to get him free from the clutches of them girls so he could drive me to the hotel. By this time, I didn't know where my godfather was, and I didn't much care. We were both staying at the Club Americana, so I figured we'd connect there sooner or later.

It was later. Two days later, in the afternoon. Pedro was waiting for me while I finished getting dressed to take off again, and my godfather phoned through from his room.

"Hey, where the hell have you been?" he said.

"Oh, around."

"Yeah. Several times, from what they tell me. So just get your ass over here. There's somebody I want you to meet."

He was a big guy with purple lips. A strong man—the kind of muscle you don't ever want to have against you because there's brains behind it. He had a big cigar between his teeth, and an even bigger .45 automatic stuffed in his waistband, under his coat.

"Say hello to Miguel Sanz," said my godfather. "This is Georgie."

"Yeah, the godson." Sanz wrapped up my hand in his, and gave me a friendly bang on the arm with the other one. "The guy who don't like airplanes."

That I didn't get, and I looked at my godfather.

"Miguel got us the DC-3," he explained. "And the pilots."

"Oh, yeah?" I said. "My godfather tell you what happened?"

"He told me. And now he says he wants his money back. For the plane."

"Well, it ain't no use to us—right, Georgie?"

"Not without that customs contact in Haiti," I said. "I'm not going to spend the rest of my life cruising around the Caribbean looking for no goddamn flotation bag."

"Well, it ain't going to be so easy to find a buyer neither." Sanz wasn't pleased about it, and I couldn't see why—unless he was going to lose his commission on the deal.

"What do we have to do that for?" my godfather wanted to know. "We just cancel the deal, that's all. You can fix it. This guy can fix anything," he said, turning to me. "No hassle with customs here, boy. Miguel knows everybody out at Maiquetía. He'll just pick up Sereni's bags himself and walk them right out of there."

"Hey, that's fantastic," I said.

"Yeah, well, he was a big man in the last government—right, Miguel? Knows everybody."

"Just a cop, Mikey. I was just a cop."

I looked at my godfather and sighed. I had to believe he knew what he was doing, but I wished he wouldn't do it. It was like Orlando with Ricardo Morales. Be friendly? Yes. Do business? No. You know where you are with crooks. *They* can't work both sides of the fence, but cops do it all the time.

The phone rang, and I was nearest.

"Red or green?" a voice said.

"Huh?"

"That Mikey?"

"Just a minute." I put my hand over the mouthpiece. "Some guy wants to know, red or green?"

"Tell him green," said Sanz, and my godfather nodded.

So I told the guy, "Green," and he hung up.

"What does *that* mean?" I said.

"It means you're not going to meet Sereni," my godfather said. "He's on his way."

"Then I better be moving on, too. I still got a lot to do."

"No sweat," said Sanz. "We'll hold the stuff here till you're ready."

"Sure."

There was nothing I could put my finger on, but I felt uneasy. I had another talk later with Orsatti, who said again he didn't see no problem about the money, and when my godfather told me he had his mules all picked out to carry the stuff over to Haiti, there was no more excuse for hanging around.

"Clear up the payment thing," I said to him, "and it looks like you got your end of this deal squared away. Now I'm going to go and take care of the rest of it."

"Okay," he said. "And good luck. Next time I see you, we'll be millionaires."

"Yeah, sure."

Pedro drove me out to the airport. We were good friends now, and looking forward to meeting again in about three weeks when he brought the 15 keys of cocaine to Haiti. If anything went wrong with the heroin deal, I was still going to be able to pay the rent.

Half an hour after getting back to Miami, I wasn't so sure. Anna wasn't home—I hadn't told nobody I was coming—and when I called Orlando to find out what had happened to the six keys due in on the *William Express*, I couldn't raise him either. So I phoned Evaristio.

"Hey, I'm glad you called," he said. "Meet me over at the shopping center in half an hour. By Zayres. We got problems."

"Oh, Jesus," I said. "I hardly got my foot in the door. What the hell is it now?"

"I'll tell you when I see you." And he hung up.

He'd sounded pretty nervous, so I turned right around and went out again. He didn't keep me waiting, either. I took the car, but I was only a couple of minutes ahead of him. When he saw me, he jerked his head toward the parking lot, and we went for a little walk.

"We got hit," he said.

My guts turned to stone. "Who got hit? What are you talking about?"

"The boat got in yesterday, and it got hit by twenty or thirty customs men and federal agents. They were all over it."

"Did they find the stuff?"

"No. They're still around, but I checked. They never found it."

I took a deep breath. No sense getting mad with the guy. "Then we didn't get hit, did we? In fact, we don't even know they were looking for the stuff. It could have been something else."

"I never see them do that before," he said. "Not so many of them. And they had pictures. They were showing pictures to the crew."

"Pictures?" It sounded political to me. Something was always happening around the Antillean Line. "What kind of pictures?"

"I don't know. I didn't see. Just the crew."

"Okay." If they hadn't found the stuff, there was nothing to worry about. "What do you want to do?"

"Well, I'll try and get it off tonight," he said. "Call me tomorrow."

"All right, Evaristio." I hadn't expected him to say that. "But don't make no hectic moves, okay? If it's got to go, let it go. We'll take it off next time around. Two weeks don't matter. We got to protect the route, that's the main thing."

"Okay, Georgie." And he went back to work feeling better.

The idea didn't do much for *me*, though. With everything else up in the air, the one thing I didn't want was a question mark against the *William Express*. I called Evaristio next day. The agents were still around, he said. He couldn't do nothing. It didn't sound like he'd tried very hard, but I let it go, and took a run by his house the day after that.

"Listen, I'm sorry," he said. "The boat's gone."

"With the stuff on board?"

"Yeah. They were watching the dock day and night."

"Okay. No sweat. I'm glad you didn't try nothing stupid. We'll get it next time."

"Sure, Georgie—you bet. You know what happened? They found 25 pounds of marijuana."

"Well, that's it, then." Suddenly I loved the man. "That's great. That'll blow the scare away."

"Yeah, right." Only he didn't share my enthusiasm. "And you

remember the pictures I told you about? The ones they were showing the crew?"

"Yeah?" Now for the bad news. He couldn't look me in the eye.

"They were *your* pictures, Georgie. Mikey's, too."

My brain stopped working for a second.

"Pictures of *me?*" That couldn't be right.

"Yeah. Yves saw them. Didn't say nothing, of course—he's a good kid. But it was you all right."

I shook my head. "No. Couldn't be. They don't *have* my picture. I never been arrested."

"They weren't mug shots, Georgie. Yves says they were like snapshots. And he thinks they were taken in Haiti. He's not sure, but that's what it looked like to him."

"Okay, okay. Shut up a minute."

I stood looking out the window and made myself think. Somebody takes my picture in Haiti. Right after that, they hit the boat. Put them together, it looks bad.

But why put them together? Miguel pulls down the heat and leaves. He turns up in Caracas, still making a noise, so naturally they watch to see who he meets. That takes care of the pictures.

Now what about the boat? They get a tip about grass coming in, and they find it. They know the boat stopped in Haiti while me and Miguel were there, so they flash our pictures at the crew.

Coincidence? Could be. In any case, what have they got? Nothing. They didn't find the load, and Yves Alexis kept his mouth shut. They're just fishing.

"Okay," I said. "It don't mean a thing. They spotted Miguel and me in Haiti and figured the grass was ours. Now they know different."

"Sure. That's it." He wanted to believe more than I did. It was pathetic. "That's got to be it."

"Right. So no harm done. And a good thing it happened on *this* trip, because now we got a really big deal coming down."

"Yeah, Mike told me," he said. "Last time I saw him, he said I'd make enough to retire."

"Yeah. Me, too. And, hopefully, it's just around the corner."

The next night, me and Anna drove over to Orlando's place and found him snorting coke with Ricardo Morales.

"Hi, Ricardo." I wasn't all that pleased to see him there.

"Hey, Georgie," he said. "How's it going, man? Hear you've been having yourself a little bit of trouble."

"Trouble? Me?" I looked Orlando straight in the eye. "You got to be kidding."

"Well, what about the cops with your picture? You don't call that trouble?"

"No." I didn't take my eyes off Orlando for a second. "Lots of people got my picture. Including my mother."

"I just thought Ricardo could find out something," Orlando said. He could see I was mad at him. "He knows a lot of big people."

Ricardo held up his hand, like he was on my side. "No, listen, Orlando—that's okay. Georgie thinks I can help him, he knows where to find me. And I'll be glad to do it."

"Yeah, thanks," I said.

"Georgie's the kind of a guy who likes to shovel his own shit," he said, "and I respect that. He's a tough kid." He took a big snort and shook his head until his cheeks flapped. "Too bad about the load, though. I hate to think of six keys of good stuff just sailing away like that, you know?"

"Uh-huh." I was still looking at Orlando. "Me and Anna figured you might want to catch a movie with us, but I see you're busy. I'll talk to you tomorrow."

"Sure, Georgie. Any time. I'll walk you to the car."

So we said goodbye to Ricardo, and Orlando came down with us.

"Look, Ricardo's a friend," he said. "Don't be like that. You can trust him the same way you trust me."

I needed Orlando, so I let him down easy. I told Anna to get in the car.

"He's *your* friend, Orlando," I said. "You want to discuss *your* business with him? Go ahead. But don't discuss mine. Not with him. Not with nobody—understand? I'm telling you."

"But Ricardo can help us."

"You want to stay in this deal? If Mikey was here, you'd be dead. Now go back to your friend, and don't tell him nothing else, for Christ's sake."

This was getting ridiculous, but that was all I could do. Orlando loved to show off. He had a big mouth, and he had breakfast nearly every day with Ricardo at Isabelita's. There was no doubt about it. The minute this deal went down, I was going to get the hell out of Miami with Anna, and just cut myself loose from all these crazy people. If Frank wanted to buy coke from me after this, he was going to have to come down to Haiti to get it.

Anyway, I now had a break from the running around, so I figured I'd lay up with Anna for a couple of days to let the dust settle. She was still bitching about the heroin, though. When I told her about the 15 keys of coke we had coming, she nearly threw a fit.

"Isn't that enough for you?" she said. "$200,000 every two weeks? Get out, Georgie. You don't need this. And it's too dangerous. You set the deal up, now let *them* do it."

"I didn't set it up yet, baby. I still got to fix things in Haiti and buy the boats."

"Well, I hope it never *gets* to Haiti," she said. "I hope they all get busted in Caracas."

I'd thought about that. With the law sniffing around, there were three points of maximum risk. One, when the shit got to Venezuela. Two, when it reached Haiti. Three, when I handed over to Frank, which I'd pretty well decided would be on the edge of Orlando, Florida. Now, if *I* was a federal agent, I said to myself, where would I make my big play? In Caracas? No. I'd let the Venezuelans take care of Miguel and the others afterwards. In Haiti? No. That was just a transit camp. They might get me and my people, but they'd have to work through the local police, same as in Venezuela. In Florida, then? Now that was something else.

No problems with extradition or nothing. All the manpower they needed. And a chance to grab off the lot—the dope, the money, the sellers, *and* the buyers.

Nothing else made sense. If we were going to get hit, it had to be in Florida. I'd convinced myself that if they *were* on to us, they would let the shipment through and go for the jackpot.

So the answer to that was to assume the worst, to go ahead as though my godfather or Frank *had* brought down the heat, and then work a fast shuffle right at the end. Once the load came ashore, we'd have to duck the surveillance and make the delivery at a place that only *I* knew about until the last moment. I wouldn't tell nobody where it would be—not my godfather, not Frank, and certainly not Orlando—until the time came to leave. And the best way to shake the surveillance, I figured, would be to play decoy—to have Frank and me lead the agents one way while the dope and the money went another.

After a little talk with Luis the Junkman and a few other guys around town, I took off with Anna in the Corvette to see the boat dealer I knew in Fort Lauderdale. If they *were* on my tail, I was pretty sure we'd spot them on the Expressway—Anna's got sharper eyes than anybody—but there was nothing. After a couple of days, we almost stopped looking. Obviously, the business with the pictures and the *William Express* had just been one of those funny things that happen now and then.

I'd been right about the Formulas, too. They were great boats—fast, handy, and with plenty of room for long-range tanks. I picked out two, told the guy to reserve them for us, and pushed on for a couple more days, spotting locations in northern Florida. Then I turned south again, with the idea of calling Frank when we got home to tell him I needed the first hundred thousand we'd talked about.

But he called me first. We'd been back about an hour, and Orlando had just come over to fill us in on what had been happening, when the phone rang. It was the operator at the Sands in Las Vegas, and she told me to hold on.

"Talk of the devil," I said to them. "It's Frank."

But it wasn't the Frank *I* knew. Something had got to him. He must have had bad news that day, or a lot of aggravation. Plus he was coked to the teeth, you could hear it.

"That you, Georgie? Where the fuck you been, man? I been calling you for days."

"Hey, listen," I said. I didn't go for that tone. "I got a lot on my plate, man. Take it easy."

"Take it easy, *shit*. You guys are fucking me around again. You're just fucking around with my money like last time. And I ain't going to stand for it."

"Nobody's fucking you around, Frank," I said, very cold. "We got people in four goddamn countries working on this deal. You got to have patience. Takes time."

"Time? What you mean, time? You had enough fucking time to grow the fucking poppies yourself, so don't hand me *that* shit. Where's the fucking load, man? Just tell me where it's at. That's all I want to hear from you cocksuckers."

I couldn't believe it. My temper just swelled up and choked me.

"You hear me, boy?"

"It's on the way." That was all I could get out.

"Bullshit." His voice had gone high, like a woman's. "I told you—don't give me no bullshit. I heard that from Mikey six weeks ago, that son of a bitch. Now I'm telling you, man. You stop fucking around with me. You get on this right now, or I'll come down there and kick your mother-fucking white ass for you, you hear?"

And he hung up.

I took a long, long breath and put down the phone. My hands were shaking, so I held them out and stared at them until they stopped.

"Something wrong, Georgie?"

"Orlando," I said, "that nigger's got to go."

16

When George Ramos flew out of Miami on August 3 to join his godfather in San Juan, Special Agent Joseph Doredant was sitting a few rows behind him. Three hours later, just after midnight, his arrival at the Caribe Hilton with Miguel Garcia and Rudolph Ostheimer was logged by Special Agent Jorge Fortunato, on duty in the lobby.

Garcia's sudden appearance in Puerto Rico on July 28 had caught the BNDD office in San Juan at something below concert pitch. Apart from Don Harper, the local agents were recent recruits who spoke little English, and though they tried to make good their deficiencies by sheer vim and enthusiasm, these qualities were not enough to outweigh in addition their deficiencies in equipment. Good communications are a prime essential in close surveillance, but the two-way radios at Harper's disposal were either obsolete or faulty or both, and, in any case, incompatible with the sets used by the FBI, customs, and other government agencies on the island. Coordinating the various units deployed in the field was therefore difficult, often entailing frantic hand signals or long, desperate sprints to find an unvandalized pay phone.

Even so, BNDD communications were in better shape than BNDD transportation. Pride of the car pool was a 1967 Pontiac Catalina, although its efficiency had been somewhat impaired by the theft of its throttle linkage. The office had been trying for months to get it fixed, but meanwhile the agents who used it had become adept at controlling the car's speed by means of a length of string tied to the carburetor lever and threaded back under the hood and in through the driver's side window. There *were* other cars, of course, but these were less favored. They were often difficult to start, sometimes because the battery or a wheel had been stolen, and, unlike the Catalina, none of them carried a spare.

But even with the most accomplished of BNDD string-pullers at the wheel, the Catalina was no match for the 1972 Lincoln that Garcia was using around town, and also for daily excursions into the countryside. Without even trying, for he was obviously unaware of their existence, Garcia shook his followers every time, which was serious. He was not known as a nature lover, and his rural rides suggested that he might be looking for a likely landing strip to fly in his load.

Appeals for help brought an immediate response from the FBI and customs, who turned over every available man and car. As many as sixty agents could then be deployed in the hunt at any one time, with half the telephone operators on the island acting as unofficial traffic coordinators to make good the absence of a reliable radio link between BNDD personnel and their reinforcements. After that, Garcia could no longer shake his pursuers in town, even if he had known about them and wanted to, but in the country no car, however well equipped, could get close enough to keep him under observation without raising a telltale cloud of dust on the dirt roads. Aerial support was clearly needed, and the Miami office agreed to send over a single-engine spotter plane.

An odd thing then happened. On the morning it was due to arrive, one of Harper's young Puerto Rican agents approached him in the Caribe Hilton and said: "I heard our plane just crashed."

"*What?*" With his communications problems, it was not unusual for important information to reach Harper in this fashion.

"That's what I heard."

"Well, who told you?"

At this, the young man looked bewildered. "I don't know."

Harper called Miami at once for confirmation, and was himself bewildered to learn that, far from having crashed, the plane had yet to take off. Hanging up, he set off to instruct the agent to check his facts in future, but at that moment Garcia emerged from the elevator, and the day's chase began. By the time Harper reached home that night, he had forgotten all about the incident

—until he was reminded of it when Miami called shortly afterwards to say the plane had just crashed. The two agents in it were unhurt, but the machine was a total wreck.

Had he known about it, Garcia would probably have claimed that the spirits were with him, but Harper counterattacked next morning. When his quarry headed out of San Juan as usual in the Lincoln, he was followed not only by a fleet of government cars, which dropped farther and farther back as they reached open country, but by a huge U.S. Coast Guard helicopter. Keeping station on a parallel course, the crew watched Garcia through binoculars and described his movements over the radio to their colleagues on the ground.

Before long, it began to look as though Harper's theory was correct, that Garcia was in search of a suitable landing place. He was now well away from the road, bumping slowly along farm tracks and stopping every so often to look over a particular field with some care. Indeed, he was so anxious to do the job properly that several times he got out of the car and walked about, bending down here and there to feel the texture of the soil—or so it seemed from the distant helicopter. After about an hour of this, he turned the Lincoln around, heading back toward the highway, and drove into San Juan at high speed, passing on the way carloads of government agents pretending to admire the view.

That afternoon, routine questioning of the hotel staff elicited a complaint from the chambermaids on Garcia's floor about the wet weeds and flowers found clogging the waste pipe of his bathtub each day. Harper puzzled over this for some time before finally matching it with another piece of information in Garcia's intelligence file. The massed resources of the U.S. government, represented by about fifty federal agents, a dozen cars, a coastguard helicopter and crew, and one written-off light aircraft, had just been deployed to watch Miguel Garcia gather voodoo herbs and flowers to put in his bath water each morning.

When the pilots Marcello Lacour and Juan Serra arrived from Caracas and checked into the room next to Garcia's, the pace warmed up. With three people to keep an eye on in a crowded hotel, it was clearly desirable to station one or more agents on the same floor, not only to provide an early warning system for their colleagues in the lobby but also to observe the traffic between the rooms. The only problem was that there were no vacancies on that floor.

Rising to the occasion, one of the Puerto Rican agents decided to create one. A distant cousin of the hotel manager's on his mother's side, he argued forcefully that a hotelier's duty to his country far outweighed his duty to his guests, working his cousin up to such a patriotic pitch that he eventually summoned two bellhops and proceeded upstairs to the sixth floor, where he summarily evicted two Chicago schoolteachers from the room they were occupying opposite Garcia's.

Caught in bras and panties, they naturally objected, standing at the door to argue the point with the agent and the manager while the bellboys threw their clothes into their suitcases. In fact, the two raised such a fuss that the pilots came out of their room to see what was happening, and the agent had to duck out of sight even more hastily than the schoolteachers, for fear that Lacour and Serra might recognize him later if they spotted him on their tail.

There was a similar sort of problem with the elevators. Sooner or later, Garcia and the pilots were bound to notice if the same people traveled up and down with them every time; somehow, they had to be delayed long enough en route for the agents to get into position before they arrived on their floor or in the lobby.

Once again, the hotel manager literally held the key—this time to the elevator controls. After another appeal to his patriotism, he gave it to Harper's men, who proceeded to damage the hotel's reputation for efficiency as thoroughly as they had already damaged it for courtesy. Whenever Garcia or the pilots stepped into an elevator, the agent on duty would allow it to leave normally but then stop it on every intermediate floor for anything up to half a minute while one of Harper's energetic young men bounded up the back stairs to reach the sixth floor ahead of them. In the other direction, a phone call from an agent in the room opposite to the effect that they were on the move would ensure that his colleague downstairs stalled the elevators long enough for him to beat them *down* the back stairs.

This went on for a week, to the mounting annoyance of those many guests unfortunate enough to share an elevator with Garcia, the pilots, or George Ramos, whose arrival in the early hours of August 4 had raised excitement in the Caribe Hilton command post to fever pitch. With four men under close surveillance, not to mention Willie Dipini, Rudolph Ostheimer, and others whom they met, the comings and goings and scurryings about the hotel became more and more reminiscent of French farce.

Assigned to take photographs of Garcia's associates, two of Harper's greenest agents hung around the lobby for days with an air of elaborate unconcern and cameras in paper bags. Whenever Garcia appeared with anybody, they would leap forward and half blind them with their flash units at point-blank range—as Harper discovered to his horror one evening when he happened to see them do it. To his even greater amazement, however, neither Garcia nor Ramos took much notice. They probably assumed that the two had a photographic concession in the hotel, for by no stretch of the imagination could government agents be expected to behave like that.

Garcia and Ramos also seemed oblivious to the disturbance they created whenever they appeared in the hotel restaurant. It might be only half full when they came down to breakfast, but within a couple of minutes, most of the available places would be taken by federal agents in resort casuals, carrying walkie-talkies in their ubiquitous brown-paper bags. And within a minute or so of their finishing breakfast, the restaurant would be half empty again, with part-eaten meals congealing at a dozen different tables.

Indeed, it seemed at times as though only Garcia and Ramos were unaware of what was going on. Perfect strangers were now stopping Harper and his men on the street to ask how the investigation was going. As for the hotel staff, they had organized a sweepstake among themselves, placing bets on the day they thought the boat would get in, for they were now quite convinced that the presence of customs and coast-guard men among the retinue of agents on Garcia's trail meant that a load was on the way by sea.

The island's telephone operators were also still following events with the closest attention. On August 4, while surveillance on George Ramos had been temporarily lost, Harper answered his phone and was told by the operator that Ramos had just called Air France to make four reservations for Haiti the following morning. Having thanked her for the tip, he then called to make two reservations himself, so that a couple of agents could go with them—only to learn that the plane was now full.

Consternation. If it had been an American airline, the BNDD would have asked it to bump two passengers off the flight to make room—standard practice among federal agencies in cases of emergency—but it was not anxious to advertise to a foreign carrier the fact that it wanted to send its agents into another country without having first notified that country's government of its intentions. Harper and his team spent half the night trying to find a way of getting somebody over to Port-au-Prince without arousing suspicion and preferably before Garcia arrived there.

They were about to give up when air traffic control came through to say that a local dentist and his wife had filed a flight plan for Haiti and were all set to leave in their single-engine private plane. On learning of the government's problem, the dentist agreed to take along a couple of its agents, provided they did not keep him waiting. Whereupon Agents Charles Schaming and Joe Fortier were driven out to the airfield with only the clothes they were wearing and the money they happened to have in their pockets, and a few minutes later were greeting the dawn at 5,000 feet. It was then that they learned the dentist had no instrument rating, and that the weather forecast for Port-au-Prince was ten-tenths overcast.

Fortunately, no great navigational skill is required to find Haiti from Puerto Rico, especially in daylight. By flying more or less due west, they eventually picked up the coast of the Dominican Republic and worked their way along to the other end of the island. The dentist and his wife had done this before, but always in good visibility. With the low ceiling, they had difficulty in recognizing their landmarks for Duvalier Airport. While they searched for them, their passengers had an even harder time keeping their composure as the plane swooped, climbed, and banked around the cloud-muffled peaks and clefts of the mountains girding the bay of Port-au-Prince.

Nor were their troubles over when they found the airfield. The Haitian authorities were not accustomed to early-morning visitors; the dentist could raise no response from the tower by radio. The agents then suggested they should land anyway, there being no other aircraft in sight, but the dentist looked doubtful. When the field shut down, he said, they left oil drums out on the runway to prevent unauthorized landings. And fifteen minutes before a scheduled flight was due in, they would send out a truck to drive up and down warning their gunners not to shoot. But after buzzing the field a few times, the dentist decided to chance it and found a long enough stretch of uncluttered runway to make a safe landing.

A few hours later, at 11:30, Agents Schaming and Fortier watched Miguel Garcia and George Ramos arrive by Air France Flight 351, and followed them by taxi to the El Rancho Hotel. As in Puerto Rico, the possibility that they might be under surveillance had evidently not crossed their minds, for they went about their business with no attempt at concealment. At 12:20, Ramos left the hotel in the same taxi that had carried him there and drove downtown to the docks, where he walked out to the *William Express* and picked up a member of the crew. After a little shopping, the two then returned to the hotel together, where they stayed for a short time before the taxi drove the crew member back to his ship. He was now carrying a suitcase.

Later that afternoon, Ramos and Garcia conferred with Alberto Perez, alias the Doctor, and his associate José Medina, in Room 29. The two agents, who had also checked into the hotel, were unable to hear any of their conversation, either through the door or from outside the window, but the meeting seemed to go well.

Then Schaming got lucky. He was lying in the sun by the pool not far from the open window of Garcia's room when Frank Matthews called from New York. Schaming would never have known this had the connection been better. As it was, the line was so bad that Garcia had to shout to make himself heard, and it was a fairly simple matter to deduce not only the identity of the caller but what he was calling about. Some big deal was going down, but "Frankie" was clearly dissatisfied with its progress. There were references to the "Frenchman," Caracas, and a plane, and something about Georgie wanting to dump the pilots, which presumably explained why they had been left behind in Puerto Rico.

At the end of the call, Garcia looked out of his window to see if anyone was within earshot, but nobody was there except a guy lying in the sun by the pool, apparently asleep.

Next day, August 6, Perez, Medina, and Ramos were followed out to the airport, where they went their separate ways—to be met at their respective destinations by surveillance teams arranged by Schaming and Fortier. And on the seventh, the two agents flew back to San Juan, a few seats behind Garcia.

Everything now pointed to Caracas, where the Anti-Drug Division of the Judicial Police Technical Corps had opened an official inquiry into the activities of Garcia, alias Cabot, on August 4. This had not gone very far because Garcia was out of the country, but the Venezuelans had already established his connection with Rolando Gonzalez, who had been under investigation for some time. As no crime had yet been committed, however, and as it was already clear that Caracas was not the final destination for the drugs—if, indeed, there *were* any—the Garcia case had a fairly low priority. It was several days after the event when the Anti-

Drug Division learned that he had returned to Venezuela with his godson, and by then George Ramos had come and gone without being noticed at all. Nor was there any knowledge or suspicion of Joseph Sereni's involvement with them, much less that by this time he was en route to Marseilles as their courier.

According to Sereni, his first trip to France on July 11 had been to prime the pump through a contact in Paris named François. François had traveled with him to Marseilles and introduced him to a man named Robert in the Cintra Bar on the Quai des Belges. On hearing that Sereni was interested in buying 20 kilos of heroin for Miguel Garcia, and another 100 kilos shortly after, Robert had told him that if the money was there, and with two or three weeks' notice, he could supply any amount required. His mission accomplished, Sereni then flew back to report this to Garcia in Caracas.

By now, Garcia had made his arrangements with Miguel Sanz for Sereni's baggage, containing the load, to be taken through customs at Maiquetía Airport without the usual inspection. He had also secretly arranged with Frank Matthews for $100,000 to be flown over from New York to Paris to pay for the first 20 kilos, but he said nothing about this to George Ramos. Garcia had his pride. It had already been dented by his godson's scorn for the plan to fly the load to Haiti in their own DC-3, and he did not intend to submit to any further criticism from that quarter for taking a "soft" line over paying for the stuff.

On receiving the "green," relayed to him by Ramos from his godfather's room at the Club Americana, Sereni returned to Paris en route to Marseilles, where he checked in at the Hotel Splendide, boulevard d'Athènes, as Joseph Massoni—a name sometimes used by his father. He then called Robert, who showed up at the Cintra Bar with an associate named Antoine and a third man, who acted as lookout.

There were no problems about taking delivery; Matthews's $100,000 had already arrived by courier. The only question was where and how to hand over the load. When Sereni told them he intended to take it to his girlfriend's place in Montargis and wait there for further instructions, they sped him on his way with true Gallic consideration for the soon-to-be-parted lovers. Antoine himself brought the suitcase out to Marignane Airport so that Sereni could catch the first available plane back to Paris.

A few days later, Miguel Garcia called Sereni from Venezuela. He was to arrange for the delivery of a further 100 kilos of heroin in mid-September and then leave for Caracas after advising Garcia of his arrival time at Maiquetía, where all was in readiness to receive the load.

In accordance with these instructions, Sereni duly placed the 100-kilo order through François and bought himself a ticket for Avianca Flight 71, departing Paris, Orly, on August 29, and arriving Caracas, via San Juan, Puerto Rico, in the early morning of August 30.

Meanwhile, things had been going less smoothly in Miami. Agents Schaming and Fortier had returned from Haiti convinced, not unreasonably, that the *William Express* was heading in with a load of narcotics, carried aboard at Port-au-Prince by a seaman in the pay of Garcia and George Ramos. Though they were not certain of being able to recognize the crew member again, having observed him only briefly and at a distance, they were confident that a thorough search of the ship would provide all the answers, and probably enough evidence to arrest those involved. When the *William Express* tied up at the Antillean Line dock in the Miami River on August 10, Schaming, Bill Warner, and about twenty other BNDD agents and customs men were waiting to seal off the vessel and work it over inch by inch bow to stern.

The only contraband they found was 25 pounds of marijuana, which had to belong to somebody else. It simply didn't make sense for Garcia, Ramos, Perez, Medina, Diaz, and all their friends and hangers-on to go running around the Caribbean for days on end just to import a few pounds of grass. Deeply frustrated, the agents then showed the captain and crew photographs of Garcia and Ramos taken, not in Haiti, as Yves Alexis later reported, but in

Puerto Rico by Harper's eager young men at the Caribe Hilton, and again they drew a blank. Though at least one member of the crew had to be lying, they all denied ever having seen either of them before.

It was a bitter disappointment. The search team withdrew with the marijuana, leaving a few men behind to make sure that if they *had* missed a load, nobody would get it off while their backs were turned.

On his mettle now, as the search had been staged on the basis of his observations with Fortier in Haiti, Schaming passed the word on the street that he wanted to see Confidential Informant No. SGI–1–0009, code name Don Juan, and met him next day in the parking lot behind Howard Johnson's on Biscayne Boulevard.

"You know Orlando Lamadrid?" Schaming asked.

"Like my own brother."

"How about George Ramos? They've been hanging around together."

"Sure. You mean the kid who lives out on Menores Avenue? Sure, I know him. He works for Miguel Garcia."

"Okay," Schaming said. "They got a deal going down? You know what they're doing?"

"Well, I know Orlando's been promising little surprises to everybody at the Ideal Restaurant," said Ricardo Morales. "We have breakfast there most days. So I guess there's some coke coming in."

17

I talked it over with Orlando, and he agreed: we had to hit him. It's too touchy a business. Once you let somebody do a number on you, tell you what to do, you're finished. Besides, you can't say things like that to a Cuban.

Frank's flamboyance was getting too damn dangerous anyway. My godfather I had to put up with; he was family. In any case, he was making his noise in Caracas, where I figured it couldn't hurt me. But Frank? No. With this attitude? With the risk of him bringing the heat down on me with these dumb phone calls or some other stupid move? No way. He had to go. Maybe he'd just been coked up at the Sands and didn't mean it, but you can't do that, not in this business. You got to be careful who you talk to, and how you talk to them.

"Maybe we'll start a war," Orlando said, like that was a plus.

"No chance. Only two guys we got to worry about. That's Nat Elder and Gattis Hinton—and we'll take care of them, too, if we have to."

"Ricardo can get us grenades. He told me."

"For Christ's sake, Orlando. Nobody's going to point the finger at us, not if we handle this right. We'll be more upset than them. We'll make it look like an accident. Or like he got it when somebody tried to rip us off."

"Well, we're still going to need weapons," he said.

"No, we don't. We got the guns and everything."

We'd just bought a brand-new .357 Magnum, a real cannon with a six-inch barrel. And there were plenty of people I could get to pull the trigger. Willie Moto for one. He was desperate. For a few keys, he would have declared war on Russia. Orlando's brother Miguel was another. He would be happy to do it—and in New York, where nobody would ever think it was us. There was

Ricardo Morales, who had this kind of deal down pat. And there was Pedro Diaz, who could blow him away in Haiti.

I was seriously thinking about that. All I had to do was tell Frank the stuff had arrived, take him out in a boat like we had to go rendezvous with the Frenchman, and boom! Ice his ass for him. He was sure to go down there alone, or maybe with one other guy, and people have boating accidents all the time. My feeling was that none of his lieutenants would do a goddamn thing about it—except try to take his place. If we handled this right, whoever took over would probably still want to go through with the deal anyway.

If they didn't, that was okay, too. Nobody except Frank's organization could buy the whole load—dealing with him made life very simple—but Zack Robinson and Henry Morgan were both pretty big, and duck or no duck, Willie Moto could take over Puerto Rico with 10 or 20 keys. So if we had to wait a little longer for our millions, we'd wind up with more money anyway. When you got a guy like Frank financing the deal up front and taking the whole shipment, you got to give him a break on price. But selling the stuff off in multi-kilo quantities to several different dealers, naturally you charge more to cover the extra handling, insurance, and overhead.

The big problem now was timing. I couldn't move against Frank till he came through with the money to pay for the stuff. But once we had the $200,000 he'd been talking about, he was dead. We could raise the other half million we needed by selling the first 25 kilos, and then the rest of the stuff would be ours, free and clear.

Another problem was the money I needed to buy the boats and set myself up to cut the load in Haiti. I couldn't ask Frank for that now. I couldn't go to Zack, either; we still owed him a bundle. But there was no reason I couldn't get it from Henry Morgan.

"You going to tell your godfather?" Orlando wanted to know.

I'd thought about that, too. Miguel was going to buy a numbers business in Caracas and retire. As long as he got his money, what did *he* care? He just wouldn't have to know about it beforehand.

"Maybe I'll give him a little hint," I said.

I got my chance next day when he called from Caracas, like he'd promised, to tell me that Sereni had picked up the stuff and was all set to leave on the twenty-ninth.

"Well, that's fine," I said. "I'm glad things are going good down there, because up here I'm having a little trouble with the man."

"Yeah? What's he doing?"

"The son of a bitch has got out of hand, that's what he's doing. He's started dishing out a few orders here and there, and I don't go for that shit."

"Ah, don't worry. He's nervous, that's all."

"Yeah. After all the bullshit you fed him. Son of a bitch figures he had the stuff coming six weeks ago."

"Don't worry about it," he said. "I'll take care of Frankie."

"No, you won't," I said. "Soon as this deal goes down, *I'll* do it."

Next day, the *William Express* came back—and the federal agents hit it again. When I called Evaristio, he said there weren't so many of them as last time, but he didn't want to touch the stuff while they were still snooping around. I told him he was absolutely right, and not to do nothing until I got there.

"Any idea what's bugging them?" I said. "You hear them talking?"

"Uh-uh. But they know *something*. And I guess they can keep this up longer than we can."

"Maybe. How about her sister ship? They hitting her, too?"

"The *José Express*? No. She was just in, and nobody bothered with her.

"Okay. Then it's simple. Here's what we do. If you have to leave the package on board again, I'll run over to Haiti and have Yves pull it out. Then I'll wait for the *José Express*."

"Fine," he said. "If you do that, the guy's name is Caterpillar.

I'll talk to him when he gets in. Tell him to watch out for you."

"Yeah, good. We're probably going to need both ships anyway when this other deal goes down."

"Right. Luis the Junkman told me. How's it coming?"

"It's coming. Next trip maybe."

"Uh-huh. Well, call me tomorrow. Around seven. Maybe things will cool off."

"Sure," I said. "But don't take no chances. You're too close to retiring."

When I called the next morning, things were the same. Maybe later, he said. There were only a couple of agents still hanging around. If anything happened, *he* would call *me*.

And he did, at about one in the morning. I jumped in the car with Anna, and we drove over to his house on North River Drive, just across the street from the dock.

"They're still there, Georgie," he said. "I could only get half of it. Three keys. I'll try for the rest tomorrow."

"Hey, Evaristio. I told you—no sweat. If you can get the other three, fine. If not, we'll do it like I said. You done a good job here. I'll see you're taken care of."

He was really trying to please. And Orlando got all excited, too, when we drove over there to stash the three keys in his apartment. He was all set to start cutting that shit right away.

"Hell, no," I said. "Just hold on to it for a couple of days. Let's see if we get the rest of it first."

I wasn't sure yet how I was going to move it. I didn't feel like calling Frank and putting up with any more of his shit, but, on the other hand, I had to keep things cool till he kicked in the two hundred thousand. It was all in the timing. What I wanted to do, if we got the six, was cut them to ten, and then go sweet-talk Henry or Zack. A few hours later, Frank himself solved my problem.

"Hey, Georgie," he said, and no bullshit this time. He was stone-cold, feet on the ground. "Don't you come up here, man. And don't call me—not till I tell you."

"What's the matter? Got company?"

"Like a hound-dog got fleas."

"Okay." Didn't make no difference to what he had coming. He wasn't calling for *my* sake. "Thanks for telling me."

I opened my mouth to ask him about the two hundred thousand, but he hung up.

"Trouble?" said Orlando.

"Not for us. Frank's pulled down the heat. We're going to have to move the stuff some place else."

I didn't like the sound of it. First the ship, and now this. Suddenly it didn't seem like such a good idea to leave three kilos lying around.

"I think I'll go have a talk with Joe Regan," I said.

Regan was a black dealer in Miami. I'd met him a few times while running around with my godfather. They'd done business together back in the sixties. But, first, me and Anna took a run over by Victoria Montalvo's house on Biarritz Drive. Miguel had asked me to make sure his old lady was okay, so I told her we were having a bit of trouble but I'd take care of her as soon as I got it squared away. That was strictly for old times' sake. She wasn't doing nothing for it now. Neither was my godfather, come to that.

As we left the house and turned at the corner, Anna twisted around and looked out the back window.

"There's a blue car following us," she said.

"You sure?" In the mirror, I could see a blue Ford, four-door, and so what?

"There's two guys in front. They look like cops."

"Well, let's see."

I kept on going, and so did they. I made a left and a right, and suddenly they turned into two guys in a gold Javelin. So I did the same number with them. Left, right—and they were still there. Then a white Ford took over as I hit the Expressway, and it stayed exactly with us. When I went fast, *it* went fast. When *I* slowed down, it did, too. Anna was right. She was never wrong about things like that.

"I'm going to Joe Regan's house anyway," I said. "Give them something to think about."

So I got off the Expressway and ran over to 35th Street NW and parked right outside his place, just by 10th Avenue. It was raining.

"Which one is it now?"

"The blue one," she said. "On the other side of the street."

"Okay. Well, you stay here. Lock the doors, and watch what they do. Anything happens, honk the horn."

I got out of the car and rang the bell like I was going to church. It was most likely the cops, but I couldn't be sure. Maybe some wise guys had heard about the 100 keys. Maybe it was a hit.

"Hey, Georgie," said Joe. "Good to see you, man. Come in. This business or pleasure?"

"Don't know yet."

"Then come in the back and let's find out."

So we went through the usual bullshit for a couple of minutes, but I didn't want to leave Anna out there too long.

"Look here, Joe," I said. "I got five keys of coke I can let you have."

"Oh, man," he said, real wistful. "Five keys? That's beautiful. But I got to tell you, Georgie—I can't handle five keys at one shot. I mean, I *can*, but it's going to take me awhile to pay you. I just don't have those kind of contacts no more. Some of my people got busted."

"That's too bad," I said. And it was. If Joe didn't have the scratch, maybe I was going to have trouble unloading the stuff for money up front. So I let him down easy. "Well, maybe I can fix it so you pay me off by installments. I'll come back and see you if I want to handle it like that."

Two more minutes of bullshit and I was on my way.

"So what's happening, baby?"

"Nothing," she said. "They're just sitting there."

I still didn't quite believe this. I never had the heat on my tail before, not that I knew of, and it didn't seem possible that they were after *me*. But they were. As I drove down to the corner, the blue Ford came along, too. Just to see what they were made of, I caught a straight street and opened up that Stingray for a few blocks, but no good. The gold Javelin was right up there with me. This wasn't no hit or nothing. It was the cops, playing cat and mouse in three cars.

So . . . Shit.

"What are you going to do, baby?"

"I'm just trying to figure it out," I said.

I was a bit flustered, but not really nervous. I had nothing with me in the car. They didn't know about the shipment or they would have tagged us with it. But somehow they had caught on I was dealing dope. And either I wasn't supposed to notice the surveillance or they were trying to crowd me into making mistakes.

"Let's go by the house," I said. "See what's going on there."

So I led the blue Ford and the gold Javelin over to Coral Gables and trundled slowly down our block. The white Ford was parked right across from the house, and a bit further along the street was a green Nova with two guys sitting up front. I didn't stop.

"Well," I said. "The Gestapo's here."

"So what can they do?" said Anna. She wasn't too worried, either.

"Nothing," I said. "Let's go see my grandmother."

She was in the Pan-American Hospital out on 67th Avenue and NW 7th Street. She had always had a bad heart, and in the middle of all this other trouble, my aunt Minerva had called to say the old lady had just had another attack. So me and Anna picked up some flowers and visited with her for a while, all bright and cheerful, but as we were leaving, I told my aunt to stick around if she could. We'd run into a bit of trouble, I said. Nothing serious, but in case it got worse, I didn't want my grandmother to hear nothing about it on the radio.

I was really worried about her, and as we drove away from the hospital with the cops right behind us again, I suddenly got tired of this cat-and-mouse bullshit. The first chance I got, I jumped a red light and took off, darting around a few streets till I lost them.

Now they knew I'd spotted them. I'd only done it to aggravate their ass, but then it hit me. I was the perfect decoy, just like I'd figured. While I kept them busy, following me around, Orlando could unload the three keys. And if they kept it up, I could also draw them off when the 100 keys came through.

"Now I got to talk to Orlando," I said.

"You want to go by his apartment?" Anna sounded surprised, and I saw what she meant. A white Corvette is a bit conspicuous.

"Maybe he's at Isabelita's."

When he wasn't home, he generally hung out with Ricardo Morales and his other cronies at Isabelita's Ideal Restaurant, down by 9th Court and 8th Street. It was a long shot, but I guess Cosmo Lacroix suddenly woke up and saw what was going on, because as we were driving down a side street near the restaurant, who should come driving up the other way but Orlando in his little white Valiant. We held a conference right there.

"I just shook off the heat," I said. "We got to get rid of that stuff. Any ideas?"

"How about Joe Regan?"

"No good. He don't got the money, and the cops followed me there."

"Okay. Then I got the answer," he said. "I talked to Elpidio Hernandez. This is a guy your godfather knows. And he's interested."

"*How* interested?"

"He's a businessman. No flimflam about it. He says he's interested, that means he'll buy if he likes the price."

"Okay. Call him. Set up a meet at your place for around twelve tonight."

"Right."

"And come back here around ten to let me know if he can make it."

"Okay. What are you going to do about the car?"

"The car?"

"Not hard to spot if the cops are looking for you."

"You're right," I said. "Tell you what. Follow me over to Coral Way. I'll leave it behind the movie house."

So we drove over to the Coral Gables Twin Theaters at 33rd Avenue, and after I locked up the Corvette, we got into Orlando's Valiant.

"Hey, I been thinking," he said. "If the cops latched on to you, maybe they're looking for me as well."

"Well, if they are," I said, "they'll have your apartment staked out. Let's go see."

He lived in a quiet, dark neighborhood on SW 27th Lane. We cruised all the streets around his place for about fifteen minutes, and there was nothing. No cars. Nobody watching the house.

"Okay, you're clean," I said. "If Anna don't see nothing, there's nothing to see."

"Well, thank Christ for that," he said. "With three kilos in there, I'm glad they're after *you*."

"Yeah, that's what I— Oh, *shit!*"

They both looked out the windows, expecting to see the cops.

"I just remembered," I said. "I got three, four ounces hid in the apartment."

Back we went again to Coral Gables. I didn't want nobody spotting Orlando's car, so he dropped me off by the bowling alley a couple of blocks from the house.

"I'll be back in five minutes," I said. "If I'm gone longer than that, start driving around. I'll wait for you here."

All around the apartment house were trees and bushes. If the cops were sitting in their cars waiting for me to drive up, I was pretty sure I could reach the entrance before they spotted me. Then, even if they had a warrant, I'd be upstairs and getting rid of the stuff before their boots hit the street. So I played Indian scout right up to the front door, and ducked inside so quick if they blinked they must have missed me. I had the key in my hand as I hit the hallway, and I was inside the apartment and had the chain on the door without hardly breaking my stride. Five seconds later, I was flushing $3,500 down the toilet, but with another 15 keys on the way, I wasn't too worried about it. In fact, now I didn't give a damn *what* they did.

I checked from the windows, but nothing was moving outside. That didn't mean they weren't there; it just meant they didn't have a warrant. I had my hand on the door to leave, when the phone rang.

"Hey, Georgie." It was Evaristio. "You want to come over? I got the rest of the load for you."

That struck me as kind of funny. I just got rid of three ounces, and here's another three kilos.

"What's the joke?"

"Nothing, Evaristio. I'm just happy you got it off. But you'll have to hang on to it for a while. I'm kind of tied up."

"No, wait a minute," he said. "That's not part of the deal. I'm not your stash, Georgie. I don't want this stuff in my house. All I do is get it off the boat, you know that."

"Sure, Evaristio, sure—take it easy. It won't be more than a few hours. And you wouldn't want me over there right now, not with the company I got."

That slowed him down. "Oh, Jesus," he said.

"No sweat. If I can't get there myself, I'll send somebody over to take care of it. Just sit tight."

Now I knew they couldn't touch me, I was even enjoying this a little. Like a game of chess. I hung up on Evaristio and called Luis the Junkman.

"Hey, Luis. You busy? I got a little job for you."

"Depends," he said.

"Well, I'd like for you to take a run by Evaristio's house and see him."

"Well, Georgie, I'd like to help you out," he said, "but I can't right now. I got some people coming over any minute. Maybe tomorrow."

"Yeah, sure." Son of a bitch. "I'll call you."

"Sure. Hear you had some trouble. They hit the boat again?"

"Luis, the only trouble I got is people running scared. Nervous people I *don't* need, not with the deal *we* got going down." And I hung up on him.

Evaristio would have to cope. Maybe I'd call the old lady in the morning and have *her* pick it up.

As I came out of the house, the blue Ford was making a slow pass down the block. I stood and watched it go by, just to aggravate their ass, then darted into the bushes as soon as it went behind a tree. When I got back to the corner, I had to wait a couple of minutes before Orlando came by with Anna to pick me up.

"Baby, we were worried about you," she said. "There's cops all over the place."

"I was on the phone."

"Well, it looks like they're getting ready to do something. They got cars coming in from everywhere."

"No, no," I said. "Everything's cool. There ain't nothing they can tag us with now."

"Except for those three kilos in my apartment," Orlando said, and he didn't sound happy.

"Okay. Drop us off by my car and go fix the meet. After we unload the stuff, maybe we'll take a little vacation until all this blows over."

I had it in mind we might go to Haiti, Anna and me. No way was I going to bring in another load just yet, not into this kind of heat. And it could be just the chance I needed to get Frank over there. So we picked up the car and went for a stroll, keeping off the main drags, and around ten o'clock met up with Orlando again behind Isabelita's.

"It's all set," he said. "He'll be over at the house around two o'clock."

"Fine," I said. "Then let's go over there now and cut this shit."

I let him go first and followed a good way behind while Anna kept a sharp lookout. After they lost us, I guess the cops figured they'd pick us up again sooner or later at the apartment, and maybe that was why she had seen all the cars up there. Anyway, we didn't see nothing, riding over to Orlando's place, and when we got there, the neighborhood was still quiet as a cemetery. To play it safe, we parked a few streets away and strolled back with Feo like a nice young couple out walking the dog. And nothing. Nobody standing around. Nobody sitting in cars. Which made me think the heat had to be coming from something my godfather or Frank had done. If they were only after me, then it had to be coming from out of town, because the local fuzz would have known Orlando was tied in with me and they would have latched on to us both at the same time.

He let us in and, with Anna helping us, we got the job done in half an hour. No fancy cuts this time. I just tipped the three keys into a big garbage bag, dumped two keys of lactose on top, and shook it like hell. Then we weighed the stuff out in half kilos, and wound up with ten chubby little green plastic packs. After that, we went out to get a hamburger. I hadn't eaten all day.

Hernandez was there on the button—always a good sign. And as soon as the introductions were over, it was straight down to business. Orlando was right. No flimflam.

"Where's the stuff?"

I took one of the half-kilo bags and put it on top of the refrigerator, right under the light. Hernandez cut it open, took a little bit out, sniffed it, tasted it.

"How much?" he said.

"I'll take eleven." I figured we could get by in Haiti for a while on $55,000.

"Drop that a point and I'll take it all," he said.

"All right." In our situation, I wasn't about to fight over $5,000. "It's all yours. You want to take it now?"

"Sure. If you want to trust me for the money."

We both laughed.

"Okay," I said. "When and where tomorrow?"

"Well, I got to go get the money at the bank. So let's say around noon, to be on the safe side."

I didn't like it. That was another twelve hours to play pat-a-cake with the cops—or the federal agents or whoever they were. But I couldn't push the guy, in case I made him nervous. If he got the idea there was heat around . . . Looked like the time had come for Orlando to earn his bread.

"All right, Orlando," I said. "It's your baby. You drop the load and collect the money. Where do you want it, Elpidio?"

Hernandez looked at me. "My partner's got an apartment on Coral Way—1860 Coral Way. First floor. Apartment 1."

"Okay. And he'll have the money?"

"Right—but not there. I'll take delivery, and then Orlando can pick up the money from my partner over by the bank. On 27th Avenue. He'll meet you on the corner there."

In the ordinary way, I wouldn't have gone for that, but I didn't have much choice. "Fine," I said. "That's it, then."

He left a few minutes later, and a little while after that, the three of us followed him out. Anna had been catching a nap in the bedroom while the deal was going down, but she was awake all right as we drove off with Orlando, who'd offered to take us around to where I'd left my car.

"You see that Chevy up the street?" she said. "With the side lights on? And the New York tag?"

"No," said Orlando. Then he kind of groaned. "Now I do. It's coming after us."

It wasn't that that surprised me—it was Orlando's reaction. As I sat there and watched him, he just came unglued. "Jesus Christ," he kept saying. Then he'd look in the mirror, shaking his head. "Oh, Jesus." He didn't know where he was going or what to do. And *I* didn't know what to say to him; it was embarrassing. He suddenly hung a wild left turn on a two-way street, snarling up both lanes of traffic, and took off like a three-bottle drunk. Then he did it again at the next intersection, missing another car by inches. I heard Anna suck in her breath as we slid around it with the tires squealing like pigs, and I had to admit, if it came down to a choice, I'd sooner do time for a first offense than kick off in a wreck with Orlando.

"All right," I said. "That's fantastic. You lost them. Now pull over and let *me* drive."

So he stopped and slid over as I ran around the front to get in behind the wheel. We seemed to have shook the guys in the Chevy—in his panic, Orlando had probably done it quicker than *I* could have done—but I figured they would have radioed in our direction of travel, so the cars would be swarming like flies up ahead. I backed around onto the driveway of a dark house and killed the lights.

"Now what am I going to do?" Orlando said, still moaning. "These guys are after me, and my house is full of stuff. Oh, Jesus."

"They don't got a warrant," I said. "If they did, they'd have hit us just now. They're just sniffing around."

"So they'll *get* a warrant." He shook his head. "You got to help me out, Georgie. That ain't *my* shit in there."

He didn't have to say nothing else. Orlando was getting ready to go to pieces. If they picked him up in this state, I'd go down with him, no doubt about that. I was going to have to try to get the five keys out of there. This just wasn't my day. But we'd drawn off the stakeout, so there was maybe a fifty-fifty chance of getting away with it—if we went back right now. It was better odds than the hundred percent certainty of pulling one-to-fifteen for conspiracy if we didn't.

"Okay. Could be they're not after us at all," I said. "Could be Hernandez brought the heat with him. But we got to get that stuff out of there. And quick."

"You mean *now?*" It stiffened him up like a slap in the face.

"You want to wait till the stakeout comes back? But God knows where we're going to stash it."

"I know a guy," Orlando said. "Over on SW 5th Street."

"Fine. Then let's go." I started the car and turned back the way we'd come. "Baby, I'm going to drop you off with Feo at the corner. I want you to grab a cab home."

"No, baby. I'm staying. Maybe I can help."

"Honey, I got a lot on my mind. You can help me by going home. I don't want to have to worry about you as well."

"I'm staying," she said.

There was no time to argue, and not much point in it either when she was in that kind of a mood.

"All right. But stay in the car. I don't want to have to come looking for you with five keys of dope in my hands."

"I'll stay in the car and keep watch," she said. Her feelings were hurt.

"You'll stay in the car and keep down," I said.

Behind Orlando's place was a vacant lot with some heavy construction equipment parked there and plenty of trees and bushes around for cover. It was also pretty dark. I rolled down the street very quietly, lights off, and pulled in by the entrance to the lot. As far as we could see, nobody was watching the back of the house.

Orlando had a hold on himself now. He slipped out on his side, closing the door without a sound, and we split up, crossing the lot in short rushes, freezing every few yards to listen out. The big danger spot was the wall we had to climb. It wasn't hard to get over, but it was just high enough to hide anybody standing in the yard if they'd posted a man back there.

I let Orlando go first. After all, it was his house, and he knew the layout better. Nothing happened, and so I followed him, coming down only inches away from a bunch of garbage cans. If I'd hit them, I'd have woken half the neighborhood.

Orlando already had the back door open and was waving me in. We zipped through the house, half expecting to find a cop around every corner, and slid into his apartment, panting like we'd run five miles instead of maybe fifty yards. As he closed the door, he stretched out his hand without thinking to turn on the light, and I knocked it down.

"You get the lactose and the rest of that shit," I said. "Better take the scale, too. I'll look after the dope."

I took a quick look at the street from the window, but couldn't see nothing moving. So I piled the ten packs into a shopping bag, and helped Orlando load up.

"I can't carry all this," he said. "I'll drop it."

"You want to come back for seconds? Suit yourself."

"Well, how the hell am I going to get over the wall with all this?"

"You don't have to," I said. So what if they found a few of his fingerprints? He lived here, didn't he? "Dump everything by the trash cans. Inside if there's room."

I opened the door a few inches and listened. All quiet in the house. So I gave Orlando the nod, and took off. I was out of that place, across the yard, and back over the wall in about fifteen seconds. Then I crouched down on the other side for a moment, making sure there was nobody waiting for us, but I could see Anna in the car—or thought I could—and I knew she would never hold still while I walked into something. I made a run for it, keeping low, and heaved the shopping bag over into the back seat as she pushed open the door for me.

"Where's Orlando?"

"He's coming," I said. But a good ten seconds went by before I heard him running toward us, and I was chewing my finger by then. As he grabbed for the door, I started the motor, and in the same instant a car appeared on the intersection behind us, signaling a right turn to come around in our direction.

"Let's go," I said, and floored it, throwing Orlando across the seat with the door still half open. He managed to get it shut just in time as I hung a left at the corner. A second later and he'd have been thrown out. A few more turns, heading away from SW 5th Street, and I lost them. Running without lights, even a white car is hard to follow in that kind of residential neighborhood, where there's lots of trees and shadows. I stopped and waited for a couple of minutes to make sure they weren't foxing around the next corner, then I put the lights on and doubled back to SW 5th, keeping to the side streets as much as I could.

We found the house, and Orlando went to the door alone to wake up his friend. They talked for a minute, then the guy started nodding his head, yawning, and I knew it was okay. We were home free. Orlando came back to the car, grinning all over his face. Anna handed him the shopping bag, and we watched him stow it under the canvas cover of a boat trailer in the carport.

We rode away from that house like kids on a picnic. We'd done it. We'd beaten them out. They could corner us now, and there wasn't a goddamn thing they could tag us with. We just had to be the smartest, toughest, goddamned unbeatablest combination in the business. I drove back to Orlando's place with the lights on high beam, windows down, and the radio going full blast.

"What about Elpidio?" Orlando said.

"That's up to you, man," I said. "You know how it goes. If there's no heat around tomorrow, go ahead and do it. If you got any doubts, forget it. Don't matter. Even if we lose the stuff, it don't matter. Better lose five than a hundred, right?"

"Right. Okay. I'll take care of it."

"Sure. Just be careful, that's all. Don't take no chances. With the stuff we got coming, who cares?"

"Don't worry," he said. "Everything's cool."

He dropped us off by my car and went on his way. Feo watered a tree. Then we set off for home—and suddenly everything was *not* cool. As I drove down the block, cars started up and lights came on all around us. I turned down Ponce de Leon Boulevard, and there had to be six or eight of them after me, strung out all over the road.

"We got a motorcade here," Anna said. She was hopping about, all excited.

"Yeah. They must have found the lactose."

"So, what now? You going to stop?"

"Stop? Hell, no. Let's give them a workout."

I leaned on it a little to open up a gap. The streets were pretty empty at that hour in the morning, so there was no traffic I could use. In the end, I would have to outrun them, which I figured I could do pretty easily when I got bored with this game. I could see nothing back there to keep up with a Corvette. But what they lacked in speed, they made up for in numbers. I'd stirred up an anthill. Every time I pulled away, I'd pick up another car at the next corner. They had a radio net spread, and the guy in charge knew his business. As soon as one of his cars lost contact with me, he'd order it into a covering position some place to pick me up if

I made a turn or doubled back. I don't know how many cars they had out. I kept losing the same ones over and over again. Maybe ten.

"I'm tired," Anna said. "Can't we go home?"

"Oh, sorry, baby." Naturally, it wasn't as much fun for her. "But we better not go to the apartment. I got a feeling they won't let us sleep too good. I'll find a motel."

"Whatever you say, baby." She yawned. "Tonight I'm *really* tired."

"Well, it's been a busy day," I said. "How about the San Juan Motel on 8th and 24th Avenue?"

"Uh-huh."

So at the next intersection I came around in a fast U-turn, burning rubber, and charged the two cars on my tail. As they veered out of the way, I hung a right, killed the lights, and cut loose in a string of turns that made *me* dizzy. On one of them, I had to climb the sidewalk at about 70 to get by a government car coming the other way, but right after that I had a clear road behind me, and I just blasted that Stingray out of sight for about a mile before switching on the lights again and sauntering, all alone, over to the San Juan Motel.

"Look, I better go tell Orlando where he can find me," I said, after I got Anna settled in a room there.

"Oh, baby. You got to go out again? Can't you just call him?"

"Better not. They may have a tap on his phone. I won't be too long."

It was taking a chance, but with all this heat around, I didn't want him taking an even bigger one in the morning, not at least without checking with me first.

The streets were all quiet again now. I saw nothing on the way over, or even around his house. Maybe they'd figured we were in for the night. Orlando came to the door in his underwear.

"I'm not staying," I said. "I just want to tell you we didn't go home. We're at the San Juan Motel. Room 3."

"Why? What's happening?"

"Nothing. Just keeping them guessing. So come and see me around eight, okay?"

"What for?"

"So we can see what's going on. Right now, they got an army on the street. Maybe things'll quieten down and maybe they won't. So don't do nothing until you check with me, okay?"

"Okay. Eight o'clock. Room 3."

As I stepped out on the sidewalk, I knew I was being watched. I could feel their eyes on me in the dark. And now I didn't think it was funny any more. I wanted to go to bed.

As I pulled away from the curb, again they started up all around me, and after weaving a few turns, I led another procession on to the Ponce de Leon Boulevard. This time, they had even more cars. They were coming out of the walls. No matter how I corkscrewed around, leaving rubber all over the street, there was always somebody waiting for me up front. And now it turned ugly. Now they weren't just trying to follow me—this wasn't surveillance no more. They were after my ass. They were looking to push me into doing something stupid, like hitting a tree, and saving themselves some paperwork.

A couple of times I nearly rammed one of their cars broadside as it came out of an intersection ahead of me, just squeezing by as their nerve failed, but then I came up against two of them, already out across the street and blocking it.

I hung a fast left, scaring myself as much as them with a real four-wheel drift to within a couple of feet of them, and found myself zipping down a dead-end street with two or three cars right behind me. So I ran into the driveway of an apartment house and stopped right outside the entrance. I figured if there was a doorman on duty, they wouldn't try nothing funny in front of a witness.

I got out and walked around the car, trying to figure out what to do next. They had each end of the driveway blocked, and several guys were already standing around looking at me and talking among themselves. I could see they didn't know what to do either, now they'd caught me.

Then one of them suddenly walked up and stopped a couple of yards away, legs apart, hands on hips. He was a chubby young guy with red curly hair.

"You mother-fucker," he said.

I laughed. I was supposed to take a swing at him now so he could shoot me through the head.

"You rat bastard cocksucker."

"Look," I said. "Either arrest me or get out of the way."

"You want me to kick your ass for you, scumbag?"

So I gave a big sigh and got back in the car. As he came around the side of it to get to me, I let in the clutch and rolled down to the exit. There I stopped, bumper to bumper with the car blocking the drive, and gave it some horn. No good. They weren't going to budge, and the red-haired guy was walking down after me.

I backed up fast. As he hopped out of the way, I swung up over the lawn and flower beds, carried away a piece of the fence, bumped over the sidewalk, hit the street, wheels spinning, and shot out of there like a champagne cork, leaving them facing the wrong way. But not all of their cars had followed me into the dead end. I picked up another one after a couple of blocks, lost him with a left and a right, found a second one waiting, and led him over to Coral Way. As I turned on to it, he was maybe two blocks behind.

I killed the lights and stepped on that Corvette all the way, just flooding it to the floor. In the mirror, I saw the guy turning after me, but by then I had 100 on the clock with the needle still moving up. His lights fell farther and farther back. As soon as they were out of sight, I whipped around on 10th, did a couple more turns, and that was it. Good night. I trundled over to the San Juan and went to bed.

Orlando knocked at the door of our room around eight-thirty. I was already up.

"How does it look out there?"

"I didn't see nothing," he said. "I looked all around, and nothing. If it stays this quiet, I'll go ahead with the deal."

"Okay. It's up to you. But remember what I said. If you see anything, don't move. Just forget it."

"Sure."

"No, wait a minute," I said. "I want you to take Anna to my grandmother's house. I got to get rid of the car. Every cop in Dade County knows it by now."

"She home? Your grandmother?"

"No, she's still in the hospital. But Anna's got a key, and nobody's going to bother her there."

As they drove off, a little white Ford Pinto started up across the street and went after them. It didn't surprise me, not after the show they'd put on. Either they'd followed him over or they'd spotted the Corvette on the motel lot. And it didn't worry me a whole lot either. I knew Anna would spot it, and after what I'd told him, he'd have enough common sense to lay back. It didn't take a college education to figure the odds.

So I let them go, and drove over to Miami Beach to sell the Corvette back where it came from. Nobody followed me. I stopped on the MacArthur Causeway a couple of times to make sure of that, but nobody else did the same, and I found that a bit strange. Why would they want to follow Orlando and not me? Unless they knew something? I put it out of my mind. What *could* they know? Quickest way to go crazy was trying to read something into every little thing that happened.

I took $5,500 for the car. That was the trade price. The guy said he could probably get me my money back if I wanted to leave it with him for a few days, but I didn't want to wait. I took the check and hopped a cab over to my grandmother's house down by 6th Avenue and 10th Street. It was around noon when I got there.

"Have you heard from Orlando?" I said.

Anna shook her head.

"Well, I guess it's too early. If the deal *is* going down, he'll be dropping the stuff about now."

"You see the Pinto that followed us?" she said.

"I saw it."

"Well, there's been a telephone company truck outside here all morning."

I went to the window to take a look. "Let's hope Orlando don't do nothing stupid."

Anna was more concerned about the dog. "Can't we go home now, baby? Feo's hungry."

Feo had to wait. I wanted to stay so Orlando would know where to find us, but the afternoon dragged by without a word, and when it got dark, I gave in. We walked a couple of blocks, then took a cab back to our apartment. There was no sign of anyone watching it, and no sign of Orlando either. I didn't know quite what to do. It was August 29. The first shipment was on its way to Caracas.

"What are you going to do about Evaristio?" Anna said, feeding Feo his dessert. Strawberry ice cream.

"Shit." In all the excitement, I'd forgotten about the other three keys. "We better go see the old lady."

Not having wheels was getting to be a pain in the ass. We hopped another cab over to Normandy Isle, and when I told Victoria Montalvo we'd drawn some heat, she wasn't too friendly.

"Don't you bring nothing down on me," she said. "I got nothing to do with it. Anything happens to me or my son, the whole ship goes down. You remember that."

"Anything happens to anybody," I said, "it'll be because your son wrecked six cars before he took off. But I didn't come here to talk about that. I came here to give you three keys of coke. If you want them, go see Evaristio. If you don't want nothing to do with it, just say so, and we'll be on our way."

"No need for that," she said, like I'd hurt her feelings. "When did I ever refuse to help out? You want something? Ask me."

"Yeah. Sure. You want the three keys, go get them. Or send Martinez. I don't care who does it, as long as you get them off Evaristio's hands."

"Maybe I'll ask Luis the Junkman."

"Good luck."

"Then me and Anna can take them to New York." Now she was full of big plans.

"I'm not going," Anna said.

"We can go as mother and daughter. Nobody'll bother us."

"She's not going," I said. "And don't bug Luis neither. I'm going to want him in Haiti in a couple of days."

"What about Orlando?"

"Good question." I looked at Anna, but she knew better than to say anything. "If he calls, tell him I'll be home."

He didn't call. And it didn't make sense to go looking for him. He could have got busted. Or Hernandez could have dusted him off for the five keys—which didn't seem too likely. He could be hiding out from the heat. Or he could have ripped me off for the fifty thousand. Whichever it was, I figured I'd hear about it soon enough. I had plenty to think about, with 20 kilos of heroin landing in Caracas in a few hours.

Next morning, there was still no word. Anna went off to Miami-Dade Junior College as usual, and I went to the bank to cash the $5,500 check I had from selling the Corvette. We had to have wheels. After shopping around a few dealers, I bought a nice little dark blue 1972 Volkswagen, and not even Anna spotted me in it when I drove over after school to pick her up at the beauty parlor. But that was mainly because she had other things on her mind.

"I called Orlando's sister," she said. "He got busted."

"No shit." I think I'd known all along. "When?"

"Yesterday. Right after he delivered the stuff."

"Oh, Jesus. Didn't I tell him? How dumb can you get?"

I walked up and down. It was my own fault. I should never have left it to his judgment, because he didn't have any.

"His sister told me he says not to worry about nothing. These things happen."

"Only when you're that fucking stupid."

I was angry, not worried. So long as he kept his mouth shut, they didn't have much to go on. Conspiracy was the most they could try for, and unless somebody talked, they didn't have a prayer.

"Is he out or what?"

"No, she says he's in Dade County Jail."

"Well, why in hell didn't Matilde call us? What's his bond?"

"She said $200,000."

"Jesus. Well, we better go see the old lady again."

This time it was the other way around. Victoria Montalvo started off friendly but turned sour when she heard what I was there for.

"I don't hardly know this Orlando," she said. "My son wouldn't want me to put up the house. It's all I got in the world. And, anyway, it ain't worth that much."

"Your son wouldn't leave nobody in the organization to rot in jail," I said. "He'd be ashamed. It's up to us to get him out, right, Mario?"

My godfather's brother gave it his close consideration. He was in the real estate business. "Well, if he's in the organization," he said, "we better see what we can do. Go find out the details and let me know."

"Ever since my son went away, it's been nothing but trouble," Victoria said.

"Yeah, he got away just in time," I said.

Before going over to the courthouse, I figured that first we ought to find out all we could from Orlando's sister, but when we got to her place, who should answer the door but Orlando himself. As soon as he saw me, he hung his head like a kid caught stealing bubble gum.

"How the hell did you get out?" I said. "We just been running around trying to put the bond together."

"Hernandez sprung me," he said. "They dropped it to fifty thousand and Elpidio put it up."

"Elpidio did? How come?"

"He wants me to say he didn't know what was in the package."

"Oh, great. Just what you need. A perjury rap. Get in the car, for Christ's sake."

He climbed in the back, and we drove off. It was all so stupid. I didn't know where to start, and neither did he.

"Okay," I said. "So what the hell happened?"

Orlando shrugged. "Well, I came over to you—nothing. I took Anna to your grandmother's—nothing."

"What do you mean, nothing? What about the Pinto?"

"I didn't see it no more after that. Just that one time. Everything was cool. So around 11:30 we went over to pick up the package at Armando's, and then we went to the drop on Coral Way. And still nothing. They must have been waiting there, because they hit me as I was coming out."

"Just a minute," I said. "Who's *we?*"

"Ricardo was with me." He laughed, shaking his head. "That guy. They must have had six cars, and still he beat them out."

I had to be dreaming. "*Who?*"

"Ricardo Morales. I offered him $2,000 to carry the gun."

18

On August 30, 1972, in the cool of the morning, Antonio Simon Orsatti-Serra drove down the Avenida Libertador in his blue and white Mustang, turned into the driveway of the Club Americana Hotel, parked, and went inside. A few minutes later, he came out again with Miguel Garcia, who had been waiting for him in the lobby. Though it was barely 6 a.m., they were laughing together as they got into the car and drove off in the direction of Maiquetía Airport.

Arriving there half an hour later, they left the Mustang on a lot near the international terminal and separated. Orsatti made his way upstairs to the glassed-in enclosure overlooking the customs area, and Garcia went to look for Miguel Sanz. He found him talking to Evelio Mijares, who was introduced to Garcia as the customs agent who would claim Sereni's baggage, and the three adjourned to the airport coffee shop to await the arrival of Avianca Flight 71 from Paris.

It landed shortly after 7 a.m. When they heard the announcement, Sanz and Mijares went through to the customs area, and Garcia went upstairs to watch. Orsatti was already there, but they did not stand together or even acknowledge each other's presence.

As Sereni came into the customs hall from immigration, he gave his baggage claim stubs to Sanz, according to plan, and presented himself to a customs agent with just his carry-on overnight bag, containing toilet things and a few small gifts. While the agent looked through it, Sanz and Mijares identified his two large brown suitcases by means of the claim stubs, lifted them off the conveyor, walked calmly past the customs agents searching the other passengers' luggage, and out through the exit to the main terminal concourse. Sereni then zipped up his flight bag and sauntered after them.

Upstairs, Orsatti and Garcia smiled at each other triumphantly. There being no further need for such extreme caution, they walked downstairs together to watch Sanz stow the first load of heroin in the trunk of his car. Everything had gone off without a hitch. They stood in the parking lot, laughing and congratulating themselves, as Sanz drove away with Mijares and Sereni.

They were so lighthearted, indeed, that Orsatti allowed the other car to get too far ahead of him. When Sanz arrived with the others at the Club Americana, they went into the hotel with the bags but found no one there to receive them. Garcia and Orsatti were caught in traffic on the outskirts of the city. Sooner than wait in the lobby, Sanz led his men out again with the suitcases, and the three drove over to the stash, apartment 7, Residencia el Castillito, at the corner of Avenida el Bosque and Avenida Libertador in the el Recreo section of Caracas. Correctly anticipating this move, Orsatti and Garcia went straight there in the Mustang, and the two cars arrived almost at the same time. The five men went up to apartment 7 with the suitcases, and came down empty-handed a few minutes later. They all then drove back to the Club Americana.

It was now eight-thirty. Around nine, Garcia, Sanz, and Mijares left the hotel again in a less jovial mood. In the interval, Sereni had reported that the load was short-weight. The twenty-four plastic bags he had brought over contained, not 24 kilos as Garcia had hoped, but only about 17. Furious, Garcia drove back to the stash to see for himself, and having confirmed that Sereni was right, returned to the hotel to take the matter up with Orsatti. The Pimp, however, had gone home by then to his apartment on the Avenida los Jabillos, not far from the stash. It was now about nine-thirty.

At eleven, everything fell apart.

Garcia, Orsatti, Sereni, and everybody else involved in the affair, except Sanz and Mijares, were arrested by the Venezuelan Judicial Police Technical Corps and charged with traffic in, and illegal possession of, narcotics, contrary to Article 367.1 of the Penal Code.

Sereni was picked up at the Club Americana. Garcia and Orsatti were arrested while arguing over the short weight in a furnished apartment they had rented next door to the stash. Another police squad, raiding Orsatti's apartment, found a couple of ounces of cocaine hidden in the waste pipe of his bidet, about fifty pornographic pictures, and two guns. Rolando Gonzalez was arrested at his office in the Centro Caprilles, and although nothing incriminating was found there, a search of his Lincoln uncovered 200 grams of cocaine hidden in a special compartment under the carpet. Pedro Diaz was picked up at home, and so were several others who had played lesser roles in the operation.

Nothing happened to Miguel Sanz—apart from receiving a commendation from the Judicial Police. After Garcia had tried to recover the $65,000 paid out for the aircraft they had never used, Sanz had gone to his former colleagues to arrange for Garcia's arrest.

As for Evelio Mijares, an officer in the Judicial Police, he was congratulated by his superiors for a successful portrayal of a corrupt customs official.

From the American point of view, the outcome was rather less satisfactory. Garcia and the others would naturally be prosecuted under Venezuelan law and thus contribute little or nothing toward building a case against their associates in the United States. Nevertheless, a new and potentially very dangerous heroin supply line had been cut, and after teleprinting the news to Miami, New York, and Washington, the BNDD office in Caracas closed its file on the case, well pleased with the result. Its agents had worked harmoniously alongside the Venezuelan police every step of the way, from Gerard Miller's early warning about Garcia's activities to the twenty-four-hour surveillance mounted on the suspects after Sanz's defection. In Washington, the case was already being talked about as a model of international cooperation.

In Miami and New York, however, the rejoicing seemed premature. A shipment of heroin had been stopped, but George Ramos and Frank Matthews were still at liberty—and at liberty to try again. After tracking Ramos all over the Caribbean, BNDD agents in Miami were not about to let him off the hook. Failing a substantive charge of possession, they were determined to bring him in for conspiracy, at least.

But progress to date had not been encouraging. Orlando Lamadrid had been well and truly set up by Morales, and they could link Lamadrid with Ramos in a way that was highly suggestive of criminal activity, but something more than suggestion and hearsay was needed to prove a charge of criminal conspiracy.

After receiving his instructions from Special Agent Charles Schaming, Morales had wormed out of the unsuspecting Lamadrid a complete picture of the cocaine-smuggling operation that Ramos had taken over from his godfather. More than that, Lamadrid had kept Morales up-to-date on the latest shipment from Haiti with daily news bulletins over breakfast at Isabelita's. During the weekend of August 12 and 13, for example, Morales learned, not only that six kilos had arrived on the *William Express*, but that Ramos was worried about the search of the ship, and also that the stuff had still been on board when it sailed. All this was duly reported to Schaming, together with the news that a further attempt would be made to get the load off the ship when it docked again in the Miami River on August 25.

Lamadrid's confidence in his friend Morales had remained blissfully unshaken by Ramos's warnings, which were more soundly based than he knew. As a front, Morales was on the payroll of Gramco International, a huge offshore mutual fund built up by Rafael G. Navarro, a Cuban businessman who had formerly represented the Batista government at the United Nations, and who, in return for advantages never clearly defined, had allowed the CIA to use his companies as a cover for its agents in the Caribbean.

Gramco's usefulness in this respect, however, was coming to an end. In 1970, when its real estate portfolio alone was valued at $850 million, Navarro had held merger talks with Robert L. Vesco, of Investors Overseas Services, but the project fell through when Bernie Cornfeld, the founder of IOS, opposed it. In 1971, with the financial community beginning to take fright at the company it was keeping, Pierre Salinger resigned as a director of Gramco, and the stage was then set for a spectacular crash in late 1972 that would ruin thousands of small investors throughout Central and South America.

A more reliable paymaster was the FBI, which had employed Morales as an informer on a regular monthly stipend since 1968. It was an association of which he took full advantage. Early in 1971, he cemented his relations with the federal government by going to work for the BNDD as well, on a starting retainer of $350 a month. This was soon increased, reflecting results. In April 1972, barely four months before informing on Orlando Lamadrid, Morales secured the conviction of two prominent Miami dope dealers —Manuel Penabaz-Tobio, and Felipe Donado-Duran—by testifying against them in open court.

How news of this failed to reach Lamadrid, Ramos, and the Cuban community as a whole is a mystery, but fail it did. On August 25, the day the six kilos returned to Miami on the *William Express,* Lamadrid discussed the situation with Morales five times, starting over breakfast at the Ideal Restaurant, and ending that night with the abandonment, for the time being, of attempts to get the load ashore.

On August 29, at their usual ten o'clock breakfast conference, Lamadrid asked Morales for help. He and Ramos had finally gotten hold of half the shipment, he said, but the Feds had chased them all over town with it. They had a buyer, though—a guy named El Pillo—who was due at Lamadrid's apartment at 11:30. (Elpidio Hernandez owned a construction company called El Pillo Development Corporation.) Now Lamadrid needed a driver and bodyguard. Was Morales willing?

Morales was willing.

Lamadrid left the restaurant much relieved at the thought of having such a formidable man on his side. A few moments later, Morales left, too. He went to the pharmacy next door and telephoned Charles Schaming at the regional office of the BNDD.

Half an hour afterwards, Morales picked Lamadrid up in his

green Chevrolet and drove him home to SW 27th Lane to meet Hernandez. Their arrival was watched by BNDD Group Supervisor Constantine Kritikos and Special Agents Jim Sweat, Bill Warner, and Philip Martin. Lamadrid seemed nervous and agitated. While he waited in the car for Hernandez to appear, he regaled Morales with a breathless account of how the previous evening he and Ramos had removed the stuff from his apartment under the agents' noses and hidden it at a friend's house. He also told Morales that he had *four* kilos to sell to El Pillo for $40,000, not five for $50,000, having presumably decided to hold one back for himself to compensate for the emotional wear and tear.

Hernandez was late. He drove on to the block around noon in his green Riviera, and Lamadrid got out of the car to give him his instructions. Hernandez was to go straight to the drop and wait for him there. Returning to Morales, Lamadrid told him to drive to 2160 SW 5th Street, which he did, taking care to use his directional signals for the benefit of Agents Warner and Martin in the car behind.

Observed by the agents at a distance, Lamadrid retrieved the shopping bag with the five kilos from under the boat cover, and rejoined Morales, who now turned south on 22nd Avenue, taking care not to lose the government car in traffic. As he approached the two-story building at 1860 Coral Way, he spotted El Pillo's Riviera outside and parked just behind it.

Now that the moment had come, Lamadrid looked into the shopping bag at his feet and compromised. Instead of a full kilo, he took out just one of the half-kilo bags and shoved it under his seat before getting out of the car and walking into the building with the other nine. Morales watched him go. He also watched Group Supervisor Kritikos and Agent Sweat, who had been following Hernandez, go into the lobby after him, and Agents Warner and Martin scramble out of their car to join them. Well satisfied with his morning's work, Morales backed up a little, drove around the Riviera, and went to find a telephone. Agent Schaming was standing by for his call.

Meanwhile, the four agents in the lobby were not certain where

Lamadrid had gone, although they could hear laughter and loud voices coming from one of the first-floor apartments. To be on the safe side, Kritikos stationed Warner and Martin outside the building, and was on the point of announcing himself as a federal agent and bursting in on the conversation, when Lamadrid saved him the trouble. He came out into the hallway, too busy saying goodbye to Hernandez to notice the agents, who had flattened themselves against the wall. Shouting out to Warner to arrest him, Kritikos thrust open the door as Hernandez tried to close it, and rushed in with Agent Sweat, guns drawn.

When Warner and Martin joined them a minute or so later, with Lamadrid in tow, they found Hernandez face down on the floor with his wrists handcuffed together behind his back. On a table at the other end of the room were nine plastic bags, one of them cut open, that were subsequently shown to contain a little over 4.5 kilos of 51.9 percent pure cocaine hydrochloride. When asked to account for this, Hernandez told the agents he had been under the impression that the shopping bag brought by Lamadrid contained fishing tackle.

Fifteen minutes after his departure from the scene, Ricardo Morales handed over the other half kilo to Agent Schaming in the parking lot behind Howard Johnson's on Biscayne Boulevard. And two days later Agent Schaming handed over to Morales a $1,000 bonus. Though the evidence against Ramos was still tenuous, the BNDD regional office was reasonably pleased with a case which offered two certain convictions at least and which had now taken on fresh significance with the news from Venezuela.

New York was still not overly impressed, however. As far as Gerard Miller was concerned, none of this had contributed much toward nailing Frank Matthews, the prime mover and principal villain of the piece. Nor did Matthews himself seem exactly stunned by events in Caracas and the collapse of his 100-kilo deal with Garcia. As the government's pressure on him had intensified, so he had become more and more preoccupied with milking the operation for cash to finance a strategic withdrawal. He was also concerned about his fast-fading friendship with Mickey Beckwith, who seemed bent on using the O.K. Corral as a base for a breakaway partnership with Charles Quarles, a leading Brooklyn policy banker and one-time dope dealer. To add to his ill humor, on the day after Garcia's arrest, Matthews went down with a touch of pneumonia that kept him at home on Staten Island over the Labor Day weekend.

During the afternoon of August 31, Gerard Miller and Roger Garay drove out there to see how he was taking these reverses. Parking well away from Buttonwood Road, they circled around behind the house, through a wooded section, and then crawled across a field on their bellies to the cover of some bushes about 150 feet from the back of the property.

Through their binoculars, they could see at once that Matthews was not happy. He and Pop Darby were arguing about something, while Gattis Hinton was locked in an equally heated dispute with another man they could not identify. Barbara Hinton was banging around in the kitchen, obviously annoyed with all of them, but, strain as they might, neither Miller nor Garay could make out a word that any of them were saying. It was very frustrating, and no recompense at all for the damage Garay had done to his striped white pants crawling across the field.

The sun went down, and as darkness came on, Miller laid the foundation for another favorite anecdote in the Matthews anthology. The back lot of 7 Buttonwood Road had not yet been landscaped. It was overgrown with weeds and long grass, offering just about enough concealment for two tall, strongly built officers to gamble on getting close enough to eavesdrop without being spotted, particularly as any sound they might make would be covered by the noise of a party in the yard of the house next door.

Inch by inch, they edged commando-style through the undergrowth toward the patio, where Matthews was still grumbling spasmodically at Darby. Progress was necessarily slow because, although it was getting darker by the minute, any unusual movement of the tall grass could easily have given them away.

Then, just as they were getting close enough to pick up a word here and there, Matthews leaned in through the sliding door to the house—and the back lot was suddenly lit up as bright as Yankee Stadium at a night game.

The two officers froze, stricken with the knowledge that not only was their cover now woefully inadequate but Matthews would have every legal justification for taking a shot at them.

Both recovered together. As Garay groped for the gun in his ankle holster, Miller threw him over on his back and mounted him.

"You say one word about this," he muttered, pumping grimly up and down, "and you're a patrolman for life."

The seconds stretched out. Garay, still trying to reach his gun, began to see the funny side of two tough cops, both family men, performing in the missionary position for the nation's number-one drug dealer, and Miller, too, found it hard to resist, even though he was first in line to get shot. Then Matthews said something to Darby, who laughed. They had evidently concluded, as Miller had hoped they would, that he and Garay were a stray couple from the party next door. A few moments later, the lights went out, and the two officers escaped gratefully into the field.

From the wiretaps, it soon became clear that Beckwith, not Garcia or the collapse of the 100-kilo deal, was the real cause of Matthews's bad temper. On September 4, Dolores Beckwith called Barbara Hinton to discuss the catering arrangements for a combined housewarming and Labor Day cookout they were holding that afternoon at Buttonwood Road. They were hardly launched on their conversation before Matthews, the mock Muslim, was threatening, via Barbara, to beat Beckwith for eating pork spare ribs, and after exchanging a few fairly jocular insults, the two men took over the call themselves.

"I'll beat your ass in anyway," said Matthews, as his opening contribution.

"What's wrong, cap?" Beckwith pretended to be puzzled.

"Because you ain't doing right."

"Captain Knickerbocker, what's wrong?"
"You ain't do right, boss."
"What didn't I do right, boss?"
"Me and you got to talk."
"Again?" Beckwith sounded weary.
"You goddamn right."
"Something happen again, boss?"
"Might be. And when I finish explaining to you, you will understand it."
"About what now?"
"What you doing."
Though guarded in what he said, knowing his telephone was probably tapped, Matthews went on to accuse Beckwith of being indiscreet in his business dealings.
"They got eyes all over the streets, man," he said. "Them motherfuckers. Eyes like cats' eyes all over the mother-fucking street."
Beckwith rejected the accusation, but Matthews was not convinced.
"If you did that," he said, "take another trip, man, 'cause that's too dangerous right now. I'll talk to you again. Come on over."
"Yeah, well. I'll come over and you can talk, man."
"Right on. We can have a long talk, 'cause you know we can always discuss things together."
"Right on."
Before he hung up, Matthews made him promise several more times to come to the barbecue, but Beckwith never showed.
"Fuck him, fuck him, fuck him," said Matthews to Darby on the telephone next day. "I didn't do nothing to him. He want to act that way, the hell with him. I ain't thinking about it."
But he was. And as it became increasingly obvious that something was cooking between Beckwith and Charles Quarles, Matthews swallowed his pride. He called Beckwith repeatedly, and even got off his sickbed to go looking for him, but to no avail. On September 11, in the course of a long, rambling telephone conversation with Pop Darby, who had been trying to mediate be-

tween them, Matthews alternately complained and raged about the way his old friend and partner was avoiding him.

"You know what it is?" he said. "I'm going to tell you exactly what it is. Mickey feels like I am superior over him, and he resent me . . . If you want to put it all down in a nutshell, this is why he keep avoiding me, don't want to see me, don't want to talk to me."

Pop Darby had to agree. "Well, I told him. I said, 'Man,' I said, 'you know that man was sick. Got out of his bed like a fool, looking for you to talk to you,' I say. 'And when he got back in, shit, Barbara had to go and get the damn doctor.' I say, 'You know that ain't right.' I said, 'Man, why don't you go and talk to this man and get this thing straightened out before you find yourself out in the street and don't know how the hell you got there.' "

The two then branched off into a highly critical analysis of Beckwith's failings as a family man, friend, and business partner, touching off yet another anguished outburst from Matthews.

"Stinking ass mother-fucker," he said. "You just tell him, whenever you see him, you just tell him—did you tell him I was upset with him?"

"Yeah, I told him, I told him . . ."

Darby went on to say that he was going over to Beckwith's place, and if he saw him there, he would talk to him again.

"Okay," said Matthews. "Tell him I said come and see me, because I am very, very upset about it, and say, lot of things to talk about . . . If he out there, just come on in the truck over here. I'll wait over here for you all."

But Beckwith never came.

To Miller, William Callahan, and Francis Sheerin, it looked like their cue. The time had come to pull in Beckwith and Darby to see if one or both could be induced to testify against Matthews and provide a backbone for the case. New York State search warrants were applied for, granted, and executed at 8:25 in the evening of September 15.

Group 12's raid on 101 East 56th Street, Brooklyn, was carried out by a squad of ten men led by Miller himself. The last of the millworkers had left the O.K. Corral about ten minutes earlier; Beckwith was known to be a gun freak, and Miller had no intention of risking his men, or his potential witnesses, in an avoidable shoot-out. They went in through the front door to the lobby, broke a pane of glass to open a locked inner door to the hallway, and then discovered there were two apartments on the first floor, not one, as they had supposed.

Both had unusual front doors. They were not wood but steel, hung on steel doorframes set in concrete between two-by-four beams. Miller decided to tackle the rear apartment first and motioned to Roger Garay, who took off his coat with a sigh. It took half an hour's steady swinging with a 20-pound sledge, and a contribution from two other men with an ax and crowbar, before the door gave way, but as soon as he stepped inside, Miller knew he had hit the jackpot. It was the first tangible proof of the size of Matthews's operation: one of the biggest and best-stocked narcotics mills he had ever seen.

His men spent the next six hours cataloguing and packing the evidence they found in the two apartments. (They were not interconnected, but Garay was spared any further exertion by a fellow officer who climbed in through an unfastened window in front of the building and opened the second steel door from inside.) When they left, they took with them no less than sixty-three boxes of exhibits.

Among the drug-cutting paraphernalia they seized were two 32-gallon mixing drums containing between them about half a pound of caked-on heroin that nobody had bothered with; seventeen large plastic mixing bags, all with some residue; 2.5 *million* glassine bags in boxes piled up to the ceiling; hundreds of rolls of Scotch tape; suitcases full of rubber bands; crates of lactose; cartons of mannite (with Walter Rosenbaum's name printed on the labels); many more suitcases—some containing bundles of street bags ready for distribution, others with packages of "weight"—and the usual clutter of strainers, respirators, scales, weights, paddles, playing cards, and other small implements.

Miller could also congratulate himself on raiding the O.K. Corral while it was unguarded. His men took away an armory of loaded weapons, including a .45 caliber submachine gun; a collection of rifles, among them two .458 caliber Magnum elephant guns that the officer in charge of the police range refused to test-fire on grounds of public safety; an assortment of pistols; and a trunkful of ammunition.

Most of the documentary evidence was found in the front apartment, which had clearly served as a recreational facility for the millworkers. The living room, carpeted in red, was comfortably furnished with a sofa, armchairs, a television set, stereo equipment, and a roll-around bar loaded with some fifty bottles of liquor. The kitchen, bathroom, and bedroom had also been used for conventional purposes, but opposite the kitchen was a closet that yielded a pillowcase containing $148,000, mostly in fifties and hundreds; Beckwith's personal papers, including his birth certificate, a New York State hunting license, the deeds to the building, gas bills for both apartments (in his own name), and a spiral-bound notebook with coded details of various narcotics transactions; yet another gun, and a selection of photographs showing Beckwith armed to the teeth like a Mexican bandit, and Matthews in bed employing *his* favorite weapon on a representative cross-section of girlfriends.

Group 12's second raiding party, led by Sergeant Jack Rawald, had meanwhile achieved less spectacular but equally effective results at apartment 7J, 130 Clarkson Avenue—the home of Pop Darby, whom they had met in the hallway as he was taking out the trash. After turning the place over thoroughly, they came up with a small quantity of cocaine, the usual collection of guns (this time, in a foot locker in front of Darby's bed), a bureau full of papers relating to various drug deals, and $14,683.

Flossie Darby told Barbara Hinton all about it on the telephone next day, doing her best to remember the code names and phrases they had adopted to confuse the wiretappers.

"They came in here and, um, found some money," Flossie said.

"Money?"

"Uh-huh. Yeah. *My* damn money . . . Where's your girlfriend?"

"Huh?" said Barbara, forgetting for the moment that "girlfriend" meant boyfriend, just as "Frances" meant Frank, and "Margaret" or "Mildred," Mickey Beckwith.

"Where's your girlfriend Frances?"

"I don't know. I've been—ah, ah, she just called here."

"Frances?"

"Yeah."

"Well, they went out the which-you-call-it place. Um, Margaret's."

"Yeah?"

"Tore it up."

"You kidding." Barbara sounded aghast.

"They was doing that while they was here."

"Which one was this, which one was this?"

"Tore it up. On 56th."

"Oh, you kidding. Where is he at?"

Flossie didn't answer. All she knew was that Beckwith had been arrested, like her husband.

"Well, are they looking for my girlfriend, too?" asked Barbara anxiously.

"Yeah. You know, they was calling his name . . ."

After describing the search, Flossie said that Darby had been told by one of Rawald's men that they had seen him go into the O.K. Corral with three suitcases, and that was when they had decided to lock him up.

"Then he asked about Margaret," she went on. " 'Oh, he's my nephew. That's my sister's son.' 'So your sister's son is going to fucking jail. We're going to bury his ass in there . . .' Shit. They know all about Philadelphia and the house, and they told him they going to keep that money, but they can forget that. I'm going down there and claim mine, because I paid taxes on it—paid a whole lot of taxes on that money . . ."

Though Flossie did not mention it, her husband had been so

shattered by the extent of the officers' knowledge that he had confessed to dealing in narcotics with Frank Matthews for years—an admission that encouraged Miller and Callahan mightily. But, even without this, Barbara Hinton was too shaken up to carry on with the conversation. It was another three hours before she called Flossie back, but Flossie could still only think about the money.

"I'm going down there to claim mine," she said, "because I don't care what nobody thinks—I sure paid tax on it . . . You heard about Mildred's hundred and seventy-six? You hear what I said?"

"Yeah. I was just trying to think what you said."

"I said, a hundred and seventy-six big ones."

"Mildred?"

"You know."

"You kidding."

"Honest to God," said Flossie. "I'm sick to death. And I was just going to one of the hotels. Good thing they didn't hit both of them."

The discrepancy between the $176,000 that Flossie claimed was taken from "Mildred" Beckwith's "hotel" and the $148,000 listed as evidence by Group 12 was obviously a mistake on somebody's part, but there was no mistaking Flossie's main concern. When Barbara expressed her understandable anxiety at being left high and dry with three kids and no word from anyone, least of all "Frances"—"I just feel like I just can't take no more"—all Flossie could say in reply was: "Worry about my little fourteen. That's a lot of money to me."

"Sure it is . . . You know, the phone is probably tapped."

"Huh?"

"The phone is probably tapped, you know?"

"Yeah?" said Flossie. "Well, I hope they tap this. If I don't get my fourteen thousand . . ."

"I know mine is. I don't know about yours . . ."

"They terrible people," sighed Flossie.

Miller, Callahan, and the other "terrible people" were jubilant.

In the space of a few days, they had cut an important heroin supply line on which Matthews had been depending; brought about the arrest of his associates in Caracas and Miami; knocked out one of his main production centers in New York; captured two of his principal lieutenants, one of whom already showed signs of cracking, and rattled Matthews enough to make him leave town.

To rub salt in these wounds, the IRS now decided to seize the *Double SS*, a 40-foot cruiser owned by Beckwith, paid for by Matthews, and used by their dealers and senior executives for drinking parties and general debauchery. Berthed in Sheepshead Bay, it had certainly not been used much for sailing. Representing ODALE, William Callahan went along as an observer and helped the agents tinker with the boat for several hours before they finally persuaded one of the twin engines to start. By then it was dusk, a thick fog was rolling in, and the rest of the crew was busy checking out Beckwith's champagne. After steering a few erratic circles, the boat returned to its original moorings and Callahan drove around to the police launch patrol station to ask for help.

The crew of Marine Launch No. 8 were having their dinner, but when they learned of the problem, they readily agreed to give the *Double SS* a tow to Governors Island, where it was to be impounded. By the time they had finished their meal, however, it was pitch-dark, and the fog had reduced visibility to a few yards. After passing a towline, they set out across the bay, but soon decided that conditions were too dangerous. The launch turned back, making for the coast-guard station, while the boarding party, keeping watch on the deck of the *Double SS*, bellowed out snatches of dimly remembered sea shanties to ward off passing shipping.

The Coast Guard was not pleased to see them at first, but after checking with Governors Island, and on being invited to join the federal agents in their investigation of Beckwith's floating cellar, the detail on duty allowed them to tie up for the night. Confident the vessel was now in safe hands, Callahan drove home to his family.

He returned next morning to find the fog had cleared, though not for *every* member of the prize crew. The coast-guard men were still on their feet, however, and when they eventually got both engines started, Callahan sailed with them around to Governors Island, where a reception committee was waiting.

In view of the importance of the case, ODALE had decided to celebrate the seizure of Beckwith's boat by the IRS. The American public, it felt, was entitled to see some of the spoils of war captured by intrepid federal agents from a major drug dealer. Accordingly, ABC television had been invited to send a camera crew to Governors Island so that the formal surrender of the *Double SS* to the U.S. government, represented by Rear Admiral Benjamin F. Engel, commandant of the 3rd Coast Guard District, could be seen across the nation on a network news program.

That night, millions of Americans watched as the *Double SS* came into view in long shot, making for the dock where the rear admiral waited, smiling, to greet its jaded crew. While the newscaster did the voice-over, reminding everybody of the raid on Beckwith's mill and what had been found there, the boat chugged steadily closer and closer, filling more and more of the screen. And as the rear admiral turned to his aide with a questioning frown, the *Double SS* chugged steadily into the end of the dock, crumpling several feet of her bow.

19

Orlando wouldn't have it. Morales an informer? He'd rather believe it about his own mother. It had to be Hernandez's partner.

"You're crazy," I said. "They wait for you. They see you park. They grab you, but *he* gets away. Forget it. They *let* him go."

No. It was Hernandez's partner. "And if things start to look rough," he said, "I'm going to take off."

"You take off and Elpidio will forfeit his bond. He's not going to like that. $50,000 is no joke."

"Well, I don't give a shit," he said. "If it looks like fifteen years, I'm going to make a run for it."

We dropped him off and went home. I had some heavy thinking to do. Anna couldn't see anybody following us, but I knew they weren't going to be satisfied just with Orlando.

There was a note pinned to the front door. "Come and see me," it said. "Your godfather's in trouble. Ana Baños."

We turned around without a word and went over there.

"What happened?"

"Imagine," she said. "They got popped."

She didn't seem too upset, but, then, things hadn't been the same between them since she caught him with his pants down in Puerto Rico.

"All of them? How'd it happen?"

"I don't know," she said. "I only know they're all in jail."

"Ooh-la-la. Well, well. Who's going to pay the rent now?"

"You better start worrying about that yourself," she said, and she was right for once.

As we drove back, Anna uncorked. She'd held herself together without a murmur so far, but now it looked like the roof was caving in. I tried to tell her, if they had anything solid to work with, how come they'd collared Orlando and not me? As long as he kept his mouth shut, they'd got nothing they could tag me with. Anyway, there was no point sitting around and brooding about it. We went out that night with Orlando and wound up at the Dairy Queen ice-cream parlor at Flagler and 54th Avenue. As we were leaving, Orlando bumped into somebody outside the pizza joint next door, and it turned out to be a Venezuelan general he knew, a political refugee but a guy with good contacts over there.

Naturally, he asked how Orlando was, and after Orlando told him, he said: "I hear Miguel was arrested, too."

"That's right," I said. "How did you know?"

"Oh, it's in all the Venezuelan papers," he said. "On television, too, over there. Biggest story they've had in years."

Orlando looked at me. "Any chance of getting Miguel out of there?" he said.

The general shrugged. "In Caracas, there's always a way to do anything."

"How?" I said. "How do we go about it?"

"Well, with $30,000, I could talk to a couple of people I know. Maybe they could arrange something. He wouldn't be able to stay in Venezuela, of course. He'd be a fugitive."

"Beats being in the can," I said. "There's plenty other places he can go to. He'll have to take his chances."

"You want me to look into it, then?"

"Sure," I said. "If he stays, he's going to face a hellatious amount of years. Let's give it a try."

"All right," he said. "Orlando knows where to find me. Let's talk again tomorrow."

So, after dropping Orlando off at his place, I went home a bit more hopeful. If we could spring Miguel, he would have to stay in South America, and if I knew anything about my godfather, he'd have that cocaine pipeline open again in no time. I didn't know whether Pedro Diaz had been popped or not, but I was already thinking of taking a run down to La Paz to find the Doctor and see about the 15 kilos I'd ordered. Henry Morgan would front the money.

Hanging around outside the house when we got home was El Gordo and his wife, the fat guy who'd told me how to borrow a car from Trail Dodge that time me and my godfather went to blow away Umberto Rojas. He often stopped by to visit and clean out our refrigerator, but Anna groaned when she saw them. She wasn't feeling so good and went through to lie down in the bedroom while I bullshitted with them for a while. I couldn't just send them away.

We hadn't been talking very long before, all of a sudden, there was a heavy knock at the door.

"Who is it?" I said, although I knew.

"Federal agents. Bureau of Narcotics. Open up."

"Anna," I called out. "Better get dressed. The Gestapo's here."

I wasn't worried. Sooner or later, they had to question me about Orlando, and better here than downtown. So I casually opened the door, and wham! They stormed the house, guns drawn. I saw men coming and coming.

"Where's the war?" I said.

They didn't take no notice. Feo was barking and snapping at their ankles, and the fat guy almost pissed his pants. They charged in, swung his ass around, and put him up against the wall.

"What you doing to him?" his wife yelled, but the agents didn't understand Spanish. "You let him alone."

Already the apartment was jammed with people tripping over each other. Then they slammed me up against the wall as well, to check my pockets, and two of them brought Anna in from the bedroom to watch. These two agents—I found out later they were Bill Warner and Jack Lloyd—had burst in with their guns out before she'd had time to move. And there she was, sitting up in bed in a Mickey Mouse T-shirt. They were gentlemen, though. They turned their backs while she put on her shorts.

"Why are they arresting you?" she said. "What are they doing here?"

"I don't know, baby," I said. "They didn't say."

Our Peke was going crazy. They had a German shepherd at the door to sniff for drugs, and Feo wanted to eat it.

"Would you pick up your dog, lady, so we can come in?" said the handler.

So Anna went to get Feo, and saw another agent going through the refrigerator.

"What are they looking for?" she said. "What do they want?"

"Don't you know?" asked another one. "Where do you keep it?"

"Keep what?" I said, as they put the shepherd into our walk-in closet. "If that dog slobbers on my clothes, I'll sue the government."

Nobody took any notice. It was like pandemonium in there.

"Look, would somebody mind telling me what this is all about?" I said. "Nobody's showed me a warrant or nothing."

"I'll tell you what it's about," one guy said. "You're under arrest for conspiracy to violate the laws against narcotics, that's what it's about."

Somebody else pulled me around. "Any weapons in the house?"

"No. No weapons. I got one, but it's over at my grandmother's house."

Expecting something like this, we had dumped everything. Anna had put the .32 down the garbage chute. The .22s we'd wiped clean and thrown out while they were chasing us around, and somebody had borrowed the .38 weeks before and never returned it. So we were clean. After they finished turning the place over, everybody gathered in the living room and looked at me. Then out came the handcuffs.

Anna hadn't expected that. For the first time, she cut loose with a few tears.

"You didn't find nothing," she said. "Why are you taking him? He ain't done nothing."

"Don't worry, sweetheart," one said, as they took me out. "We'll be back for you later. Where's the Corvette?"

"What Corvette?" she said, and I could have kissed her. "We got a Volkswagen. A blue Volkswagen."

El Gordo hadn't moved off the wall since they put him there. "Officer," he said, "is it all right if I leave now?"

"No," said the agent. "You stay there. I'll be back."

"What's his bond?" I heard Anna say as I went through the door. "How much will it be?"

"More than *you* can raise, honey," somebody said. "So don't worry about it."

They pushed me into the back of a 1967 Buick, and a black agent read me my rights.

"This the best the government can do for you?" I said, meaning the Buick.

"Sorry," he said. "I know it ain't what you're used to. Where'd you get the money for that car?"

"The Volkswagen?" I said. "I saved up my green stamps."

"The Corvette. The white one."

"What Corvette?" I said. "You got the wrong guy. I own a blue Volkswagen. Want to see the registration?"

"No, no." He figured he had me talking now. "Where's your godfather? We ain't seen him around lately."

"Oh, haven't you heard? He's in jail."

"Yeah? In jail? What for?"

"For being careless." And that was when it finally hit me. *I* was under arrest.

"How do you know that?" he said. He was trying to tie me in with the guys in Caracas.

"Because I read the goddamn newspapers." Jesus. How could this have happened to me? Where was my million dollars? "Now don't talk to me no more."

"There ain't *been* nothing in the papers. So how do you know? Who told you?"

"Take a look at the Venezuelan newspapers," I said. "Now leave me alone. I got a right to remain silent."

They left it at that until we reached the old Bureau of Narcotics building right off Biscayne Boulevard. As soon as we got upstairs, they started in with the needle.

"Well, for a while there you were doing pretty good for yourself, kid. Now you got to pay your dues. Like for the next fifteen years."

"What's my bond?" I said.

"Okay." One of them looked at the clock on the wall. "It's now Saturday. Court don't sit till Monday. How about $250,000?"

"I want to make a phone call. I got a right to make a phone call."

"Later. First you got to play the piano for us."

So while Bill Warner took my prints, the other agents kept up with the bullshit.

"You sure got a stupid partner, you know that? All that voodoo crap in his house. You got to thank him for this."

I just looked at them. They weren't going to get nothing out of me until I figured everything out and knew exactly what I was doing.

"Your godfather's talking, too. That goddamn bastard son of a bitch Miguel Garcia—they're twisting his balls in Caracas, you know that? He's going to put all you mother-fuckers inside for life."

I made like I was deaf, and one agent—a little Mexican guy—got so mad, he came up and poked me with his finger.

"You goddamn son of a bitch," he said. "You suck dick, mother-fucker."

"Hey," I said. "You know? We got to listen to this fucking bull-shit? Man, you got me. I'm here. I got to take this shit, too?"

"Okay," Warner said, like he was bored with the whole thing. "Lay off, you guys."

They were trying to con me into taking a swing at one of them so they could turn around and kick my face in. And they kept it up until they finished booking me and took my picture. Then they put the cuffs back on for the ride over to Dade County Jail, and as we were going downstairs to the car, somebody pushed me. I managed to save myself from falling, and ran down the rest of the stairs before they could do it again.

"Hey, I'll make a deal with you," one of them said when he caught up with me on the sidewalk. "Let's save the taxpayers a couple of bucks. I'll take the cuffs off and give you fifty yards before I start shooting, okay?"

It was so stupid it made me feel better. If that was the best they could do, I had to be able to beat this.

When we got to the jail, I sat in the tank for an hour before they took me upstairs to a cell. On the way, I asked again about my bond, figuring the guards would tell me the truth, and they said no bond had been set, as far as they knew. That was bad news. So then I asked to make the call I was allowed. I'd been saving it until I knew where I stood. I phoned Anna, but she wasn't home.

It was Sunday before I got to talk to her, or anybody, and by then I was pretty uptight. Visiting times over the weekend were split according to the prisoners' last names: A to M on Saturdays, and everybody else on Sunday. But Anna hadn't wasted no time. She'd knocked herself out trying to get help, starting the minute they'd taken me out of the house.

"We went to Orlando's," she said. "El Gordo drove me. I wanted to go see Victoria Montalvo, but they wouldn't take me. I was going to say to her, 'Either you bail him out or I'll talk to the agents and tell them the whole story.' "

"Oh, Jesus, baby," I said. "You can't *do* that."

"No. Orlando told me. 'You crazy?' he said. 'You could get yourself killed, talking like that.' So I called her on the phone. Woke her out of bed."

"What did she say?"

"Well, I told her what happened, and she hung up on me. 'You shouldn't have called me,' she said. 'It's got nothing to do with me.' "

It was like a big hand reached up in my insides and squeezed the breath out of me. I could hear my heart thumping in my ears.

"So then I really wanted to go over there," Anna said, "but nobody would take me."

I should have known, but it hadn't never crossed my mind that the old lady would turn her back on me. If *she* was going to act like that, how much help was I going to get from people like Martinez? We had around $20,000 I could lay my hands on, but I didn't want to use that for bail money and have nothing left when I got out. Property was better, anyway. And when I thought about what those people owed me, the money I'd earned for them to buy their new houses and everything, I damn near choked.

"So what did you do then, baby?" I said, because I didn't want to frighten Anna with none of this. She was crying already.

"I called my sister, and she came over to stay with me," she said.

"Yeah, that's good. Okay. Well, now we got to get a lawyer."

"No, baby. I did that already."

"Hey!" The kid was fantastic; had more balls than all of them put together. "Is he good? How'd you find him?"

"Someone Orlando knows told me about him. His name's Melvyn Kessler. And he says they're going to arraign you tomorrow."

"Yeah, they got to do that."

"Then he'll see about the bond. Told me not to worry. He won't let them set it too high."

"Sounds like a nice guy," I said.

"Yeah," she said. "*I* thought so."

Come Monday afternoon, around two o'clock, they drove me over to Federal Court in the post-office building, and Mel Kessler came to see me in the holding cell. Anna was right, as usual. With her instinct for people, she'd picked a good one. He was tough, businesslike, and human. No bullshit.

The government side seemed very confident, he said. Looked like I was in a whole lot of trouble. But the first thing was to make bail. Did I own any real estate? No, I told him. And as of right then, I didn't know nobody who *would* put up collateral for a bond. Okay, he said. In that case, we'd have to fix something quick. His investigator had a house to sell, so he'd send him in to see me.

At this point they took me into court, in front of Magistrate Peter Palermo, and right away the government attorney started firing questions:

"What do you do for a living?"

"I sell jewelry."

"You have a license?"

"Yes."

"Where did you get the money for the car?"

"My godfather gave it to me."

"You ever been to Haiti?"

"Yes."

"You ever been to Venezuela?"

"Yes."

"Why?"

"My godfather invited me to go."

"Your honor, this man's godfather, Miguel Garcia, also known as Marcello Cabot, has a long record of narcotics violations. He was arrested recently in Caracas and is awaiting trial on charges of narcotics violations. A large amount of heroin was seized there en route to the United States, and—"

"Your honor," said Kessler, jumping up. "Are we considering the case of my client or trying his godfather?"

I liked the man's style. He kept picking them off like that, and by the time the hearing was over, it didn't sound like they had much. He'd given me a lot of confidence, and it wasn't shook when Palermo set bail at $50,000.

"You want my advice?" Kessler said afterwards. "Don't make it. Don't even try. Let's wait. If that's all they've got, it's too steep. I'm going to ask for another hearing."

"When?"

"I'll try for Friday. They're going to have to come up with something more solid than that. And it'll give us a little time to work something out for the bond."

So. Two days in jail hadn't killed me. Four more probably wouldn't either.

Kessler's investigator came over to see me next day. His name was Aguedo Lugo, and he knew Ricardo Morales from way back. They'd been in the Congo together for the CIA.

"So what do you think?" I said. "Was it him?"

"Got to be," he said. "That's your problem, right there. Orlando really fucked up when he picked Ricardo. I also heard he was over in Caracas two, three days before your godfather got busted."

"Ricardo was? No shit." Now I'd have to kill the son of a bitch.

"Yeah, but you don't got to worry too much about that. Right now, there's a lot of holes in this conspiracy deal, so let's hang tough. It looks good."

But a couple of days later it didn't look so good. He came over to tell me they'd fixed for Anna to buy the house, with my brother-in-law co-signing the paper because Anna was underage.

"Now for the bad news," Lugo said. "The government's filling in a lot of those holes. Morales is doing it. Looks like he's telling them the whole story. They know a little more about this thing every day."

"Yeah, but they can't convict on *that*," I said. "He'll have to go to court and testify."

"Well, I don't know. He might just *do* that. You see the papers—the Spanish papers? There's a whole big splash about this heroin coming in from a Communist country."

"Oh, Jesus," I said. "So that makes him a fucking hero?"

"Listen," he said. "I got to ask you this, so don't be offended or nothing. You thought about doing a deal?"

"A deal?"

"With the government."

"No." I looked at him a long time. "No, I haven't."

"Okay. I got to ask you, because that's a possibility you ought to consider."

"No, no," I said. "That's out."

Anna was trying to spring me another way. She went to see a voodoo queen—not Raquel Dumois, but another one, who'd never laid eyes on her before. And right off the bat, she told Anna she had come about the man she was living with—Anna hadn't said a word. He was a man who traveled a lot, but what he did was against the law, she said. Now he was in jail, and Anna wanted to get him out.

Naturally, Anna was impressed. The *santera* told her a lot of other things, too, including that Anna's mother was still in Cuba, and so she listened real good when the old woman laid out what she had to do. First, she had to take a bath with white flowers and Florida water. Then she had to get a white pigeon and smear cocoa butter on its back and wings. After that, she had to tie green, yellow, and red ribbons to its legs, take it into a cemetery, walking backwards, and release the goddamn bird over her shoulder. As it went free, so I would go free.

To be on the safe side, Orlando also took her to see his *palero*, a real spooky guy who kept a human skeleton in his room. This one had a different answer to the problem. He blew smoke on top of a glass of water and told Anna my bail would soon be reduced, and I'd get out. All she had to do was take four eggs, coat them in cocoa butter, and smash one at each corner of Dade County Jail. The doors would then open, he said.

She did that on Thursday. On Friday, I went to court again and they turned me loose.

The government attorney didn't have nothing new to say. It was the same old run-around. Where did I get the money? What about the traveling? Why was I consorting with drug dealers? In the end, Magistrate Palermo got fed up with it and dropped my bond to $20,000. Kessler gave me a nod, and I was out.

Lugo drove me and Anna home in his car.

"No doubt about it," he said. "Ricardo's their ace in the hole. I don't see how we can beat that."

"Well, how much can he know?" I said. "He just went along on this one deal, and I wasn't even there."

"He knows enough. He knows about the ship. He knows about it sailing again with the stuff still on board. He knows about the heroin deal. Face it. Anything you told Orlando, Orlando told Morales."

"And now Morales is telling the agents," I said. "Great. Just wait till I see Orlando."

It wasn't long. He was there at the house to congratulate me on making bail.

"Thanks a lot," I said, after sending Lugo on his way. "If it wasn't for you and Morales, I wouldn't have been in the slammer in the first place."

"Hey, take it easy, man." I'd hurt his feelings. "I did just like you told me."

"In a pig's eye," I said. "Did I tell you to shoot off your mouth about how rich you were going to be? Did I say, bring Morales in on the deal? I must have warned you fifty times about that guy."

"Ah, come on, Georgie," he said. "Talk on the street says it's all kind of loose."

"Don't feel loose. Ricardo Morales has fucked us up good."

"Man, you got him all wrong." Orlando shook his head. "You know what he did? When you were inside? He came to see Anna. He came all the way over here to help her, right, Anna?"

"Yeah, baby. He said he could get passports for the three of us. With different names."

"Jesus," I said. "Orlando, you believe that shit?"

"He can do it. He knows how to get them."

"Sure he does. He cleans us out to pay for them, then tips off the agents. For Christ's sake, that's his business. The man works for the fucking government. He's an informer."

"Man, I find that hard to believe," said Orlando, still shaking his head. "You really got it in for the guy."

"Believe it. We know they had an undercover in on the deal—they told Kessler."

"Well, for my money, it's Hernandez's partner. You think it's funny how Ricardo got away? Well, ask yourself. How come they ain't got that guy either?"

Orlando just wouldn't have it, and I couldn't stay mad at him. Except for Anna, he was the only one who'd stuck by me. After she talked to them on the phone, Anna went out to see the old lady and Martinez and the others, and all of a sudden they didn't know us. "Oh, no. We can't. Sorry to hear about your troubles, but we can't." So it was now down to just the three of us.

Plus Cosmo Lacroix and the spirits, of course. As a payoff for getting me out of jail, Anna had to make an offering of *panatelas*—little soft, syrupy cakes. She arranged a bunch of them on a plate, put butterscotch candy all around the edge, poured honey on top, and put them in the bathroom behind the toilet so Feo couldn't get at them. He caught a whiff of them, though. He followed her in there, wagging his tail, but suddenly stopped dead in his tracks and backed out, very suspicious.

Then a funny thing happened. The bathroom door jammed. It had never done that before. The key was on the inside, so it wasn't locked, but I just couldn't turn the handle. In fact, I damn near tore it off before I finally gave in and called the locksmith.

He couldn't budge it either.

"Funniest damn thing I ever saw," he said. "Looks like this is going to cost you a new door."

He was right. We had to break it in. And when Anna went to look at the *panatelas,* three of them had gone—from the middle of the plate. Feo couldn't have done that. Even if he'd sneaked in there without us seeing him, he would have messed up all of them and got his fur sticky. And it wasn't.

Things were getting very sticky in other ways, though. After having his lunch of *panatelas,* Cosmo Lacroix must have gone on vacation. Along with Orlando and Hernandez, I was due in court soon to enter a plea on the conspiracy charge. Naturally, it was going to be not guilty, but Kessler didn't like the odds.

"I'll give it to you straight," he said. "They've pieced the whole thing together. They've been to Haiti. They've got witnesses there. They've got you with your godfather in Puerto Rico. They can show you've been hanging around with Orlando for a year or more. They've got you meeting with Hernandez. They've got the five kilos, and they say they've got a witness. So it's tight now. Looks like they've got a good, solid case."

"This witness," I said. "Is it Morales?"

"Does it matter? We can go to court with this, but I have to tell you: if they've got all they say they have, I don't think we can win. You could get fifteen years. Maybe less, as it's a first offense."

"Oh, Jesus." I heard what he said, but it still wasn't real to me.

"And then again, maybe not," he said. "They're also working hard to connect you with this heroin deal."

That tied in with the rumors I'd been hearing. In Caracas, Sereni was talking for a fact, and although he didn't know me, he sure as hell knew *about* me. There'd been a lot of talk over there about Mikey's godson. I'd also heard that Orsatti and Mikey were having the shit beat out of them in jail, and they were only human. Sooner or later, they'd tell what they knew.

"If I was ready to plead guilty," I said, "what would happen?"

"Well, they might take a more lenient view, I don't know. I'd have to see. But lenient could still mean eight years."

"Oh, Jesus."

"Better than fifteen," he said. "Trouble is, there's been so much publicity. And now they're talking about a guy called Matthews, a big dealer up in New York City."

"They arrested him?"

"No. But they say he's involved in some way, and if he is, that'll only make things worse. So I want you to think very carefully about this. If we fight them and lose, you're at the mercy of the court. But if you're ready to plead guilty, maybe we've got something we can bargain with. It's up to you. I'll play it any way you want."

"Okay," I said. "And thanks. I'll let you know."

Before I made up my mind, I took a last run over to Victoria Montalvo's house with Anna. It looked pretty good, with the paintwork sparkling in the sun.

"You shouldn't have come," she said. "They probably followed you here."

"Why would they follow me? They busted me already."

"I don't want nothing to do with this," she said. "You shouldn't have come."

"I figured that when Anna told me you wouldn't help with the bond."

"How could I?" she said. "My son wouldn't want me to pledge the house. It's all I got."

"What about the three keys I gave you?"

"You didn't give me nothing," she said. "I can't help you. I'm sorry. I got to go now."

And she closed the door on us. I drove Anna home and went to see Kessler.

"How about if I cooperate?"

"If you really mean that, I'll find out," he said.

"Will it hurt my godfather?"

"They caught him with 17 kilos of heroin. He's in a Venezuelan jail. How can you hurt your godfather?"

"What about Orlando?"

"Georgie, they got Orlando on ice. It can't make any difference to him either way."

"All right," I said. "Then ask them."

He called me back next day.

"No more than five for sure. Perhaps less. Depends what you can give them, of course, but, with remission and parole, that's pretty light. You won't do better."

"Okay." I didn't like it, but if they pinned the heroin on me, too, I was in line for thirty years. "Then I'd better sit down and tell these people a story."

And that was all I meant to do. I'd tell them a story to fit what they knew, and toss in just enough of what they didn't know to make it seem worthwhile.

Aguedo Lugo took me over to the headquarters of the Federal Strike Force in Miami, a quiet little building with a fence around it in the North-West section of town. Jack Lloyd met me out there with Bill Warner and another agent named Jim Sweat. They couldn't make no promises, they said, but if I told them the whole story they'd make a strong recommendation for leniency.

"That won't do me no good if I'm dead," I said. "If I tell you the whole story and you put me in prison, I'm going to get myself killed."

"You've violated the narcotics laws, and you'll have to go down," they said. "But if you cooperate, the court will go easy on you, and you'll get all the protection you need. We might even put you in the federal witness program so you can do your time in a safe house. But that's all according to how much you can tell us and how much it's worth."

So I laid out the bones of it for them, changing the characters around. I didn't even mention the old lady, Martinez, or any of those. When they asked me who else had been in on the deal, I gave them the names of people they knew already or else couldn't catch. I was not too fond of playing informer, but this way I could hack it, and it seemed to work.

"You know Frank Matthews?"

"Yeah, I know him."

"You dealt with him?"

"Sure, I've dealt with him."

"Tell us about it."

"Why don't you just tell me to feed myself into a meat grinder?" I said. "With a guy like that, there ain't no such thing as a safe house."

"Don't worry about it," Lloyd said. "You're no use to us dead. Whatever needs to be done will be done—you're dealing with the U.S. government now. And, anyway, nobody will even know you've talked to us until we're ready to go to trial."

That was good to know. "Nobody here in Miami will get to hear about this? That I'm cooperating with you?"

"Absolutely not. Not until the trial comes up."

"Not even Ricardo Morales?"

They looked at one another. "Nobody will know except the three of us and the U.S. Attorney in charge of the case. Figure it out for yourself. The more you tell us, the more valuable you are, so the more we'll take care of you."

"I'll stay out on bail?"

"Of course. Now what about Frank Matthews?"

"Why don't I tell you about him later?" I said. "After you got him inside."

"Georgie, let me make this clear. Either you level with us or it's no deal—it's as simple as that. If we even *think* you're holding out, now or any time, all deals are off. You got that? You'll just be another defendant, and we'll hit you with everything we've got. And that's plenty."

"Okay, okay. I get the picture."

So I gave them a little taste of what I knew, acting like I still wasn't happy over what I might be letting myself in for, and needed to be coaxed. It wasn't a formal statement—I told them I wouldn't sign nothing until I'd thought things over some more—and they were happy with that. They just wanted some idea of what they would get as *their* end of the deal.

"Now what about Anna?"

"*What* about her?" I said. "You leave her alone."

"She's at risk, Georgie. There are a lot of people involved here. If somebody testifies against her, we'll *have* to take her in."

That was something I *hadn't* thought of. It set me back for a minute, and I guess it showed.

"Talk to her, Georgie. Bring her with you next time."

I didn't say nothing.

"When shall we make it?"

"I'll call you," I said.

Now I was *really* in trouble. Forget about the government. Never mind what Frank would do to me if he found out. I had to face Anna. I hadn't told her yet I was even *thinking* of making a deal, because I knew what she'd say. Anna belonged to the old school: better to be torn in a thousand pieces than sacrifice your honor. I hadn't been looking forward to the fight we were going to have when I told her *I* meant to cooperate. Now I had to talk *her* into doing it as well.

I decided to speak to Kessler first, but that only made it worse. He said Anna and me should get married. Then neither of us would ever be pressured to give evidence against the other, and anyway, it would look better.

"But Anna doesn't *want* to get married," I said. "She told me."

"Well, talk to her, Georgie. You're in this thing together."

The next few days were a nightmare. It started as soon we went to bed.

"We're in this thing together, right?"

"Sure, baby," she said. "You know it."

"Suppose they hit me with thirty years. You'll be an old lady by the time I get out."

"Baby, if you think that's going to happen, we got to make a run for it."

"And be fugitives all our lives? Never a minute's peace? Uh-uh. We got to beat this some other way. Maybe I ought to plead guilty, like Kessler says. Young kid, first offense—maybe I'll draw a light sentence."

"How light?"

"Who knows? Depends what sort of impression I make in court."

"Well, you're good at that. You can make a good impression."

"Think so? Kessler says it would look better if we got married."

"Married?" She pulled away in surprise.

"Yeah. You know how judges are. You don't mind?"

"Mind? Well, I don't know, baby. No, I guess not. Not if you think it's going to help."

"Okay. Fine. I'll get the license tomorrow."

That was the easy part. I let things settle down a bit, then zeroed in again.

"Of course," I said, very casual, "if I *did* plead guilty, Kessler thinks there's a way I can make *sure* of drawing a light sentence."

"Yeah? Well, why didn't you say so, baby?"

"Well, I'm not too keen about it, but they'd probably make a deal. He says it happens all the time in these cases."

"A deal?"

"Right. You know. If I cooperate a little bit, they'll let me plead guilty to a lesser charge, and I'll get off light."

"Then cooperate, baby. What do you have to do?"

"Well, it's not just me. It's got to be both of us. I mean, people know we ran stuff up to New York together and everything."

"Okay. So what do *we* have to do?"

"Well, we'll have to tell the agents what they want to know, for a start."

"You mean, about what we been doing?"

"Right," I said. "And who we've been doing it with, and like that."

Silence. I felt her fuse burning down. Four, three, two, one—blast off. I tried to hold on to her, but she fought me off.

"No."

"Baby, I don't have a choice."

"I don't want to hear about it. Don't talk to me."

"I don't like it either, but what can I do? It's that or thirty years."

"I'm not listening. I don't care what you say to me, so forget it. Just leave me alone."

"Baby—"

"You want me to inform? Don't even *think* about it."

"Well, do me a favor. Talk to the agents. Maybe you'll listen to them."

"I don't want to listen to *nobody*. And I don't want to get married either."

It went on like that for a week. Then, on September 20, we got married in Kessler's office.

Not that she liked the idea any better, but she started to listen when I told her what I had in mind. The agents believed I was ready to testify against Orlando and Hernandez when they came up for trial, but there was no way I was going to do that. I was going to keep everybody happy while we got our shit together and then pick the right moment to take off. So it didn't matter what I told them, I said. If we weren't there to say it in court, it didn't mean a thing. They couldn't use it.

"But then you'll be a fugitive," she said. "You told me you didn't want that."

"I know. But I've had an idea. If I can rip Frank off for a couple of hundred thousand, we might just make it."

Three days later, we met Lloyd, Warner, and Sweat in Howard Johnson's on Biscayne Boulevard, Room 515. Luckily, I'd told Anna to listen to what I said and take her cue from me, because this time they brought a tape recorder. So I went through the story again, switching things around like before, only this time I did it so much I even confused myself. But the only new names I gave them were Yves Alexis and Evaristio Santiesteban, and I had to do that because there was no way they were going to believe I didn't know how the stuff was brought in. Otherwise, it was just the people they'd seen me with in Haiti and Puerto Rico—my godfather, Diaz, Medina, Perez, and Ana Baños. Plus Matthews, but only Bill Warner seemed really interested in him.

Anna cooled off a lot after that. She'd seen what I was trying to do, although she still wouldn't talk to the agents much. Whenever they asked her anything, it was always "yes" or "no" or "I don't remember." A few days later, we had to go through the whole thing again for Gerry Miller, who came down from New York with Jack Rawald. I guess Bill Warner had called them.

Had I dealt with Matthews? *Yes.* How many times? *Four or five times.* How much stuff? *Oh, 20, 30 kilos.* Coke or smack? *Coke.* How about the heroin in Caracas? *Well, it didn't get through, did it?* Had I been in on that deal? *In on it? Me and Frank planned it.*

After that, they went into a huddle with the Miami agents, and I went home to Anna. Next day, Bill Warner and Jim Sweat came over to see us at the house. They were worried about our safety, they said. They thought we ought to move out of town for a while, just as a precaution.

"Fine," I said. "Nothing holding us in Miami."

The family knew the whole situation by now—all except my grandmother, who was still pretty sick. She'd been told I'd joined the army and was doing my basic training.

"No," said Anna. "I won't go."

"It's for your own good," Warner said. "Like a little vacation on Uncle Sam."

"I don't care. I'm not leaving. I'm going to stay with my sister."

"Baby," I said.

"I'm not listening. I don't want to talk to these people. I got nothing to say. Not to you, not to nobody. You do what you like. I'm not leaving this house."

A few hours later, we packed our bags and followed the agents over in the Volkswagen to a motel in Miami Beach. But, as soon as they left, we drove right back across the causeway to see Orlando. I didn't want to disappear and maybe give him ideas.

"Hey, listen," I said. "This case is closing in on us. Me and Anna are moving up to Fort Lauderdale for a few days. See how things work out. If we have to take a walk, we'll have the jump on them."

"Good idea," he said. "Maybe I'll blow town myself. My lawyer says somebody's talking for sure. Got to be."

"Right. Morales."

"Come on, Georgie. I had breakfast with the guy this morning. It's Hernandez's partner."

"Have it your way. But I got a feeling I ain't going to be around at the trial to find out."

Two days later, the agents came by the motel to move us up to a housekeeping cabin at West Palm Beach.

"You'll be more comfortable," Warner said. "You can stay up there till the trial."

"When's it to be?"

"November 6."

It was getting close. About four weeks.

"What about our apartment?" Anna said.

"That's okay. We'll pay the rent and keep an eye on it for you."

So we drove up behind them to West Palm Beach. There they settled us into a nice little efficiency cottage and gave me $140, a week's living expenses in advance. It was all very friendly now.

"Listen, will you do me a favor?" Anna said. "Will you take Feo back with you? Give him to my sister? I'm frightened he'll get lost up here if he runs out."

"Okay," they said. "Sure."

Warner put him on the back seat, handling him careful because he knew how that dog loved chewing on cops. The agents used to say that, for what he'd done, Feo should get ten years in the pound.

"What'd you do that for?" I said, as they drove away. I knew how she was going to miss him.

"I wouldn't want to see his face on a wanted poster," she said. "We're getting out of here, right?"

"Yeah, baby. But not yet. It's too soon. If they're going to catch us, I want them to catch us *after* the trial."

I figured on leaving in another two weeks. Anna hadn't been indicted, so she had nothing to lose, but I knew there'd be a warrant out for me the minute I didn't show. What I needed was a clear forty-eight hours with nobody looking for me.

That first week, the agents came out nearly every day with new questions. It didn't look promising. But on Friday afternoon they gave me another $140 and said, "So long. Have a good weekend. We'll see you on Monday."

"Sure," I said. "You, too."

It was simple as that. We'd leave the following Friday and *not* see them Monday.

We needed some money, though, and also more clothes. It was going to be cold up in New York. On the Tuesday, as Warner and Sweat were getting into their car to drive back to Miami, I asked them for a day off.

"Hey, listen," I said. "Anna's going stir crazy. You guys got anything for me tomorrow? I want to show her Cape Kennedy."

They looked at each other. "Nothing that can't wait till Thursday," said Warner.

Next morning, I drove down to Miami. I didn't want to go to our main bank, in case anybody spotted me, so I could only get the $4,000 we had in a safe-deposit box at another branch, but I figured that would tide us over until I clipped Frank for our getaway money. After that, I darted over to the apartment, sneaked in the back way, packed a suitcase full of warm clothes, and sneaked out again.

The only thing left to do now was see Orlando.

"I've had it," I told him. "We're splitting. Friday night."

"Me, too," he said. "Where are you going?"

"New York."

"Yeah. That's the best place. I'll see you up there."

It wasn't likely, but I didn't want to make the guy feel bad. "Where will you be?" I said.

"Don't know. Tell you what. You can reach me through that number I gave you when I took the stuff up there."

"Okay," I said. "Good luck. And do us both a favor. Don't say nothing to Morales."

At about four o'clock on Friday afternoon, I signed for another $140 and the agents left.

"Take care," they said. "Have a nice weekend."

"Thanks," I said. "We will."

At about eight, we took off in the Volkswagen and drove very carefully to New York City, obeying the speed limits and signs all the way.

It was Sunday when we got there, and I took a room in one of those rat-bag hotels on the West Side in the low Forties. Anna was tired, so I left her there to take a nap while I went uptown to find Ricky Acosta, who usually hung around a place called Va Cuba at 157th Street and Broadway. I asked for him in there, and he showed up a few minutes later.

"Hey, man," he said. "Good to see you. I heard all the screaming and hollering about Mikey and that. What's going on?"

"Nothing," I said. "We all got popped, too."

"Oh, Jesus. I didn't know. Hell, man, I'm sorry."

"Yeah. Well, that's how it goes. And that's why I come up here—to get lost."

He shook his head, looking doubtful. "Well, I don't know, man.

Things are bad up here, too. If they're looking for you, you ought to take a run down to Haiti or some place like that."

"I aim to," I said. "But first I got to get some money. I'm going over to see Frank. Tell him I got 20 keys lined up but I need a couple of hundred thousand to front the deal. You want to come?"

"Oh, no." He whistled, and pretended to wipe sweat off his forehead. "Not me, man. I wouldn't do that if I was you."

"Why not?"

"The word we got up here is, Mikey's talking. They say he's spilling the whole story, so Frank's liable to be a little hectic."

"Shit."

That did it. That meant Zack was out, too. I'd finally come to the end of my rope. And it was still a couple of weeks to the trial.

"I got to find a place to stay," I said.

There was a store on 157th with a lot of little ads in the window. One of them was for a room just down the street at $20 a week, so I went to have a look. It was clean and nice. I drove downtown to fetch Anna, and half an hour later we moved in.

Now I had to do something about the Volkswagen. As soon as it got dark, I drove higher uptown and parked on 181st Street. I took off the Florida tag, left the door unlocked, with the keys in the ignition, and went to buy a cup of coffee. Fifteen minutes later, I walked back and the car had gone.

We lived very quietly for the next ten days, eating all our meals in and only going out after dark. I hadn't told Anna about my talk with Ricky. I was waiting for Cosmo Lacroix to come up with a miracle, but he didn't. The trial was due to start on a Monday. On the Friday before, I called Melvyn Kessler in Miami.

"Where the hell are you?" he said. "The agents think you're dead. They think you were shot."

"No, no. We're okay. But I'm thinking of taking off."

"Don't be a fool," he said. "Now you listen to me. You haven't done anything wrong yet. You're still out on bail. So you come on over here to my office, and I'll straighten this out with the agents."

"Well, it's not as easy as that. And, anyway, they don't need me —not for this trial. They got another witness."

"For God's sake, Georgie. You had a deal with them. If you welsh on it, they'll lock you up and throw away the key. Now goddammit, be sensible. I told you—five years tops. Less remission. Plus parole. What more do you want? You're young. It's nothing. Where are you? New York?"

"Well, maybe you're right."

"No maybes about it, Georgie. I'm *right*. Now listen. Catch the next plane down here and check into the Holiday Inn at Coral Gables. You got that? I'll get in touch with you there."

"Well, I don't know."

"Trust me, Georgie. *Do* it."

"Well, I'll think about it. I'll let you know."

I went back and told Anna what he wanted me to do.

"It makes sense, baby," I said. "If I could have got the money, it would have been different, but without it, we don't stand a chance. I'm not going to hide the rest of my life and jump out of my skull every time somebody knocks on the door. I'm not going to have you do it, either. I got to go back."

"You mean, you're going to testify? Against Orlando?"

I looked at her. I couldn't do it. "No," I said. "I mean *after* the trial."

One second she was happy; the next she was down again. "Baby, they'll crucify you. I'm scared."

"Don't be scared. I still got a card or two to play," I said, acting very nonchalant. "I just got to watch how I do it. And I don't want to have to worry about you. You got a couple of uncles living up here, right?"

"So?"

"So I'll give you half the money, and you go stay with them. Say you're on vacation or something. And I'll send word as soon as I know what's happening."

She started to cry. "No, don't go, baby," she said. "I'm really scared."

"Well, I'm not too happy about it myself," I said, and I gave her a hug. "But it's the best thing. And, anyway, I'm not going yet. We got another four, five days."

I stretched it into seven and tried to make them count. On the next Friday, I figured the trial ought to be over, so I called Mel Kessler again.

"You son of a bitch," he said. "What happened?"

"Nothing happened. I couldn't testify against Orlando, that's all. So where does it leave me?"

"Way out in left field," he said. "Judge Fulton issued a bench warrant. Plus now you're on a bail-jump charge as well."

"Suppose I surrender."

"That's your only chance. I'll try to set it up—a voluntary surrender. And you better pray you get to me before they get to you."

"Okay. Monday morning. I'll call you when I get in."

"No," he said. "Tomorrow."

"Can't. Got things to do. Was it Morales?"

"What? Yes. Georgie, make it tomorrow."

"See you Monday," I said.

Things weren't working out so bad after all. Soon everybody would know that Morales was the informer, and that would hold me cool for a long time.

Now I had to see my family. I said goodbye to Anna, which wasn't easy, and flew down to Miami to spend the weekend at my mother's house. On Monday morning, I called Mel Kessler, and he took me in to surrender.

Nobody said much.

"Do we still have a deal?" I asked the agents, and they just shrugged. They didn't seem to know.

We sat around while Kessler had a session with Sam Sheres, the new federal prosecutor on the case, and then they took me over to Dade County Jail. I was left there to stew for a whole week.

On the Monday after I surrendered, I came up in front of Chief Judge Fulton for a hearing, and after listening to what Sheres had to say, he released me into his custody. Jack Lloyd joined us as we left the court, and we all got into a car waiting outside. I figured they would take me over to the BNDD building, but instead we hit the Expressway and headed out toward the airport.

"Hey, where are we going?" I said, although I knew already. Cosmo Lacroix was back on the job.

Gerry Miller and Roger Garay met us at La Guardia, and we checked into the Ramada Inn. It was all very friendly. They bought me a drink.

"You're in a lot of trouble, Georgie," Miller said.

"Yeah, I know."

"Yeah, but do you know what you've got to do for us now?"

"I got to give you Frank Matthews—right?"

"*Right*," they said.

20

For those eight million Americans who regularly resort to pharmacology for pleasure, stimulus, or relief, cocaine will probably always remain an occasional self-indulgence, an expensive treat with which to reward or compensate themselves for life's ups and downs. Held back from excess by its price, they are more or less safe from the psychological dependence that cocaine induces in heavy users like Frank Matthews.

Matthews loved cocaine. It was not just his business; it was breakfast food, quick lunch, and nightcap—a complete life-support system. Indeed, dependence is not quite the right word in his case, for it suggests that he needed cocaine in order to carry on a normal life. In fact, cocaine had imposed such a pattern of its own on his behavior that his normal had become abnormal by any conventional standard. By the autumn of 1972, Matthews showed all the classic symptoms of chronic cocaine abuse, shuttling between extremes of euphoria and irritability in an almost continuous macho-delusional-power trip.

He seemed possessed by a sense of invincibility, of a godlike mastery over his own fate that was not to be shaken for long by such setbacks as the raid on the O.K. Corral or the collapse of a 100-kilo deal. What was one heroin mill or heroin source more or less to Black Caesar? The loss was annoying, but it taught him nothing. It was an affront, not a lesson. Afterwards, he went about his business as blatantly as ever, still salting millions away in preparation for retirement. He was not to be hurried or intimidated by anybody, not even by the federal grand jury investigating his affairs.

Anyone else in his position might have felt it prudent to use his network of informants to keep an eye on the proceedings, at least to the extent of finding out who were being called as witnesses, but Matthews seemed indifferent to the danger. For all the effect it had on his behavior, he either did not know or did not care that George Ramos had testified against him on November 22, and that his days were consequently numbered. Had he known or cared, he might well have numbered George Ramos's days instead.

Except that Miller, Callahan, and Sheerin were taking very good care of their star witness. They kept him in New York for about a month, guarded around the clock by federal marshals, first at the Skyline Motel and then, as he was needed less often for questioning in Brooklyn, at another motel in Saddlebrook, New Jersey. Ramos was there when he heard, on December 5, that Orlando had been arrested and that Anna had been picked up as a material witness.

A week or so later, Callahan and Sheerin decided that he had given them enough. Now formally inducted into the federal witness program, Ramos was sent out of harm's way to Portland, Oregon, and on December 20 Magistrate Max Schiffman issued a federal warrant for Matthews's arrest. The hope was that, with Matthews's fall, a half dozen more potential witnesses then sitting on the fence—men like Dickie Diamond and Donald James—would also come down on the government's side and agree to testify against him at his trial.

The *fear* was, however, that Mob lawyers would quickly spring Matthews on bail and the government's witnesses would all clam up again. To minimize this risk, the time and place of Matthews's arrest had to be carefully engineered. After waiting nearly a year and a half for this moment, Miller was not anxious to see it bungled by precipitate action. He wanted his man collared in circumstances that were as compromising as he could make them, and preferably not on his home turf, where Matthews could most easily mobilize his defenses. Miller was even willing to forgo the pleasure of making the arrest himself if it would fasten the handcuffs on him that much more tightly.

As unhelpful as ever, Matthews spent Christmas quietly at home with his family on Staten Island. He had a few friends over, including Vinny Moore, the owner of Brownee's, but spent most of the time parceling up money in Christmas wrapping paper. Although the government attorneys and agents could not know it, and fretted impatiently, Matthews was getting ready for another trip to the laundry.

He left by air for Las Vegas on New Year's Eve with several suitcases and a new girlfriend, Cheryl Denise Brown, the beautiful twenty-three-year-old daughter of a New York City schoolteacher. He planned to spend about a week in the casinos and then move on to Los Angeles in time to catch the Super Bowl game between the Washington Redskins and the Miami Dolphins. Federal agents in Las Vegas were duly warned to pick up the trail as Matthews arrived at McCarran International Airport, but promptly lost him. By the time they found him again, Matthews had registered at the Sands, unloaded most of the gift-wrapped money in safe-deposit boxes around town, and rented a car.

Not used to the suddenness of his movements, the agents lost him several times more after that, but could always count on finding him sooner or later at the tables, where they watched him drop $170,000 in a few days. Their performance was making New York nervous, however, and toward the end of the week they were told to take Matthews into custody. When the orders arrived, he was missing again, but on January 5, 1973, they spotted him driving out toward the airport with Cheryl Brown.

Spotting them at the same moment, Matthews shook off the pursuers as easily as ever, but the agents now knew he was on the move and staked out the terminal building. The two were picked up there shortly afterwards while attempting to board a Los Angeles flight, and minutes after the news reached New York, Miller, Callahan, and Sheerin were on their way to Kennedy to catch the next plane out.

Matthews had offered no resistance. He was found to be carrying about $25,000—for him, hardly more than loose change. As there was no warrant out for Cheryl Brown, he tried to give her $5,000 to cover her expenses back home, but the agents confiscated that as well. To make doubly sure she would stay in town, they decided to hold her for questioning, and the two were taken to Clark County Jail.

A few hours later, as Sheerin conferred with Devoe Heaton, the U.S. Attorney in Las Vegas, about arrangements for a hearing, Miller and Callahan came face to face with Matthews for the first time, amid a crowd of other federal agents, marshals, and local deputies.

"I've been waiting for you," said Matthews calmly.

"Yes," said Miller. "I've been kind of looking forward to this, too."

"When my lawyer gets in, I'll be leaving here," Matthews went on. "And the next time you come looking for me, you better bring a shotgun."

"Oh, I will, Frank, I will. But I'm afraid there isn't going to *be* a next time. Not for forty or fifty years anyway."

"Man, you're dreaming. You got nothing on me."

Callahan smiled. "I think we've got a pretty good case."

"Yeah? We'll see what you got when my lawyers get through with it."

"Frank," said Miller. "Face it. You're through. You got an empire now, but I'm going to pull it down around your ears."

"If you can do it, do it." Matthews was suddenly bored with the conversation. "Hey, can you lend me a few bucks? They took all my money."

Miller searched his pockets. He had left New York in such a hurry he had forgotten to bring any with him. Callahan loaned him a dollar.

"Here you are, Frank." Miller handed it to him. "And don't forget to pay me back."

"Thanks a lot," he said. "I may not be around."

"In that case," Miller said, "I'll be taking it off your dead body."

When Matthews was brought before Magistrate Joseph L. Ward, his bail was set at $5 million—the highest bond ever required by an American court.

As for Cheryl Brown, when Callahan said he would like her to be held for the time being, the sheriff of Clark County looked through the contents of her purse, found a motel-room key, and charged her with possession of burglary tools.

Though relieved to have him behind bars, the government attorneys were uncomfortably aware of the fact that Matthews was quite capable of posting a $5 million bond. Fortunately, the next day, January 7, was a Sunday, but another hearing was set for Monday morning, and Stanley J. Kaufman, who had meanwhile arrived from Brooklyn to represent Matthews, was certain to ask in any case for a substantial reduction in bail. In New York, U.S. Attorney Robert A. Morse ordered members of his staff in the Eastern District to work through that Saturday preparing extradition papers, and in Las Vegas, Callahan and Miller went into a huddle with the IRS agents assigned to the case under the IRS Narcotics Traffickers Program.

On Monday morning, Kaufman duly asked Magistrate Ward to reduce Matthews's bail to $100,000. His client was a gambler, he said, who always carried large sums on his person, and who had paid taxes in 1971 on a declared income of $200,000. The government was quite free to examine Matthews's safe-deposit boxes and bankbooks. Furthermore, his client was prepared to waive extradition and return voluntarily to the Eastern District of New York.

Though grateful for that, U.S. Attorney Heaton vigorously opposed any reduction in Matthews's bond, citing the prisoner's gambling losses as evidence of how little $100,000 would mean to him, particularly as he was believed to have at least a million dollars salted away in Las Vegas banks alone.

Magistrate Ward was impressed by this argument but showed himself willing to meet Kaufman halfway. Matthews's bail, he ruled, would be reduced from $5 million to $2.5 million.

It was still an enormous sum, but not nearly big enough to suit Miller, Callahan, and Sheerin, who knew that Matthews would hardly notice it. Upon his return to New York, he would almost certainly have gone free but for the countermeasures they had cooked up over the weekend. It was absolutely essential to show their prospective witnesses that they could keep Matthews behind bars in spite of his money, his power, and his political influence.

As Matthews left the courtroom handcuffed to a black federal marshal, a small, plump, shortsighted man in a rumpled suit, carrying a government briefcase, detached himself from the waiting crowd of reporters and rubberneckers and planted himself in their path. Peering up into Matthews's face, he identified himself as an IRS official and presented him with a piece of paper.

"What's this?" asked Matthews suspiciously.

"It's a termination assessment," he explained. "We estimate that your taxable income for the year ending 31st of December 1972 was approximately $10 million. The tax now due therefore amounts to $7,009,165. Plus a $6 lien fee."

Matthews looked bewildered. Then he laughed. "Little man," he said. "How in the fuck do you expect me to pay that?"

The other adjusted his pebble-thick glasses and stared up at him gravely. "Preferably in cash," he said.

Game, set, and match. In effect, Matthews's bail had been raised to $9.5 million, of which $7 million would have been forfeited immediately had he cared to produce it. And even if he *had* considered making a present of $7 million to the government, he would at the same time have convicted himself of tax evasion on a huge scale, for how could anybody with a declared annual income of $200,000 amass such a sum? Miller, Callahan, and Sheerin flew back to New York confident that their prisoner would now stay safely in jail until he was brought to trial.

In fact, they all flew back together on Saturday, January 13: Matthews, guarded by federal marshals; Barbara Hinton, who had left the children with her mother and flown out to be with Matthews as soon as she heard of his arrest; Cheryl Brown, seated at the other end of the cabin (the sheriff of Clark County had dropped his charge against her); the IRS agents; and Matthews's lawyer, who sat with the government attorneys for much of the flight, to Barbara Hinton's undisguised annoyance.

Matthews himself was listless and apathetic. Deprived of coke for several days, and knowing he had been outmaneuvered in the matter of bail, he had little to say to anyone, although he did talk briefly to the three men mainly responsible for bringing him down, and even hinted at his readiness to consider a deal.

"A deal?" said Miller. "What have you got to deal *with?* We know all your people. We'll get them anyway."

"You don't got the Italians," he said.

They looked at one another.

"I don't know," said Callahan. "Even if you gave us your connections, the best we could do would be, what? Ten years?"

The others agreed.

Matthews shook his head. "Forget it," he said. "No way. I can't do time."

But he had to do a little. On their arrival in New York, he was taken to the West Street Detention Center. In the weeks that followed, a string of indictments was handed up: on January 18, for federal income-tax evasion; on the twenty-fourth, for conspiracy to distribute cocaine in the Eastern District of New York; on the twenty-sixth, for conspiracy to distribute heroin in the Eastern District. After that, various superseding indictments were also filed, as Callahan and Sheerin felt able to name and prosecute Matthews's co-conspirators.

Indeed, the investigation kept widening the scope of the case to such an extent that the government began to feel some reluctance about going to trial before all its leads were run down. In February, the Attorney General advised everybody concerned in the Justice Department that no further indictments were to be handed up or unsealed without his prior approval. It was a move toward coordinating a case which now involved literally scores of law-enforcement agencies across the country and which was bringing new suspects into focus almost every day.

For his part, Matthews replaced Stanley Kaufman with Gino Gallina, of Lenefsky, Gallina, Moss & Hoffman, a sharp New York law firm with a special reputation for defending difficult criminal cases. A frequent visitor to West Street, Gallina concentrated on reducing Matthews's bail, helped to some extent by the government's caution about proceeding before Matthews's empire had been fully explored. The longer the delay, the less defensible could it be made to seem for the government to hold him without trial by asking for bail to be kept at a level which, he maintained, was beyond his means.

While awaiting results from this line of attack, Matthews ran his business from jail, conferring daily with Pop Darby, whose own trial had also been postponed; Donald Conner, who had taken over the day-to-day running of the organization; various other key executives; and Barbara Hinton, who continued to stick by him despite his now public infidelity. Brought before the grand jury in February, a few days after Matthews's twenty-ninth birthday, she refused to cooperate after a grant of immunity, and was now liable for prosecution on a perjury charge, as well as for conspiracy.

Not that her loyalty made much difference to Matthews's situation, one way or the other. Having learned that George Ramos and others would testify against him, he was not sanguine about his chances. He was also worried about what might come out at Mickey Beckwith's trial, which was due to start before his. If convicted, Matthews knew he faced fifty years at least.

At this point, he had about $15 million stashed safely overseas. It was not enough.

On April 9, some three months after his arrest, Gallina won a bail-reduction hearing before Judge Anthony J. Travia in federal court. As soon as the date was set, the government attorneys sensed what was coming and urgently warned their superiors in Washington that Matthews would probably now make bail and jump it to avoid trial. If any high-level attempt *was* made to influence Judge Travia's decision, however, it had no effect. He ordered Matthews's bail reduced to $325,000, subject to two conditions: that he stay within the jurisdiction of the Eastern District Court and report regularly to the U.S. Attorney's office.

Matthews's people knew what the amount would be at least a week beforehand. On April 2, a meeting had been held in Durham,

North Carolina, between a delegation led by his aunt, Marzella Webb; representatives of Georgia Surety, a bail-bond firm in Atlanta; and Edward L. Stanton, representing the interests of the insurance company asked to underwrite the bond. After examining the real estate deeds offered as collateral by Matthews's friends and relatives, Stanton told the meeting they were insufficient and that he would require $100,000 of the $325,000 to be put up in cash.

Mrs. Webb excused herself to make a phone call.

Shortly afterwards, Stanton received a call himself. It was from a young woman who asked him to meet her in the parking lot behind the First Union Bank. When he did so, she handed him a plastic hold-all, which he took into the bank and opened in a confidential booth. It contained five bundles of $100 bills, each amounting to $20,000, wrapped in Christmas paper.

With the necessary arrangements thus completed in advance, three surety bonds issued by the Public Service Mutual Insurance Company in the sum of $325,000 were lodged with the court on April 9, and Matthews went free. To celebrate his release, he bought a new Cadillac—a white convertible.

Indeed, he picked up pretty much where he had left off. Technically, he was now living at 2785 Ocean Parkway, Brooklyn, an apartment building into which Barbara Hinton had moved with the children when the IRS seized his house on Staten Island. His lieutenant Donald Conner also lived there, but Matthews was too busy getting his money together to spend much time at home. Paying scant attention to travel restrictions, he was seen several times in conference with leading New York narcotics dealers.

At this stage, Group 12 had no manpower to spare for keeping watch on a man already arrested and booked for trial. All their efforts were now properly directed against Matthews's executives, with the object of dismantling his empire. For news of Matthews himself, they had to rely on occasional reports from other agencies. On May 9, for example, an IRS investigator spotted Matthews with Big Robbie and several other big dealers at an after-hours club at 356 West 145th Street, one of the biggest gambling joints in Harlem. There was a lot of money on the table.

Miller and Callahan were in Venezuela at the time. They had flown down to interview Miguel Garcia, Joseph Sereni, and Antonio Orsatti in jail. The key witness against Matthews was still George Ramos, safely tucked away in Portland, and now reunited with Anna as a belated twenty-second-birthday present, but the testimony of Sereni, for instance, who had met and discussed the 100-kilo deal with Matthews in Caracas, could have made the heroin conspiracy case virtually watertight. Encouraged by the Venezuelan reaction to the idea of sending Sereni up as an additional witness at Matthews's trial, Miller and Callahan flew home on May 10 to set the diplomatic and legal wheels in motion.

But they turned too slowly.

On July 2, 1973, Frank Matthews was due in Brooklyn federal court to plead to a fresh indictment superseding one of the six already handed up against him. He failed to appear, and has not been found since. Nor has an estimated $20 million in cash.

Gattis Hinton and Cheryl Brown disappeared at about the same time. They have not been found either, despite the biggest international manhunt in history.

POSTSCRIPT

Frank Matthews

On July 1, 1973, two men appeared at the offices of the Public Service Mutual Insurance Co., in Great Neck, New York, with a briefcase containing $225,000 wrapped in Christmas paper. Added to the $100,000 in cash already advanced for Matthews's bail bond, this relieved the company of any necessity to foreclose on the real estate put up as collateral by his friends and relatives.

Aware that Matthews had been transferring huge sums of money overseas (it was thought to Algeria), the police and federal agents assumed at first that he had left the country. A month after his disappearance, however, Detective Michael Bramble happened to spot him in Brooklyn at the wheel of a white Cadillac convertible and gave chase in his own car. Unable to summon help, for he had no radio, Bramble tried to cut in ahead of the Cadillac, but Matthews forced him off the road.

The Cadillac was later found abandoned with traces of blood on the front seat. These were presumably meant to suggest that Matthews had met a violent end, but plainly there were some sacrifices that neither he nor his men were prepared to make, for it was not *human* blood.

The focus of the manhunt now shifted back home. Thousands of reward posters were circulated, and federal switchboards were jammed with callers claiming to have seen him. One such tip mobilized a small army of police, state troopers, and federal agents in Syracuse, New York. After sealing off the area, an assault group armed with riot guns and automatic weapons filtered into a downtown rooming house and burst in suddenly on an eighty-year-old man watching television. When he had recovered from the shock, they asked him his name.

"Frank Matthews," he quavered.

Other, more reliable sighting reports placed him in Minneapolis, Los Angeles, Atlanta, and Chicago, but always too late. Within months, most of the tips were coming from overseas: from the Bahamas, Bonaire, and Bogotá, and then, as time went by, from much farther afield—from London, Paris, Tel Aviv, Bangkok, Hong Kong, and even Okinawa.

On January 25, 1974, the Drug Enforcement Administration increased the reward for information as to his whereabouts to $20,000. The only other fugitive ever to have had such a price on his head was John Dillinger in 1931.

The police forces of the world are still looking for him. By now his features have probably been changed by plastic surgery, but hardly a week goes by without at least one report of a sighting somewhere reaching Roger Garay at Task Force headquarters. As these have never led to anything, one school of thought has it that Matthews is dead, dumped along with Gattis Hinton and Cheryl Brown by the Mob or by the Corsicans or by some enterprising rip-off artist inspired by his millions, but no one close to the investigation thinks so. After five years, they are still picking up his characteristic vibrations.

Some think he may still be running the narcotics business in the United States by remote control, like a black Luciano. Others picture him at the head of a private army of former Chinese Nationalist troops escorting caravans of raw opium down from the hills in the Golden Triangle. But wherever he is and whatever he is doing, Frank Matthews can be sure of one thing: Gerard Miller has his shotgun ready.

GEORGE RAMOS

On July 5, 1973, George Ramos was taken from Portland by federal marshals to appear before Chief Judge Charles B. Fulton in Miami. Having already pleaded guilty to one charge of conspiracy, he was sentenced to four years' imprisonment, with credit for time served. In all, he was to spend twenty-nine months in custody, appearing in court from time to time to testify against former associates in Miami and New York.

Paroled on March 17, 1975, he and Anna were given new identities by the federal government and resettled in another part of the country to start a new life. As he is still the government's chief witness against Frank Matthews, he remains under federal protection.

Gerard Miller

The new Drug Enforcement Administration, formed in 1973, gave Miller virtually carte blanche on the Matthews case. He relinquished command of Group 12 to Sergeant Jack Rawald and took Roger Garay with him to Washington, where he formed Central Tactical Unit No. 2, a personally chosen team of federal agents who worked exclusively on the case with unlimited access to government funds and facilities until well into 1974. By then, Centac 2 and the Brooklyn grand jury had assembled enough evidence against Matthews's closest associates for the U.S. Attorney, Eastern District, New York, to bring them to trial, which he did in 1975. Miller was then posted to Atlanta, where he remained until reassigned to Miami at the end of 1977.

As one of the most experienced federal agents on the active list, he lectures to at least a thousand police officers a year on the subject of organized crime. And he never fails to remind them to look out for Frank Matthews, who still owes him a dollar.

William Callahan

Upon the formation of DEA, Callahan was appointed Regional Counsel, Narcotics Task Forces. With Miller's departure for Washington to run Centac 2, Callahan took on the additional responsibility of "prosecutorial coordinator" for the Matthews case, as there was a real danger that it might otherwise be fragmented among several different regions.

Its center of gravity remained in New York, however, where Callahan brought some eighty witnesses before the Brooklyn grand jury before handing the case over to the U.S. Attorney's office in December 1974 for prosecution in federal court.

He was then transferred to the Antitrust Division of the Justice

Department and in October 1977 left government service to become president and director of UNITEL, the New York international investigative agency and security consultants specializing in "white-collar" crime.

The Miami Conspiracy

Orlando Lamadrid was returned to Miami after his arrest in December 1972 and pleaded guilty to charges of conspiring to violate the narcotics laws and to bail-jumping. He was sentenced to eight years' imprisonment.

José Martinez, Victoria Montalvo, Ana Baños, Raquel Dumois, and José Medina were brought to trial on April 26, 1976. Dumois was in due course acquitted, but the rest were convicted and sentenced to various terms of imprisonment.

The Cocaine Connection

Alberto Perez, also known as the Doctor, was arrested in Costa Rica in 1976 and imprisoned for possession of cocaine.

José Medina was arrested in Miami in 1973 for smuggling cocaine, jumped bail, and upon his recapture was tried on a number of narcotics charges and sentenced to a total of seventeen years in prison.

Pedro Diaz was said to have been released by the Venezuelan authorities after his arrest in Caracas on August 30, 1972, but has not been heard of since.

The New York Conspiracy

William Beckwith was convicted on October 31, 1973, of violating the narcotics laws, and is serving a twelve-year term in Atlanta Federal Penitentiary.

Nathaniel Elder was arrested in Atlanta in March 1974. He had been hiding but "got tired of it." He pleaded guilty to violating the narcotics laws and was sentenced to three years' imprisonment and five years' special probation.

Barbara Hinton, William Beckwith, Charles William Cameron,

John Wesley Carter, John Darby, Thelma Darby, David Clement Bates, Marzella Steele Webb, and others were brought to trial on August 4, 1975, before Chief Judge Jacob Mishler, U.S. District Court, Eastern District, New York, on a total of nine counts of conspiracy to break the narcotics laws. As Francis Sheerin was no longer with the U.S. Attorney's office, the case was prosecuted by Assistant U.S. Attorney David De Petris.

More than forty witnesses, including George Ramos, were called during the trial, which lasted for two months. On October 8, 1975, the jury acquitted Marzella Webb, but the others named were found guilty and sentenced to various terms of imprisonment. Barbara Hinton's conviction was subsequently reversed on a technicality.

The Victims

In 1972, the most conservative official estimate put the total of heroin addicts in the United States at half a million. In 1977, the National Institute on Drug Abuse estimate the total at 560,000—the cruelest of all commentaries on the prodigal outpouring, year by year, of money, manpower, and technology in the War on Drugs. Taking into account the figures for drug-related crime and the costs of law enforcement, the Institute's most recent (1975) assessment of the overall social cost of heroin addiction was $10.3 billion a year.

The fact is that government is waging an unwinnable war on human weakness, a war absurdly expensive to keep up, ridiculously profitable to the enemy, and insanely destructive of American city life. Every penny of the billions spent by government and "earned" by men like Frank Matthews is taken from ordinary Americans, either in taxes or by addict criminals. No junkie can support his habit legally, and very few can support it honestly. At the time of writing, heroin is fetching $1.65 a milligram on the street, or about $1.5 million a kilo after allowing for losses in cutting and bagging.

In February 1977, the House Select Committee on Narcotics

Abuse and Control attracted abuse of another kind by recommending that "the U.S. should offer to purchase the entire world supply [of opium] for eventual destruction."

A better idea might be to buy it and dispense it free, in the form of heroin, to registered addicts at government clinics. If America were bold enough to call off the war, it might find there was no one left to fight.